FINLAND'S RELATIONS WITH THE SOVIET UNION, 1944–84

FINLAND'S RELATIONS WITH THE SOVIET UNION, 1944–84

Roy Allison

St. Martin's Press New York

ISBN 0–312–29066–7

Library of Congress Cataloging in Publication Data

Allison, Roy.
  Finland's relations with the Soviet Union, 1944–84.

  Bibliography: p.
  Includes index.
  1. Finland—Foreign relations—Soviet Union.
2. Soviet Union—Foreign relations—Finland.
3. Finland—Foreign relations—1945-   · I. Title.
DL1048.S65A44   1985   327.4897047   84–17694
ISBN 0–312–29066–7

Contents

Acknowledgements

This book is the product of several years of research, which have included four visits to Finland, and my debts to individuals and institutions are numerous. I am particularly grateful for the assistance and encouragement which I received in England from Dr Richard Kindersley, Dr David Kirby and Mr Adam Roberts. I remain indebted to many others in both St Antony's College, Oxford, and the School of Slavonic and East European Studies, University of London, who contributed directly or indirectly to the completion of this work. In Finland my special thanks are due to Dr George Maude, whose comments and advice at all stages in my research have been invaluable. I am also beholden to Professor Osmo Apunen for stimulating discussions and for granting me the use of the facilities of the Department of Political Science at the University of Tampere during 1981–2. Many other colleagues in Tampere and Helsinki sustained me with their active interest in and sympathy for my work. The Embassy of Finland in London has also provided me with much useful material over the years.

I would like to acknowledge the financial support I have received from the Social Science Research Council, Oxford University and the Leverhulme Trust.

For providing me with incentive when the will was weak my final debt is to friends and relatives in England and throughout Finland.

ROY ALLISON

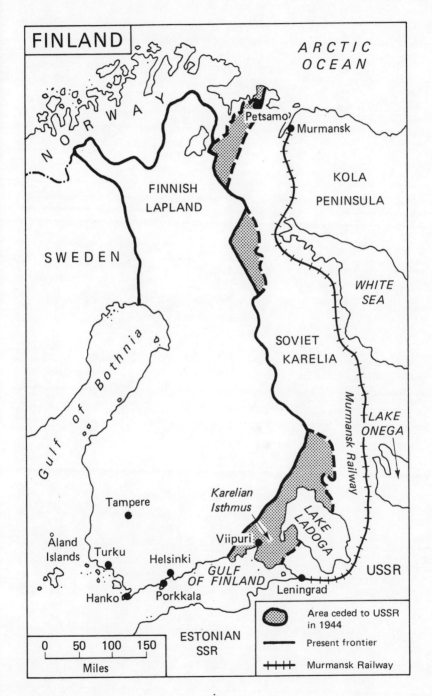

FINLAND

ARCTIC OCEAN

NORWAY

FINNISH LAPLAND

SWEDEN

Petsamo

Murmansk

KOLA PENINSULA

WHITE SEA

SOVIET KARELIA

Murmansk Railway

LAKE ONEGA

Gulf of Bothnia

Tampere

Karelian Isthmus

Viipuri

LAKE LADOGA

Åland Islands

Turku

Helsinki

GULF OF FINLAND

Hanko

Porkkala

Leningrad

USSR

ESTONIAN SSR

	Area ceded to USSR in 1944
	Present frontier
+++	Murmansk Railway

0   50   100   150

Miles

ix

Introduction

THE 'FINLANDISATION' ARGUMENT

After the dust created by the post-war division of Europe had begun to settle many Western observers were surprised to find that a small North European state, which had fought two bitter and unsuccessful wars against the Soviet Union since 1939, and which possessed a long land frontier with this giant neighbour, had retained not merely its independence but its Western political and economic system. Soviet behaviour towards Finland after 1944 did not appear to conform with widespread views about Soviet motivations and objectives drawn from Soviet conduct elsewhere in Europe. In short, Soviet–Finnish relations were regarded as a special case, as anomalous, with few relevant parallels for other states bordering on the USSR.

Finland was a constitutional democracy, with a market economy and political freedoms like its Scandinavian neighbours. But since Finland had accepted certain military-political commitments in her post-war treaties with the Soviet state it was unclear whether she should be regarded politically as an unqualified member of the Western camp. Such doubts appeared to be less relevant in the 1950s and 1960s as the ideological confrontation between East and West in Europe abated and as Finland's neutrality became internationally acknowledged. Already in this period Soviet leaders praised their relations with Finland as a model of peaceful coexistence, but few in the West attached much importance to the broader significance of these relations for Western Europe as a whole.

Towards the end of the 1960s Finland's Eastern relations were brought into international prominence by the popularisation among Western journalists, politicians and academics of the expression 'Finlandisation'. This term purported to describe a process discernible in post-war Finnish–Soviet relations which incrementally has led to the loss of Finland's national autonomy, and which illustrates, by analogy, a danger posed to Western Europe much more broadly by the Soviet Union in a period of *détente*. Although the worries

1

underlying the concept of Finlandisation had been expressed as far back as the early 1950s in an internal debate in Austria, and the term *'Finlandisierung'* emerged in academic dialogue in West Berlin in the 1960s, it was not until Willy Brandt became Chancellor of West Germany in 1969 that Finlandisation became a catchword used by those fearing or opposing Brandt's *Ostpolitik,* and in particular the withdrawal of American troops from Europe. These fears and uncertainties reflected claims or speculations about Soviet intentions and the effects of her physical power which had been arrived at independently of an investigation of Finland's position. But regardless of the question of whether Finland has actually been Finlandised in the sense meant by the proponents of this term, some prominent Western politicians, like Franz-Josef Strauss, have propagated an image of the Finlandised state which in their view has a potential and dangerous general applicability for Western Europe. This image has assumed considerable political significance, although there have been few attempts to convincingly flesh it out, at least by reference to the Finnish–Soviet relationship itself.

Finlandisation is understood as a covert, protracted and insidious process leading to the loss of a nation's independence in policy-making. Although the Finlandised state may remain outside its powerful neighbour's bloc it is assumed to lie within its 'soft sphere of influence'. A soft sphere relationship is created by a weaker state accepting or suggesting a series of political accommodations to a stronger state in order to establish, formally or informally, a level of dependence which it is willing to tolerate rather than risk conquest or more direct domination.[1] It is undeniable that Finland has been prepared to make some political accommodations since the war in response to the proximity of Soviet power, but those supporting the Finlandisation hypothesis often argue that Finland has clearly overstepped the line dictated by her geopolitical position.

From his study of Finland the Norwegian strategist Nils Ørvik has drawn perhaps the fullest picture of the Finlandised state.[2] While Ørvik accepts that such a state may retain its traditional institutional structure, in his view it will adapt the personnel in its government and its foreign policy decisions to Soviet demands or to the anticipated desires of the stronger state. This kind of anticipatory deference eventually undermines the national will of the state involved and breaks down resistance to further pressures. The Finlandised state in Ørvik's analysis becomes subject to 'remote-control'. It is characterised by isolation, inability to repel territorial infringements or occupation, joint borders or free access for foreign armed forces, a lack of national unity and common objectives, the strength of Communist or left-wing parties, and economic dependence. All of these conditions have been predicted of a Western Europe bereft of American support. A Finlandised Western Europe, it has been argued, would then be liable to a covert process of Sovietisation.

The parallels made with Finland's Eastern relations have not been restricted to Western Europe. A former Soviet international relations specialist argued in 1980, for example, that Afghanistan during the Cold War had been an example of how peaceful coexistence should be conducted between the Soviet Union and a country of the Third World: 'as Finland in Europe, Afghanistan was in Asia'. If the term Finlandisation is to be used in Europe, he suggested, one could have talked of 'Afghanisation' in Asia.[3] A Western specialist on Asia has proposed that Soviet leaders might accept a formula for Soviet military withdrawal from Afghanistan 'if it provided for Finland-style arrangements'.[4] Another view comes from David Vital, who has described Finland's position as 'a paradigm for the future' of successful relations between a small and great power. Vital was thinking primarily of future power relations in the Middle East.[5]

These views reveal one of the problems of the Finlandisation theory, as the specialist on Finland George Maude has shown, namely that 'Finnish experience is torn out of its context and thrown into a world of generalised experience, that of tyranny in general, that of Soviet policy in general, that of fate of small nations, that of the fate of Western Europe.'[6] The long-term Finnish president, Urho Kekkonen, tended to stress the special character of Finland's Eastern relations, which, he told an American journalist in 1973, meant that Finlandisation however it is defined 'is not a commodity for export'.[7] But from a different angle Kekkonen has argued that if by Finlandisation is meant trustworthy and constructive cooperation between states with different social systems, then 'we even recommend for general use this new term originally coined in foreign parts as a disparagement of Finland'.[8] He accepted the term Finlandisation as a description of Finland's post-war policy of reconciliation with the Soviet Union.[9] Many Finns have pointed to the implications of Finnish–Soviet economic cooperation. In a book entitled *Finlandisation* one writer has presented the Finnish case as a model of pioneering forms and habits of cooperation between socialist and capitalist countries.[10]

In this broad sense it remains true that the Finnish case represents something of a model. The American exponent of Finlandisation Walter Laqueur has been correct, therefore, in claiming that if Poland or Hungary constitute one example of a close relationship between the Soviet Union and its smaller neighbours, Finland provides another, and Soviet leaders regard it as such. But Laqueur, among others in the West who refer to Finlandisation, does not view the Finnish–Soviet relationship in general terms as a paragon of reconciliation between former belligerents, or between socialist and capitalist states; he has a far more specific and negative interpretation of these relations in mind. He makes a conceptual leap, therefore, for which he supplies no evidence, by going on to claim that under 'certain conditions' this kind of relationship might spread to other parts of the globe.[11]

Laqueur has a very difference notion of Finland's position to Kekkonen or to most Finns, since he believes that Finlandisation exists at the least as a condition in which a country can no longer exert full sovereignty. This view does relate, however, to some criticisms of Finnish policy which have been voiced by a few figures on the margins of Finnish politics.[12] Laqueur has outlined the 'price' which he believes Finland has paid to avoid the fate of the Baltic Republics. In the field of foreign policy he views Finland's neutrality as compromised by the country's special obligations to the USSR: it cannot oppose any major Soviet foreign policy initiative nor enter any commitments without Soviet approval, and it is expected to render active support for some aspects of Soviet foreign policy. He claims that Finland is expected to have close commercial relations with the Communist bloc. The Finnish army is purported to work under Soviet restrictions. Laqueur accepts that there is no Soviet interference in Finland's internal affairs, but alleges that only political parties, prime ministers, and a president approved by the USSR can enter the government or assume office. He claims that the Finns are expected by this tacit arrangement to exert self-censorship and deny the existence of the whole condition of Finlandisation.[13]

The broad examination of Finland's relations with the Soviet Union which follows provides the material to judge how far those features or consequences of this relationship which are assumed in the description above correspond to reality. It is quite another question whether such features, even if they do reveal some degree of Finlandisation in Finnish–Soviet relations, can be duplicated in other interstate relations. This will depend on the extent to which they are determined by conditions unique to the Finnish case.

THE INTERWAR AND WAR YEARS

For over a hundred years, from 1809 until the Bolshevik revolution in autumn 1917, the Grand Duchy of Finland was the northwesternmost part of the Russian empire. The collapse of the imperial regime in Finland was followed in close succession by the restoration of Finnish autonomy, a declaration of independence by the Finnish parliament on 15 November 1917, and the recognition of the independent Finnish republic by the Bolshevik government on 31 December. Lenin anticipated a socialist seizure of power in Finland and was prepared, therefore, to concede Finnish independence to nullify Finnish bourgeois claims that the Finnish identity and freedoms were under threat from Great Russian chauvinism. He trusted that this move would augment the determination and ability of the Finnish proletariat to conclude decisively the class struggle underway in Finland. It appears that Stalin, as Commissar for Nationalities, expected a reunification of the future Finnish Socialist Republic and the Russian regime within the USSR.[14]

In the event a civil war broke out in Finland, which raged until spring 1918 when Finnish White Guard forces under the former imperial Russian officer General Gustav Mannerheim inflicted defeat with German assistance on Finnish Red contingents partially supplied by the Bolshevik regime. This bloody episode, and an attempt by Mannerheim to fulfil an old Finnish nationalist dream and 'liberate' regions in East Karelia from Soviet rule, confirmed a pro-German orientation in Finnish policy and left a legacy of hostilities and suspicions with the new rulers in the East. Those of White persuasions were to remember the 'War of Liberation' as a struggle against Soviet Bolshevism.[15]

Although after the collapse of German power Finland signed a peace treaty with the USSR at Tartu in October 1920, this was only intended to establish frontiers and did not alter the Finnish Establishment's view of Russia as *perivihollinen*, the 'hereditary enemy'. The interwar years were expended by Finnish politicians in a search for a policy to resolve Finland's basic security dilemma, which was conceived of as a threat to Finnish territorial integrity from the East. The Tartu treaty granted few territorial concessions to the defence of Leningrad, despite the view of the chief Finnish negotiator, J. K. Paasikivi, whose appreciation of *Realpolitik* would be crucial to the successful reappraisal of Finland's policy towards reconciliation with the USSR a quarter of a century later. Although as Prime Minister in 1918 Paasikivi had sought security from Russian pressure through a reliance on Germany, by 1920 he was one of the few Finnish politicians who appreciated the consequences for Finland of the changes of the power balance in Europe in favour of the USSR; he already foresaw the need to accommodate Soviet security needs.

The Soviet Union had lost all the advanced bases of the old imperial Baltic fleet and did not become a party to an agreement in 1921 which confirmed the demilitarisation of the Åland Islands in the Baltic Sea. But for most Finns Soviet insecurities were overshadowed by the Karelian question. They regarded the creation of a Finnish Communist inspired and Soviet sponsored Karelian Workers Commune in East Karelia as an immediate ideological threat. The Soviet government believed that this act and a frontier agreement with Finland had resolved the issue of Karelia, but Finnish eyes remained fixed on East Karelia and on the fate of the Finnish-speaking Ingrians in the Leningrad area in the 1920s and 1930s.

Finnish diplomats in the 1920s sought to counteract the perceived threat on Finland's eastern frontiers through participation in the League of Nations and reliance on the sanctions of this body. They had no sympathy with the idea of an eastern security system constructed by Moscow, although they were induced at a time of more vigorous Soviet diplomacy to sign a non-aggression pact with the USSR in January 1932. But the entry of the Soviet Union into the League in 1934 and the increasingly overt hostility between the USSR and Germany forced a reappraisal of Finnish policy on Finnish statesmen in the mid-1930s. They aimed at a closer identification with the Scandinavian neutrals and a withdrawal from great power politics, although the goal of neutrality became merged later with the possibility of entering some kind of defence alliance in the Nordic region. Involvement in a Nordic bloc could then perhaps be used to enlist Western support.

Finland's professed desire and ability to remain neutral in a European conflict was treated by Soviet spokesmen in the mid-1930s as a delusion if not an outright deception. Influential figures in the USSR connected Finland with German plans for aggression and remained unsatisfied by Finnish statements to the contrary.[16] The Finnish President for much of this decade (March 1931 to March 1937), P. Svinhufvud, was known to hold pro-German sympathies, which in Soviet eyes could be linked to the continuation of a fierce campaign in Finland for the elimination of domestic communism and the toleration of a small but vociferous fascist-inclined party, the People's Patriotic Movement. Against the background of these unpromising signs in Finland, in 1938 Soviet diplomats initiated negotiations with Finland to secure the western approaches to Leningrad. Both Finland's strategic position and its Nordic connections inclined Soviet negotiators still to view Finland in a separate category to the Baltic states. But the Finns turned down offers for a military assistance pact with the USSR and for the further provision of Soviet military assistance if necessary. They did not share Soviet fears about the likelihood of German aggression via Finland, and so were unwilling to cede a defence base to the USSR in the Gulf of Finland and to be drawn into a Soviet security system.

The breakdown of the Soviet–Finnish talks in 1938 was crucial, since Soviet demands were to be renewed and enlarged next autumn after the USSR had been fortified by the Nazi–Soviet pact in August 1939. This non-aggression pact included a secret protocol which now placed Finland alongside Latvia and Estonia in the Soviet sphere of interest. Even at this stage it is unclear whether Stalin entertained designs on Finnish independence. But during discussions in Moscow in November, Finland's special envoy, J. K. Paasikivi once again, was instructed by the Finnish government to reject Soviet demands for the establishment of bases in the Gulf of Finland and the readjustment of the frontier on the Karelian isthmus in exchange for territory in Soviet Karelia. Upon the pretext of a border incident the Red Army subsequently attacked Finland on 30 November 1939.

Stalin may have been persuaded to resort to military force by the hard-line faction led by A. Zhdanov, the Party leader in Leningrad. If Zhdanov expected the Finnish working class to greet the Red Army as liberators his hopes were dashed, but the ideological groundwork for this was carried out by the creation of a puppet government under the exiled Finnish Communist O. W. Kuusinen in the border town of Terijoki. Once the 'Terijoki government' concluded terms with the USSR Finnish sovereignty was clearly at stake in the 'Winter War'. But the 'People's Republic of Finland' was dispensable, since unexpectedly successful Finnish military resistance, and the fact that Finland was not of primary strategic significance, persuaded Soviet leaders to conclude a peace treaty with the Finnish state in March 1940. After over three months of unassisted fighting Finland lost the Karelian isthmus, the entire province of Viipuri, and border territory to the north. The Hanko peninsula also had to be leased for thirty years for the USSR, although Finland received back the Arctic territory of Petsamo.

The shock of the Winter War, which left 25 000 Finnish dead, had the effect of polarising Finnish attitudes. Many Finns, especially those from the Karelian regions and on the Right, could not conceive of the peace conditions as permanent. The Finnish government did little to discourage the bitter anti-Soviet mood, which was fuelled in August 1940 by the incorporation of Estonia, Latvia and Lithuania into the USSR and by the harsh conditions imposed on the subjects in the new Soviet republics. In this atmosphere a closer association with Germany could be regarded even by prominent Finnish figures as a precondition to the possible recovery of the lost Finnish territories. In August 1940 Finnish leaders concluded a secret transit agreement with the Germans allowing the passage of German troops through Finland from German Baltic ports to northern Norway. By December Hitler's plans against the USSR required Finnish participation, which the Finnish military command may have surmised over the next few months, although Finnish leaders were neither committed to nor informed of these plans until shortly before the German invasion of the Soviet Union in June 1941. The Finns found a *casus belli* in an ill-timed Soviet bombing raid and on 26 June declared war on the USSR as a co-belligerent of Germany.

The Finns did not regard themselves as allies of Nazi Germany but as participants in a defensive war to regain their former frontiers, which were reached by the end of August. This view is expressed in the Finnish term for the war – the 'Continuation War'. The degree to which Finnish statesmen felt committed to the overall German objective of the military destruction of the Soviet state remains an open question. But it is undeniable that Finnish nationalist ideals lured the Finnish army further into East Karelia than defensive lines warranted. Once again the hankering for a 'Greater Karelia' found expression during conflict with the Soviet regime, although the Finnish army was not universally acclaimed as a liberating force by the remaining inhabitants in the occupied regions beyond Finland's eastern frontiers. Significantly, however, Mannerheim stopped short of advancing on Leningrad, and the front was stabilised.

Eventually some 150 000 German troops were deployed in Finland. But it was not until June 1944, confronted with a major Soviet offensive on the Karelian isthmus, that Mannerheim urged the Finnish government to commit Finland to a political treaty with Germany to ensure further supplies of troops and *matériel*. In the event all that Germany achieved was an informal personal assurance from the Finnish president, Risto Ryti, that Finland would not conclude a separate peace. In August when Mannerheim, who was directing the Finnish defence forces, was persuaded to become head of state to lead Finland out of war he repudiated this agreement. This paved the way for an armistice with the USSR which preserved Finnish independence and provided the conditions for a radical reorientation of Finland's post-war security policy outlook.

THE FINNISH POLITICAL SYSTEM

When the Finnish–Soviet armistice was signed in September 1944 Finland retained her political institutions intact, unlike other eastern European countries after the Second World War. Finnish leaders were obliged to press for some modifications in the arrangement of political forces under the terms of the armistice, and they witnessed a general radicalisation in Finnish politics, but for nearly twelve years the conservative heads of the Finnish state manipulated the powers of their office and relied on strong constitutional safeguards to control and direct these changes. In this fashion Finland's constitutional democracy survived the years of political flux and uncertainty after the war unimpaired.

By the Finnish constitution of 1919 the president both directs foreign policy and acts as commander-in-chief of the armed forces. He also appoints and dismisses governments, although these need to enjoy the confidence of the two hundred member Finnish parliament. This is a unicameral legislative organ, to which ministers of the government are responsible, and which contains representatives from numerous parties. The constitution lays down that the president resolves matters of war and peace with the consent of parliament. But the primary importance of the president in determining foreign policy has permitted him to exercise his power in this field, for example in the late 1940s, even with minority backing in parliament. Moreover, the significance accorded to foreign policy in post-war Finnish politics has enhanced the president's role in general. These features of the president's office act to modify Finland's parliamentary system.[17]

Constitutionally the Finnish president should be elected by the people via an electoral college every six years, although since the 1944 armistice the Finnish parliament has enacted legislation twice to allow this election to take place in parliament – 1946 and 1974.

Finnish governments, which have usually been formed from a coalition of parties, have lasted in office for an average of only a year. The president is expected to provide a degree of continuity in policy, in particular in foreign policy, but many Finnish politicians have served in ministerial capacities for long periods and have ensured a degree of continuity in government.[18]

After hostilities with the Soviet Union ended in 1944 the aristocratic Marshal Mannerheim remained president of the Finnish republic, although his role became increasingly symbolic. He was succeeded by the veteran politician and diplomat J. K. Paasikivi, in March 1946. Paasikivi, who since November 1944 had served already twice as Prime Minister under Mannerheim, held the office of president for a full decade. Paasikivi was an old Conservative whose long experience, nevertheless, gave him the judgement to recognise that the new constellation of power in the post-war world, and in particular the influence of the USSR, compelled Finland to make limited but substantial adjustments in policy. But the rightward swing in Finland domestically after 1948 indicated that he was not committed in the longer term to the radicalisation of Finnish politics and society of the immediate post-war years. In this he differed to Urho Kekkonen, who as Minister of Justice after the war and as the head of five governments in the early and mid-1950s, was closely associated with the implementation of Paasikivi's *Realpolitik*.

Kekkonen was a bourgeois politician of the Centre (the Agrarian Union), but he believed that a process of domestic radicalisation in Finland was desirable as a necessary precondition of post-war cooperation with the USSR. Kekkonen succeeded the aged Paasikivi in March 1956, and his tenure lasted for a remarkable twenty-five years. In the 1960s Kekkonen's foreign policy expertise gradually earned him the support of all the major political parties in Finland, although he was also criticised for exploiting his role as guardian of the nation's foreign policy to increase his own power and authority to an excessive degree. In January 1982, after Kekkonen had retired on grounds of ill-health, the Social Democrat Mauno Koivisto was elected as Finland's first left-wing president.

After the war the Finnish political left divided into the Social Democractic Party (SDP), which purged itself and moved to the Right, and an umbrella organisation, the People's Democratic League (SKDL), which was used as a parliamentary front by the Finnish Communist Party (SKP). Since the Finnish civil war the SDP had provided a focus for those in Finland seeking a peaceful and constitutionalist path to socialism, but it had taken a strong stand against the USSR in Finnish governments preceding the Winter War and during the war years. By the late 1940s the SDP was controlled by men whose experience of wartime national solidarity had been translated into an uncompromising anti-Communism and hostility to the Soviet Union. This stand was dropped finally only in the mid-1960s. The Finnish Communist Party was legalised in 1944; it had succumbed to nationalist and anti-Communist fervour in 1930. But from the first post-war election the Finnish Communists were committed to a popular front strategy rather than a revolutionary programme. This included a determination to eliminate all vestiges of 'fascism' from Finland.

Right-wing authoritarianism had gained little popular support in Finland since the early 1930s, although the People's Patriotic Movement (IKL) which embraced this outlook had participated in the Finnish government of January 1941 to March 1943. Such fascist-inclined parties and organisations were banned in Finland by the 1944 armistice. Traditional and conservative Finnish values continued to be championed by the National Coalition (or Conservative) Party. While the latter has been regarded as a party of large capital with international links, the Agrarian Party (the Centre Party after 1965), traditionally a representative of Finnish agricultural interests, has remained very much an indigenous Finnish product. The flexibility of the Agrarians and their position in the political centre have enabled them to participate in most of the post-war ruling coalitions, and often to determine their composition. It was this bourgeois party which, for reasons to be explored later, Soviet leaders eventually came to rely on most heavily among the political forces of post-war Finland.

1 The Reconstruction of Post-war Finnish–Soviet Security Relations 1944–56

FROM ARMISTICE TO PEACE TREATY 1944–7

The fundamental premise of Finnish security policy since the wars of 1941–4 has been that Soviet security interests in the north-west can be reconciled with the existence of an independent sovereign Finnish state. The issue of the political independence of Finland after the Second World War was brought up by the Western Allies already during the Teheran summit conference in December 1943. The views expressed at Teheran showed that the Allies had not considered Finland after summer 1941 simply as an Axis state. The United States in fact had not declared war on Finland. At the conference Stalin, by offering assurances that Finnish independence would be preserved in the final settlement between Allied and Axis powers, opened the door for a conditional negotiated peace between Finland and the Soviet Union. Under pressure in other quarters the Western powers approved the main features of the conditions for peace with Finland which Stalin presented at Teheran. This mutual understanding allowed Finland to remain largely outside the territorial controversies in Europe which were already discernible at the Yalta conference in February 1945, and which were to fuel the Cold War hostilities of the powers after the war.

At Yalta the Soviet Union demanded explicitly that the states on the Soviet western borders, according to the post-war settlement, should act in cooperation with the USSR against any possible future German aggression. There is some evidence that as early as April 1945, even before the defeat of Germany and Japan, Stalin had concluded that another war was only a matter of time. Nevertheless, earlier during the course of the war the United States had accepted the argument that the Soviet Union would require governments on its

12

western frontier which were prepared to maintain good relations with the Eastern great power. Thus, upon the conclusion of the war the United States representative in Finland told the Finnish Foreign Minister that it was 'especially important that Finland develop good neighbourly relations with the Soviet Union'.[1] Differences in the approaches of the Western Allies and the USSR to the security of east Europe surfaced at Yalta, however, although Finland remained a side-issue, and Soviet leaders did not feel compelled to reconsider their security priorities in the north-west as outlined at Teheran.

The timing of the conclusion of the 1944 Finnish–Soviet armistice depended on certain military and strategic considerations. After the loss of the town of Viipuri Finnish resistance to the Red Army's drive in Karelia stiffened and it became evident that the Soviet troops employed in Karelia were required elsewhere; the race to Berlin was already underway. Finnish military resistance in the closing months of hostilities with the Soviet Union was, therefore, no negligible factor. At least until these months, despite Stalin's assurances at Teheran, the forward plans of the Red Army may have included the occupation of part of Finland for the minimal need to guarantee that future war reparations would be discharged.[2]

The military priorities determining Soviet attitudes towards Finland in 1944 were stressed by United States ambassador Hamilton in answer to a State Department enquiry about Finland. This report provides not only an astute contemporary analysis of Finland's particular position, but also indicates the official American understanding of the strategic priorities operative in Soviet policy towards Finland. Hamilton observed that Stalin's long-term strategic objectives demanded full Soviet concentration on crushing the German armies and reaching Berlin before the other Allies. Any occupation of Finland would have been a military diversion outside the long-range plans drawn up by Stalin, since Finland was not on the main military route to Berlin. In Hamilton's opinion the Soviet decision not to attempt to occupy Finland was also influenced, although to a lesser extent, by Soviet respect for the Finns as fighters, as demonstrated in particular during the Winter War. He believed in addition that a Soviet occupation would have weakened the Finnish will to produce war reparations. Soviet leaders already understood in 1944 the future need for industrial equipment from abroad for the post-war reconstruction of Soviet industry.[3]

The presence of German troops on Finnish soil crucially influenced the armistice negotiations in 1944. Some years earlier, soon after the

German attack on the Soviet Union, Hitler had pressed the Finns to participate in the siege of Leningrad and the German general Jodl had tried to persuade Marshal Mannerheim to use Finnish troops in an attack on Leningrad. Mannerheim refused to comply despite Leningrad's clear military vulnerability to such an attack. Similarly, Mannerheim refrained from attacking the Archangel–Murmansk railway line, the Allied supply line to the USSR. These examples of restraint illustrated the Finnish contention that the Finnish objectives in the 1941–4 Continuation War were not inseparably allied with those of the German war effort. The Soviet negotiators considered it possible, therefore, to demand that the Finns break off relations with Germany and expel German troops from Finnish territory as a precondition of the armistice with Finland. A similar precondition had been raised on the Soviet side already earlier that year when a secret meeting had been arranged in Stockholm to ascertain the terms under which negotiations could be initiated. Since the Finnish–Soviet armistice was concluded in September 1944, eight months before the war ended in Europe, the Finnish preparedness to drive German troops from Finnish soil meant that Soviet troops formerly tied down in the Karelian region could be redirected to Central Europe where the core security interests of the Soviet Union lay.

The terms of the 1944 armistice resolved the problems of local security which Soviet leaders had perceived in the direction of Finland. The issue of the defence of Leningrad had involved two basic security considerations: the defensive zone of the Karelian isthmus, and the Finnish coast which formed part of the narrow approach to the city. By confirming the border which had been drawn between Finland and the Soviet Union by the 1940 Moscow Treaty, the 1944 armistice transferred the entire Karelian isthmus to the USSR. In addition, the Petsamo region, which had provided Finland with an Arctic Sea outlet, was relinquished to the Soviet Union, the provisions of the 1940 treaty concerning the demilitarisation of the Åland Islands in the Baltic Sea (*Ahvenanmaa*) were reaffirmed, and the Porkkala peninsula on the southern coast of Finland was leased to the USSR as a naval base for a period of fifty years. The latter secured the approaches to Leningrad but it cast a shadow over Finnish independence for many years, and therefore the Soviet security thinking behind the demand for Porkkala deserves close attention.

In the armistice negotiations of September 1944 the former Finnish Foreign Minister Carl Enckell told the Soviet delegation that the

Finnish authorities had been convinced that 'the course of the war had entirely changed the views about the need to protect the Soviet Union from the west'. In other words, he argued, through its victory the USSR 'had eliminated the danger of a new attack from the west'. Enckell told Soviet Foreign Minister Molotov bluntly that Finnish public opinion would not understand that the demand for Porkkala merely reflected military concerns and that there was a danger that the Finnish public would see 'a political requirement in this demand, which will make Finland's existence as an independent state much more difficult'. He reminded Molotov that when the issues of Porkkala had been raised in October 1939 the Finns had expressed their concern over the proximity of Porkkala to Helsinki and had pointed out that other means existed to safeguard access to Leningrad through the Gulf of Finland.[4] In reply Molotov stated that 'we still place great significance on the fact that Leningrad has to be protected from a visit by uninvited German guests', and continued:

> The narrowest point of the Gulf of Finland is between Porkkala and Naissaari, and therefore this is just the point that can be put to best use as a forward zone for the protection of Leningrad from danger which threatens from the sea . . . the question of the security of the whole of the Soviet Union and above all of Leningrad forces us to bring forward the issue of establishing a naval base at Porkkala . . . Only the security perspectives of Leningrad dictate this demand, and we have no other intentions.[5]

Enckell queried whether the Soviet government would be satisfied instead with the Hanko peninsula in the extreme south-west of Finland. But Molotov revealed the pressures behind him by noting curtly that the Soviet military and naval authorities required Porkkala.[6] In fact Molotov informed British diplomatic sources that he had not intended to demand Porkkala but had been unable to divert the persistent demands of the Soviet general staff.[7]

Military pressures within the USSR may well have determined the fate of the Petsamo region also, which in Molotov's words had been used 'as a springboard for attack on the Soviet Union'. Petsamo, he argued, was important for the security of the Murmansk line and for the unexplained need for the USSR 'to have a joint border with Norway'.[8] The possession of Petsamo would reduce the opportunities for exploiting Finland as a military bridgehead against the Soviet Union. With the development of the Murmansk naval base this territory would become still more strategically significant for the USSR.

The Finnish government hoped for some amelioration of the harsh territorial provisions of the armistice agreement before the conclusion of the final peace treaty. These hopes included the detachment of the Helsinki–Karjaa railway line which went through Porkkala from the area of the lease and a Soviet concession of the Finnish right to use the Saimaa canal region of Jäniskoski against territorial compensation in the north of Finland. For strategic reasons Soviet military leaders were unprepared to relinquish the Saimaa canal, although already in 1945 Western diplomats had heard of a possibility of allowing the Finns its use through an arrangement after the peace treaty.[9]

Finnish diplomats were aware of the feelings of the dispossessed Karelian population and of a general expectation that the abandoned area of Karelia would be returned up to the line of Vuoksi. In a moment of pessimism at the end of 1946 the Finnish president Paasikivi remarked to a Western journalist that although the Finnish government had 'full reason to believe that the Soviets will not present us with further demands . . . any peace with the Soviet Union cannot be really durable if it takes land from Finland which the Finns have settled for a thousand years'.[10] Paasikivi hoped to show the Soviet government the significance of Karelia to Finland by referring to economic facts, and to argue that it would also be in the Soviet interest to improve Finland's economic base out of regard for future Finnish–Soviet trade.[11]

In April 1946 a Finnish government delegation, which went to Moscow to discover whether concessions could be agreed to by the Russians before the formal peace treaty conference, was informed by Stalin that none of the territorial provisions of 1944 could be revised. The Soviet Deputy Foreign Minister, Vyshinski, warned both the Finnish Prime Minister and Foreign Minister that if the Finns were to attempt to side with other states against the USSR in the treaty negotiations 'they would certainly see what will happen to them'.[12] As a consequence, the Finns suppressed their hopes for revisions of the provisions concerning Porkkala and Karelia at the Paris peace conference.

At the peace conference limitations on the size and scope of the Finnish defence forces were demanded by the British but opposed by the Soviet delegation. This appeared to reflect British suspicions at the time that Finland, together with the Balkan states, would sooner or later automatically augment the Soviet defence potential.[13] In fact the USSR wished to impose reciprocal controls, both quantitative and qualitative on Italy's armaments. The Finnish defence forces were eventually permitted an army limited to 34 400 men, a navy with a maximum tonnage of 10 000 tons, and a air force of no more than sixty aircraft (see Articles 13–18 in Appendix 1).

The Paris peace treaty renewed a provision already contained in the 1940 peace treaty which obliged the parties 'to refrain from any attack upon the other and to make no alliance and to participate in no coalition directed against either of the contracting parties'. It also complemented the 1940 treaty through an article intended to prevent the participation of Finland in the rearmament of Germany and Japan and the development of their military industries. The treaty was signed on 10 February 1947 although it did not come into force until 15 September 1947 when it was ratified by the USSR and Britain.

The conclusion of the armistice in 1944 had forced a radical reappraisal of Finland's security policy upon her political leaders. The Finnish Minister of Justice, Urho Kekkonen, was among the first to espouse a policy of 'national realism'. In a speech broadcast on Armistice Day he argued that 'the Soviet Union's own interests are related to the independence of Finland', and underlined that 'mutual enduring reconciliation' between the former belligerents could only be achieved through the creation of 'a new mental attitude in relations between our nations'. In practice this meant that Finland's independence could only be ensured through 'winning (Soviet) confidence and the creation of good-neighbourliness'.[14] Prime Minister Paasikivi upheld Kekkonen's views when he spoke a couple of months later on Finnish Independence Day. When he had been the Finnish minister to the USSR in 1940–1 his reading of power politics had led him to the view that Finland's interests required her to rely on Germany as the strongest European power. But by 1944 Paasikivi recognised that these basic national interests compelled Finnish leaders to conduct their country's foreign policy in such a fashion that it would never again run against the Soviet Union. To gain Soviet confidence in this basic premise of post-war Finnish foreign policy Paasikivi declared that 'the term "hereditary enemy" has to be forgotten once and for all'.[15]

Paasikivi believed that the Soviet policy toward Finland remained as before Finnish–Soviet hostilities, 'a defensive policy aimed at the security of the state'. Paasikivi recalled asking Stalin and Molotov during negotiations in autumn 1939 why they feared that Finland would attack the Soviet Union. In Paasikivi's words, Stalin answered 'we do not fear Finland, Finland is an altogether too small state to attack the Soviet Union, but some great power could use Finland against the Soviet Union'. In retrospect Paasikivi considered Finland's decision not to accept the Soviet conditions for territorial exchanges in 1939, based on 'legitimate security concerns', to have been a political mistake, since Soviet leaders then felt compelled to use other means to arrange 'realistic guarantees that Finland would not be taken advantage of by any great power'. For Paasikivi the lesson to be learnt from history was that the Soviet Union had to be able to trust that Finland 'will never again side with the enemies of the Soviet Union'.[16]

The conclusion of the armistice did not automatically dispel Soviet suspicions about Finnish intentions. The chairman of the Allied Control Commission, which had been set up in Finland to ensure the execution of the armistice terms, Colonel-General Zhdanov, reacted openly and unequivocally to the news that arms caches had been laid down in Finland in autumn 1944 and spring 1945. He repeated that the USSR did not fear Finland militarily, but he did not consider this the issue. He told Paasikivi:

> We Russians consider that the arms caches show that there are people in Finland, within army circles as well as outside them, who would be ready to rise to fight against the Soviet Union if, for example, a situation were to arise which would break into a dispute with the Western states.[17]

The officers implicated were prosecuted by the Finnish authorities for preparing illegal armed activity, although the charges originally levelled against a former chief of the Finnish general staff, General A. Airo, were eventually dropped.

The views expressed by Captain Haaksalo, the adjutant to the commander of the Finnish defence forces, at the beginning of 1948, which may well have reflected broader feelings among Finnish military circles, seem to lend credence to Zhdanov's beliefs. From a Western diplomatic report of discussions with Haaksalo, on the outbreak of a war between the great powers the Finnish army would initially have to fight on the Soviet side, but it would wait until the Western states were to attack the Soviet Union by way of Murmansk and then join this attack. Finland would attempt to defend its territorial integrity for as long as possible, but, in an evident allusion to Finnish resistance, Haaksalo added ominously: 'if long trains were to arrive in Finland from the Soviet Union, it would be clear that they would not return empty'.[18]

Paasikivi was aware already in 1946 that there were rumours current about the possibility of war between the Western states and the Soviet Union. Such a war, he explained at a news conference, 'would be a grave misfortune for us since we can judge well enough what measures the Soviet Union would begin against Finland to safeguard its position in this quarter'.[19] In these circumstances it appeared to be in the Finnish as well as the Soviet interest to fix some kind of security arrangement between the two neighbouring countries, which already in peacetime would remove Soviet doubts about Finland's likely behaviour in time of crisis or hostilities in the Nordic region.

THE 1948 FINNISH–SOVIET TREATY OF FRIENDSHIP, COOPERATION AND MUTUAL ASSISTANCE

Origins

A proposal for a joint Finnish–Soviet defence agreement to provide against a possible attack by Germany had been made by the Soviet government in April 1938. But the talks had broken down, and when the idea of a defence alliance had been broached the following autumn the Finnish government had been unwilling to pursue the matter further. In an interview in Feburary 1947 Paasikivi disclosed that during those earlier discussions he had assured Stalin that the Finns would not permit an attack on the USSR through Finnish territory. In the changed post-war conditions Paasikivi reaffirmed: 'were someone in the future to attempt an attack on the Soviet Union through Finland, we must fight, together with the Soviet Union against the attacker as much and for as long as we can'.[20] Finland 'will defend itself by every means', he predicted, 'however if its strength should not suffice for this help would have to be sought from the Soviet Union'.[21]

Paasikivi's declaration was undoubtedly a response to earlier Soviet enquiries. A few months after the armistice with Finland Zhdanov had asked President Mannerheim his views about the conclusion of a cooperation agreement similar to the one concluded with Czechoslovakia in 1943, and Zhdanov had taken up the matter with Prime Minister Paasikivi in May 1945.[22] But the initiative for the creation of some kind of Finnish–Soviet security pact was not taken unilaterally by Zhdanov. In discussions with Zhdanov in winter 1944–5 Mannerheim had observed that since there existed joint Finnish and Soviet security interests in the Gulf of Finland this created opportunities for broader cooperation in security policy. The former White general even drew up a draft treaty in summer 1945.[23] Mannerheim's initiative aroused interest in Moscow, and it may have been an important factor encouraging early Soviet diplomatic recognition of Finland, since it dampened down Soviet suspicions by indicating that at the highest level a real change was taking place in Finland's security policy thinking. But an attempt to conclude such a treaty on security issues before the conclusion of Finland's peace treaty would have created political and legal problems.

In spite of Mannerheim's previous initiative Paasikivi gave the impression to Western diplomats that his statement in 1947 was intended to act as a substitute for the creation of a formal security arrangement with the USSR.[24] On the Soviet side, however, Paasikivi's words were taken to indicate a willingness to assume firmer commitments. In November 1947 the Soviet government brought up the subject of a military treaty in discussions between Molotov and the Finnish Prime Minister Pekkala, and Molotov extracted a promise from Pekkala on behalf of the Finnish government for the conclusion of some kind of military treaty intended to promote 'still closer cooperation with the Soviet Union'.[25] Pekkala acted without the authority of the Finnish president, but his promise raised Soviet expectations, and in mid-February 1948 the new Soviet ambassador in Helsinki, General Savonenkov, suggested to Foreign Minister Enckell that the Finns should publicly take the initiative for a Finnish–Soviet security arrangement. A Finnish initiative would be less likely to create tension in Scandinavia and affect the security policy choices of the Scandinavian countries in a fashion adverse to Soviet interests.

Under growing Soviet pressure Enckell resorted to the argument that Finnish public opinion had not yet matured sufficiently for the conclusion of a military treaty with the USSR. By 18 February he viewed the situation as one of 'extreme gravity', since he believed 'Finland was now faced with a choice of accepting a treaty which, in time of war, would put the Soviet army on the country's western frontiers, or of refusing a treaty and being occupied by [the] Soviets in time of peace'.[26] The speaker of the Finnish parliament, K. A. Fagerholm, judged it to be very difficult for Finland to prevent a 'defence friendship' pact with the USSR in view of the pressure which the Soviet leaders could apply on Finland in connection with reparations deliveries and the interpretation of the peace treaty.[27]

Finnish anxieties were raised to a new pitch by the personal intervention of Stalin. On 22 February Stalin sent Paasikivi a letter containing the framework for a Soviet–Finnish mutual assistance treaty, 'which would be similar to the treaties between Hungary and the Soviet Union and Romania and the Soviet Union'. Stalin proposed such a treaty 'against a possible attack by Germany', and as a means 'to create the conditions for a fundamental improvement in relations between our countries for the purposes of peace and the strengthening of security'.[28]

Paasikivi's immediate impression on receiving Stalin's letter was said to have been that the Russians planned to bring Finland under their military control.[29] Mannerheim also reacted very pessimistically. He considered any decision to negotiate the Finnish–Soviet treaty 'merely the beginning of the end', since although 'the Finns might be able to obtain some surface concessions . . . the Soviet Union would obtain everything it wants and use the treaty plan . . . [as a] wedge to take over the country'.[30] In this context Mannerheim claimed that Soviet forces had been strengthened in the Viipuri region and at Porkkala. In a cabinet session Paasikivi brought forward legal objections to an immediate conclusion of a military treaty with the USSR. He presented these as a diplomatic rearguard action to create a tactical delay. The pessimism with which he and Mannerheim greeted Stalin's proposal compared with their approval in principle of such a treaty in 1945–6 should be understood in terms of the radical change in the international context. By the end of 1947 the wartime alliance between the West and the Soviet Union, which had still influenced Finland's peace treaty negotiations, had disintegrated, and Finland was left to fend for herself in the harsh division between the great powers.

The military provisions

Paasikivi's fears about the results of negotiating a mutual assistance treaty with the USSR proved to be unfounded. The causes for Soviet leniency over the negotiation table with the Finns will be assessed in the context of Nordic regional conditions. The present intention is to describe the initial reception of the 1948 Treaty of Friendship, Cooperation and Mutual Assistance (FCMA), and outline how the military provisions of the treaty, which have been the cornerstone of post-war Finnish–Soviet security relations, were officially interpreted.

Stalin described the treaty with Finland effusively as 'a great turning point for trust and friendship between our countries', although he recognised that attitudes of distrust which still existed could not be removed overnight.[31] A *Pravda* editorial argued that the provisions of the treaty proved false claims that the USSR had been trying 'to obtain military bases from Finnish territory' or that the treaty would oblige Finnish troops to be sent outside the borders of Finland.[32] Molotov, the principal Soviet negotiator of the treaty, merely remarked that the treaty was 'aimed at a repetition of German aggression'.[33]

A Soviet writer later recognised that in 1948 'in some more pessimistically minded circles [in Finland] the Treaty of Friendship aroused doubt and uncertainty', since they feared that 'in the future the treaty would lead to a change in the foreign policy course of Finland, to compel it to join the "Eastern bloc"'.[34] The Finnish Social Democrat organ, for example, predicted that the general significance of the treaty 'independent of an interpretation of its individual articles', would be 'a change in our foreign policy position', since it may fix Finland 'into belonging to a determined power group' in the post-war world.[35] But Foreign Minister Enckell emphasised the distinction between the security commitments of the Finnish FCMA-Treaty and those of the other FCMA-treaties the Soviet Union had concluded in East Europe, a distinction which had resulted from Finland's 'particular geographical position'.[36] In his view Finland was unlikely to fall into a cohesive great power bloc after signing the 1948 treaty as the Social Democrats feared, and as would probably have taken place had the Hungarian or Romanian treaty models actually been used as the basis of the Finnish treaty.

A speech broadcast by President Paasikivi on 4 April 1948 constitutes the essence of the Finnish understanding of the military articles of the 1948 treaty and still defines the framework within which Finnish security policy operates. These articles read as follows:

Article 1
In the eventuality of Finland or the Soviet Union through Finland,

becoming the object of an armed attack by Germany or any state allied with the latter, Finland will, true to its obligations as an independent state, fight to repel the attack. Finland will in such cases use all of its available forces for defending its territorial integrity by land, sea and air, and will do so within the frontiers of Finland in accordance with obligations defined in the present treaty and, if necessary, with the assistance of, or jointly with, the Soviet Union.

In the cases aforementioned the Soviet Union will give Finland the help required, the giving of which will be subject to mutual agreement between the Contracting Parties.

Article 2

The High Contracting Parties shall confer with each other if it is established that the threat of an armed attack as described in Article 1 is present.

In addition to these articles the treaty parties confirmed in Article 4 the pledge contained in Article 3 of the Paris Peace Treaty 'not to conclude any alliance or join any coalition directed against' the other party.

Paasikivi considered the first part of Article 1 merely to describe the action Finland would undertake in any event 'true to its obligations as an independent state'. 'If our country or the Soviet Union through our territory were to become the object of an armed attack by Germany or its allies', he explained in reference to this article, 'we will defend our territorial integrity to the extent that we are able'. But since Finland would act in this manner anyway, Paasikivi found if difficult to understand 'how the proclamation of the matter . . . would bring about a change in the position of our country'. Paasikivi described the function of resisting an attack on the Soviet Union through Finland as 'in the first place the business of us Finns and only in the second place that of the Soviet Union'. It was for this reason, in his opinion, that the treaty referred to Soviet assistance only arising 'if necessary'. He identified three stages in the process leading to consultations: initially the existence of a situation demanding consultations is established, then consultations follow, which decide when the measures provided for in Article 1 are to commence. Paasikivi underlined that the object of consultations was strictly defined by the conditions set forth in Article 1, unlike the

Romanian, Hungarian and Bulgarian FCMA-type treaties, in which the consultations obligation is of a different kind and is extended to concern all important international issues. The East European treaties also stipulated joint action to prevent a future renewed threat from Germany, and military cooperation in the event of attack, which created far wider responsibilities for the treaty parties than did the Finnish–Soviet FCMA-Treaty.

Paasikivi viewed the provisions of Article 2 of the 1948 treaty as a natural outgrowth of the circumstances described in Article 1. He believed that looked at realistically it was 'inconceivable that the Soviet Union would sit with arms crossed when the existence of a threat of attack directed at Finnish territory is established'. In such an event Finland naturally would confer with the USSR on the means to repel the attack. Paasikivi defined the word 'established' as 'an expression of mutual will'. He observed that the provision of Soviet assistance, if required and 'subject to mutual agreement', could be understood to mean separate Finnish–Soviet joint discussions to decide the form in which and under what conditions the assistance would be given to Finland.[37] Finally, although he did not spell this out, Paasikivi was aware that the treaty offers alternatives, since the USSR may either 'assist' Finland in its military operations or Finland may defend itself 'jointly with' the Soviet Union.

The Constitutional Committee of the Finnish parliament addressed the question of how to determine when Finland's forces would be inadequate to repel the attack described in Article 1. The committee laid down that the need for Soviet assistance 'has to be confirmed by both states'. This act of 'confirmation' or 'establishment' was conceived by the Finnish authorities in 1948 as an active step rather than a tacit agreement. The committee confirmed Paasikivi's view that the threat of armed attack referred to in Article 2 'has to be established mutually', but added the important point that 'there are no obligations defined in the treaty intended to prepare for military activity in our country in time of peace other than the obligation to begin consultations in accordance with this article'. Consultations could certainly take place in peacetime, although they would presume that a threatened attack was imminent, but any military recommendations arising from such consultations could only be implemented at a later stage once hostilities had begun. The specialists on the committee determined that detailed provisions concerning the rights of foreign troops on Finnish territory could only be prescribed with parliamentary approval.[38]

In the Soviet theory of international treaties the interpretation of treaties is considered important to establish the true meaning of the treaty within 'the given specific, concrete conditions of international relations'.[39] The authoritative Finnish views outlined above about the circumstances, as defined by the 1948 treaty, leading to consultations with or military assistance from the USSR, have determined the character of Finnish security policy since 1948, but it should not automatically be assumed that these Finnish interpretations have been shared in every respect by Soviet leaders. The presumption of 'mutual understanding' over the provisions of the treaty has prevented the treaty parties from publicly expressing divergent views about them on an official level. President Kekkonen later admitted privately, however, that since 1948 the Soviet authorities had disapproved of the Finnish view that the need for Soviet assistance, as referred to in the FCMA-Treaty, should be jointly established. He called this a 'unilateral interpretation' by the Finns, which 'had not been added to the [treaty] text itself'.[40] This basic divergence in opinion has remained unresolved, notwithstanding Soviet behaviour during the 1961 Note Crisis (see chapter 2) when, as Kekkonen later underlined, the USSR acted as if the need for assistance should be established by both treaty parties.[41]

The Finns have presumed that the independence of their state would not be compromised by possible joint military operations with the USSR. Already in 1948 the Foreign Affairs Committee of the Finnish parliament specified that since the FCMA-Treaty was based on the sovereign equality of the parties, whatever the specific character may be of the preparations for wartime military cooperation which may take place under the terms of the treaty, they 'will be directed by the authority of the Finnish state' and 'the Finnish defence forces shall act in all eventualities in their own country, as their own military units, forming their own leadership, and under their own officers'.[42] These assumptions were to form the basis of Finland's post-war defence policy, and were to enable Finland to maintain an independent defence stand, despite the obligations held jointly with the USSR in the 1948 treaty. This statement was intended primarily to allay fears and suspicions within Finland about the practical consequences of the FCMA-Treaty. The changing fortunes of Finland's wartime collaboration with Germany had given the Finns good cause for doubts about military cooperation with the great powers.

THE GREAT POWERS, FINLAND, AND NORDIC SECURITY DURING THE COLD WAR YEARS 1947–52

The strategic importance of Finland to the dominant Western powers in the post-war world, the United States and Britain, was relatively minor considered purely in bilateral terms. Finland's role was believed to be much more important, however, from the vantage point of the strategic situation in Northern Europe as a whole. The basis premise of Western thought in this respect was that any change in Finland's position would affect the political and military alignment of forces in the Nordic region. A further assumption underpinning Western security thinking was that the Soviet Union was deterred from advancing into the smaller West and North European countries by the individual or collective political and military strength these countries possessed or could muster. Until late 1947, Western political-strategic interests in Scandinavia were largely an extension of wartime involvement in the area. But the British chiefs of staff were pointing out already in summer 1947 that the Nordic area would be of great strategic significance in a war between the USSR and the Western powers.[43] An examination of Soviet attitudes to the north-west frontier region of the USSR reveals that it was just such a regionalisation of the strategic significance of Finland for the Western states in the late 1940s and early 1950s which created the strongest Soviet anxieties about the position of Finland.

The Western powers were aware of Finland's exposed geographical position and were not oblivious to the sensitivity of the Soviet Union to developments in the Nordic region. In autumn 1947 the British Northern European Affairs Division argued that the formation of a Scandinavian bloc 'would have disastrous results for Finland, since the Soviets would unquestionably regard such a bloc as hostile and therefore take steps to speed up the complete absorption of Finland as a countermeasure'.[44] The American State Department considered Finland a special case, and felt that she could be relied on to set definite limits on Soviet influence. In a review of July 1947 the director of the Office of European Affairs told the Secretary of State that Washington should refrain 'from acts in Finland which might reasonably be regarded by the USSR as a challenge to its essential interests'.[45] It appears that Washington made no attempt to induce Finland to become associated with Western security arrangements in the late 1940s. Although the State Department was inclined to support the Finns, even after the conclusion of the Finnish–Soviet treaty in April 1948, care was taken that this was done in an inconspicuous manner to avoid antagonising the Soviet Union.[46] The Finnish ambassador was told in Washington in March 1949 that the 1948 FCMA-Treaty would not affect Finnish–American relations and that the United States fully understood the special position of Finland, which it did not wish to disturb.[47]

The 'Finnish argument' may have had some influence on the American attitude to Swedish neutrality. The Swedes contended that if Sweden were to join the Western alliance system this would lead to changes in favour of the USSR in Finland. In October 1948 the Swedish Ambassador in Washington, Boheman, argued to the acting Secretary of State that a major reason for the mild Soviet policy towards Finland was based on the theory that a harsh policy would frighten Scandinavia into close military cooperation with the West.[48] The American Ambassador in Moscow, General Bedell Smith, had to admit that there might well be some truth in the argument that Moscow's policies towards Finland were moderated by a desire to prevent Sweden from joining the Atlantic Alliance. This also seemed to be implied indirectly in a National Security Council report which observed that the United States should 'refrain from forcing Sweden into an attitude which would be provocative toward the Soviet Union'.[49] Even in August 1949, once Denmark and Norway were formally committed to NATO, the American Ambassador in Moscow (now Kirk) expected 'Moscow's strong desire to keep Sweden neutral would continue to influence the Soviets to proceed cautiously with regard to Finland'.[50]

American policy does not, however, seem to have been strongly influenced by the 'Finnish argument'. The general belief was that if Soviet leaders decided that it would be in their interest to draw Finland further into their orbit, relations with Sweden would not bar them from such an action. The Soviet proposal for a Finnish–Soviet FCMA-Treaty was interpreted in this way. The British Foreign Office considered the Soviet proposal in terms of its likely implications for the security position of the rest of Scandinavia. It was believed that if the USSR were to decide to take control of Finland, pressure would subsequently be directed towards Sweden, which would be still more adverse to British interests.[51]

The issue of Norway provoked even stronger reactions in Britain. In spite of being a signatory to the 1947 peace treaty Britain regarded Finland relatively passively, but Norway had belonged to the area of traditional British military-political interests. Britain had had only chance historical interests in the Baltic Sea. On 8 March the Norwegian Foreign Minister, Lange, informed the American and British ambassadors that he expected the USSR to make a treaty proposal to Norway corresponding to that made to Finland, and he enquired about possible Western assistance if the Soviet Union were to attack Norway upon the rejection of such a proposal. Already on 13 January a British proposal from Foreign Minister Bevin had been left with the American Secretary of State, Marshall, which aimed at extending an anti-Communist league to Scandinavia. In Bevin's opinion, Soviet action in Czechoslovakia, then in Finland, and soon in Norway, would form not only a strategic but also a political threat to the West.[52]

The American reaction to the Soviet treaty proposal to Finland was similar to the British. In Congress President Truman declaimed that 'the tragic death of the Czechoslovak Republic has caused a shock throughout the whole civilised world'. 'Pressure is now directed towards Finland', he continued, 'in a threat to the whole Scandinavian peninsula'.[53] On 1 March Ambassador Bedell Smith demanded immediate guarantees of Western support from the American government. He urged support for Finland 'in anything short of war, in particular by taking the matter up in the United Nations in a very firm way'.[54] On the evening of the same day Secretary of State Marshall requested the American Legation in Finland to enquire from the Finnish government whether it was aware that if it felt 'Finland's national independence and territorial integrity' to be 'under definite threat or menace of armed force', the way would be open for Finland to bring its case before the UN Security Council under Article 35 of the Charter. In this event the United States would support Finland 'within the limits of the Charter of the United Nations.'[53] Truman's declamation and the United Nations issue may best be understood as attempts to use Finland in the American propaganda drive to stiffen the general Truman line, which had little interest in Finland itself. Both Britain and the United States were prepared to proclaim their verbal support for Finland in diplomatic channels, against a perceived Soviet threat, out of consideration for regional or global security concerns.

Towards the end of March 1948 the Finnish Foreign Office enquired whether Roosevelt had abandoned Finland to the Soviet sphere of influence through an agreement at Teheran. Marshall's immediate response took the form of an emphatic denial: the Department had 'no, repeat no, knowledge of any agreement regarding Finland of this kind'.[56] The American State Department repeated its denial of any knowledge of a secret agreement placing Finland in the Soviet orbit in October 1950, and Finnish ministers were told the following month that an understanding with the USSR of this nature would be 'contrary to our [US] basic policy'.[57]

The closer American and British contacts with Finland were, however, the stronger were Soviet suspicions about Finland's security policy priorities. On 5 March 1948 General Savonenkov accused Finland of having been in contact with Western states about the Soviet FCMA-Treaty proposal. The Soviet government, he told Foreign Minister Enckell, 'was aware that Paasikivi and members of the cabinet were seeking contacts for an orientation with the Anglo-Saxons for purposes unfriendly to the Soviets, and the Finns should not expect the Soviets to permit it'.[58] Savonenkov's blunt words about Finland's choices were followed a few days later by an article in *Izvestiya* which, noting that the FCMA-Treaty proposal was formally directed against Germany, claimed that 'Germany is linked to the European "reconstruction" planning of the Americans, and this being so the treaty offered to Finland is directed also against the United States.'[59] Throughout the late 1940s Soviet articles strongly condemned supposed Finnish attempts to extend economic contacts with the United States through joining the 'marshallised Europe'.[60]

As previously observed, however, America tried to be discreet in its material support of Finland after the conclusion of the FCMA-Treaty. While the Office of European Affairs favoured 'modest loans to Finland for sound economic projects' in June 1949, it opposed large loans 'since they would undoubtedly alarm the Russians and might be provocative'.[61] A State Department policy statement in December recognised that if Soviet policy were different 'there is every evidence that the Finns would cooperate fully in plans for European economic recovery', but as things were 'we must consider the effects of any US move on Finnish–Soviet relations'.[62] Nevertheless, the US State Department felt disposed to give Finland support in the United Nations, if asked, 'in resisting any sweeping interpretations or unreasonable proposals' under the FMCA-Treaty with the USSR.[63]

Although the American ambassador in Moscow, Bedell Smith, believed during the negotiations for the Finnish–Soviet FCMA-Treaty that Soviet leaders would pursue a policy of the military integration of Finland in one form or another,[64] the results of the negotiations indicated, in the words of the Finnish Minister of Defence, that Soviet leaders had decided to consider the Finnish issue 'less as an element in the integration of perimeter states than as a factor in the Scandinavian area'. The Finnish minister believed that had the Soviet Union attempted to absorb Finland territorially there would have been immediate repercussions in Norway and Denmark, and that this had been an important factor in affecting Molotov's decision to withdraw the initial Soviet demand for a treaty identical to the treaties of Hungary and Romania and to agree to base the negotiations instead on Finnish counterproposals.[65]

There is in fact no evidence that any Soviet desire existed to absorb Finland through an FCMA-Treaty. Molotov's uncustomary leniency behind the negotiation table, which led to the text of the treaty being written largely by the Finns themselves in the form, as Kekkonen described it in a brave joke to Stalin, of 'a dictate by Paasikivi',[66] was not without explanation. The Foreign Affairs Committee of the Finnish government had deliberately, 'as a diplomatic secret', leaked information to the USSR that any negotiations for a FMCA-Treaty were, from the Finnish view, 'very serious and our demands unconditional'.[67] The pressure Molotov brought to bear on the Finnish delegation may have been affected by advance knowledge about the likely latitude of the Finns in the negotiations. He was aware of possible problems in securing the acceptance of the Finnish parliament for the treaty, and he was apprehensive lest Parliament failed to ratify it in the form eventually agreed upon.

The timing of the FCMA-Treaty negotiations was crucial. The Communist takeover in Czechoslovakia had sent out a wave of suspicion and uncertainty into West Europe and Scandinavia. Soviet leniency towards Finland could act as a reassurance. In discussions with the American ambassador in Moscow, Molotov pointed to the Finnish treaty in May 1948 as 'a convincing example of the lack of aggressiveness in Soviet foreign policy'.[68] The other Scandinavian states were still in ferment over which of the various security options to adopt, and the conclusion of a Finnish–Soviet FCMA-Treaty on the Soviet initiative and after the pattern of the other East European FCMA-treaties would have resulted in a firm anti-Soviet security stand throughout Scandinavia west of Finland. Molotov was too careful a diplomat to neglect the broader implications for the USSR of any local security arrangement with a border state.

The Soviet appraisal of Finland in regional Nordic terms compelled a keen interest in Finland's attitude towards a Scandinavian defence alliance, which was under negotiation in 1948–9. In the Soviet view a neutral Scandinavian defence alliance was a practical impossibility, and for this reason the Scandinavian negotiations were regarded as a bifurcation of plans to establish an Atlantic military alliance. In January 1949 Radio Moscow argued that the military alliances under preparation in the Nordic area meant a threat to the security of Finland, and that American agents were trying to transform Finland into a bridgehead against the Soviet Union. 'These circles', this broadcast alleged, 'use Finland as a tool in attempting to expand their influence in Europe'.[69]

After the failure of the Scandinavian defence alliance negotiations Soviet critics turned against a perceived Atlantic orientation in Finland's policy. Already in December 1948 a Soviet article had condemned attempts 'to scare the Swedes, Norwegians and Danes with the idea that they will not be accepted into the Atlantic conclave unless their military plans take account of the strategical importance of Finland for the USA'. The writer claimed to detect an 'olympic indifference [among] Finland's rulers to plans which would turn the Northern countries into a base of operations for the American expansionists'.[70] The membership of Denmark and Norway in NATO from spring 1949 reinforced the earlier Soviet belief that a neutral Scandinavian alliance was impossible. Swedish neutrality was treated with great suspicion, since Swedish generals ostensibly were insisting 'that Sweden should in good time build military bases which the American armed forces will need in the event of war', and since Swedish leaders had 'bound the country to the enslaving Marshall Plan . . . [and] joined the so-called Council of Europe, which is an auxiliary implement of the North Atlantic treaty.'[71]

Inspired by this set of beliefs Soviet leaders were most unwilling to accept any closer military cooperation between Finland and the other Northern countries. 'The history of Finland's independence', *Pravda* noted in 1951, 'is full of examples of how the "idea of the North" is used in aggressive policy against the Soviet Union.' The Finnish people, the Soviet Party organ asserted, should not be deluded by such 'Northernism'. Since the present Finnish government led by the Social Democrat Fagerholm 'unrestrainedly extolled the so-called "Northern cooperation" ', there was evidence, in the Soviet view, that 'Finnish ruling circles completely approve the adventurist foreign policy which the Scandinavian ruling circles are pursuing at the behest of the American–British warmongers.'[72] This specific attack on the policy of the Finnish government occurred at a time of exacerbated Cold War polemics, when the 'bridgehead' view of Finland's security position was confirmed in Soviet thinking by the former Finnish Communist leader, Soviet theoretician, and eventual member of the Central Committee Presidium, O. W. Kuusinen. Kuusinen proclaimed that 'the American and British imperialists, who are making preparations to launch another world war, would very much like Finland to place her territory at their disposal as a base for attack on the Soviet Union'.[73]

At the turn of the decade President Truman was indeed thinking in terms of reviewing American policy towards Scandinavia, 'looking toward a closer alignment of those countries with the West'. Secretary of State Acheson still believed, however, that 'any efforts in the direction of Finland would be most dangerous to the Finns'.[74] But in the years immediately after the conclusion of the 1948 FCMA-Treaty the unremitting Soviet preoccupation with Western strategic intentions and activities in the Nordic region led to a series of unwarranted claims about Finland becoming enmeshed in such plans. This preoccupation can be illustrated by a number of specific attacks to be found in Soviet articles.

In spring 1949 Finland gave information to the Transport Committee of the Economic Commission for Europe in connection with plans for the establishment of an international road network. In the USSR this was interpreted as an indication that the West, in cooperation with Finland, wanted to improve the strategic roads running to the Soviet border for a possible future conflict. From the Soviet perspective, since 'one of these roads leads to Vyborg [Viipuri], another northward to the Soviet frontier . . . this whole business looks very suspicious, especially in the light of the aims of aggressive NATO'.[75] In the same year much was made of an extensive wolf hunt arranged in the proximity of the Soviet–Norwegian border, which Soviet observers interpreted 'in reality' as 'an expedition that had to investigate and carry out the initial preparations to find a suitable place for a military base'. 'In this way', the Soviet army journal argued, 'the presence of English and American observers is understandable.'[76] In 1950 *Izvestiya* cited a Finnish Communist newspaper which drew attention to the transport of military equipment to Finnmark province and observed that during the last war the Germans had concentrated their equipment in these same places, 'in order to transport it later to Finland and via Finland to troops operating against the Soviet Union'. The paper claimed additionally that 'military preparations in Scandinavian countries are closely connected with military preparations going on in Finland itself'.[77]

The Soviet Union was not particularly vulnerable militarily in the region of Finnmark. In January and February 1949 reports were published on the concentration of Soviet troops at the Finnish border and military exercises held close to this border.[78] The head of the Swedish army reported an increase of Soviet forces in the Salla and Vilno regions, but did not attach any significance to these movements.[79] Soviet military exercises were aimed more probably to influence Norway than Finland, with the possible intention of warning Norway against membership in NATO. Yet Soviet statements continued to indicate a hypersensitivity towards American associations with Finland. 'All kinds of representatives and advisers from NATO are visiting Finland for the umpteenth year', *Izvestiya* bemoaned in 1951.[80] A couple of years later *Pravda* went further afield to disclose that Finnish officers who had fought in the Winter War against the USSR 'are playing a significant role in training American troops for action under arctic conditions'.[81]

The clearest illustration of how Soviet security perceptions in the North in the late 1940s and early 1950s affected Finnish territorial concerns can be found in the interesting but little examined case of the so-called Åland guarantees. The Geneva international treaty of 1921 had resolved that the Åland Islands (Ahvenanmaa) belonged to Finland, although both this treaty and the Finnish–Soviet treaty of 1940 affirmed that the islands were to be demilitarised. In response to an initiative on the part of the islanders a Finnish committee was set up with the intention of clearing up the jurisdictional boundaries of the state and the province, and of renewing the self-government law. At this stage Soviet interest was aroused and in November 1946 the Soviet Ambassador, A. Abramov, told the Finnish Foreign Ministry that the USSR was unable to accept the guarantee clause. By the Soviet interpretation this clause could not be reconciled with the armistice treaty and would limit Finnish sovereignty on the Åland Islands, which would then increase the opportunities of foreign states to interfere in the affairs of the islands.[82] In response to these Soviet claims the Foreign Affairs Committee of parliament suggested withdrawing the clause under dispute.

This episode illustrated the Soviet preoccupation with the means by which the Western powers could project their influence in an area of considerable regional strategic significance to the Soviet Union, the Baltic Sea; in this case under cover of guaranteeing the status of the Åland Islands. The legal relationship of Finnish guarantees with the Finnish–Soviet armistice was peripheral to the main Soviet interest – control of the Baltic Sea.

In August 1948 the Fagerholm Government set up a new committee to prepare the self-government law for the Åland Islands. The old proposal for international guarantees was left out of the subsequent committee report. But according to a new proposal a clause in the old guarantee law of 1922 would be left in force, which had ensured the islands the right of appeal to the Council of the League of Nations. This proposal would have left the islanders at least a symbolic guarantee, although the League of Nations had been dissolved. The Soviet press responded before long by citing a Finnish Communist paper's claims that 'the Scandinavian Defence Committee, which acts under the instructions of American and British experts, has included the Åland Islands in the strategic plans of the Scandinavian military alliance'.[83] A couple of months later *Izvestiya* asserted that during the previous summer representatives of the American armed forces accompanied by Finns had made frequent tours of the islands.[84] For the USSR the reasons for Western interest in the Åland Islands were clear: 'the Åland Archipelago has important strategic significance – it closes the passage to and from the Gulf of Finland'. The Soviet preoccupation once again was with foreign military bases in the North. 'Those seeking naval and air bases near the boundaries of the Soviet Union', it was observed in June 1951, 'do not want to renounce the "Åland card" '.[85]

In summer 1950 the Soviet Union acted more forcibly. The Soviet Ambassador, General Savonenkov, informed the Finnish government that the USSR considered that to leave the clause of the old guarantee law in force would be contrary to both the 1944 armistice and the 1947 peace treaty.[86] He argued that this clause would restrict the full sovereignty of Finland contrary to the peace treaty which emphasised the independence of Finland. In reality the 1947 treaty restricted Finnish sovereignty appreciably more than the obsolete League of Nations clause. The Soviet view was determined by the fact that unlike in the case of the 1947 treaty the USSR had not been a signatory to the Åland Convention in 1921.

Soviet attacks on the self-government bill became more virulent after summer 1950. The bill was described as a continuation of the wartime policies of 'Finnish reaction' aimed at using the Åland Islands 'in the future as a base for an attack on the Soviet Union.'[87] In Stockholm Soviet pressure on Finland over the islands was instead believed to portend future Finnish–Soviet negotiations about changing them into a Soviet military base. Ultimately in June 1951 the chief Finnish parliamentary committee revoked the guarantee law completely under prompting from Prime Minister Kekkonen and Foreign Minister Gartz.

Soviet pressure on Finland to revoke the disputed clause may have had some rational grounds. To have left the clause in force may have been considered dangerous in the event that the United Nations Security Council, dominated by the Western states, were to adopt the functions of the League of Nations Council. Under such circumstances the Western states would have had a good legally vested reason to become involved in the affairs of the Baltic Sea, which may subsequently have been reflected in NATO strategy. Furthermore, the USSR was absent from the Security Council sessions at that time owing to the dispute over the rights of the Formosa China delegate.

One further example of how Soviet views of the Nordic region in the early 1950s acted as a constraint upon Finnish policy-makers was the issue of Finnish membership in the Nordic Council, a body which was established in 1952. The Soviet Union adopted a hostile attitude to the Council on similar grounds to its opposition to the creation of a Scandinavian defence alliance. It argued that the formation of both organisations would be calculated to bolster the political and military unity of the Northern countries under United States' leadership. The NATO member majority in the Council was taken to indicate the dominant policy course of the body.[88] Finland did not join the Council in 1952, and over the next three years Soviet comments about the adverse affects of Finnish participation in the body were unremitting. In September 1955, for instance, *Izvestiya* proclaimed that 'the supporters of the Nordic Council are striving to make all the North European states, including Finland, allies of the West German militarists . . . [united] against their real friends, the Soviet Union and the People's Democracies'.[89] In a statement some days later, Prime Minister Kekkonen argued to a Swedish audience that 'of course the suspicions of the Soviet Union toward the Nordic Council can be shown to be groundless'. But 'because that suspicion is still there, despite the arguments we consider to be convincing, and it influences Soviet policy, we have to take account of it as a reality and act accordingly'.[90]

Kekkonen's argument characterised the cautious, anticipatory approach adopted by Finnish leaders in the first post-war decade in the formulation of policy which had a regional Nordic dimension.

Soviet views about such policy were generally exaggerated rhetorically and often quite misplaced, but for Finland they had to be treated with particular respect so long as uncertainty still existed over the political character of Finnish–Soviet relations. This uncertainty, which gradually abated in the mid-1950s, was a legacy of the period which many Finns recognised as the 'years of danger', 1944–8.

In the years between the armistice and the FCMA-Treaty the Soviet Union failed to pursue a consistent, clearly communicated policy towards Finland. Soviet leaders could not yet commit themselves to trusting the intentions of a neighbour state situated in a strategically sensitive region, which had been a co-belligerent of Nazi Germany, in which exponents of fierce ideological anti-Communism had formerly held political platforms, and in which revanchist sentiments over the lost Karelian territories were still widespread, if not publicly expressed. Finland's expulsion of German troops had been a precondition of any political dialogue with the USSR, and Finland's independence was tolerable to the USSR in a military-strategic sense after this act principally because the Baltic Republics had become part of the USSR and since Sweden was maintaining her neutrality despite Western pressures. The Porkkala base acted as a further guarantee of Soviet strategic interests.

The Nordic region was still peripheral to Stalin's main concerns in central Europe. The issue of Finland could be resolved in due course. In the meantime the priority was to prevent extra-regional Western powers from establishing a strong presence in the Nordic region and Baltic Sea, whether politically or militarily. Despite the explicit anti-German clauses to be found in Finland's peace treaty of 1947, Germany remained weakened and divided and the main Soviet concern in the North at this time was with Britain and the United States. A second Soviet goal was to prevent the Nordic states from combining in an anti-Soviet stand, under the aegis of the Western powers. The ambivalence in Soviet policy towards Finland, if managed carefully, could be used to exert influence over the other Nordic states.

After 1948 the fluid alignments in the North began to take firmer shape. Soviet leaders decided to force through some kind of serious bilateral security arrangement with Finland, which would ensure Soviet security in the north-west border region in the long-term. This reflected a recognition that Communist and socialist political forces within Finland in fact were unlikely in the near future independently to offer more substantial gains to the USSR through gaining sufficient influence to promote a genuine alignment between Finland and the Soviet state (see chapter 6). The 1948 treaty marked the real beginning of an independent, stable Soviet policy towards Finland, albeit one influenced, especially during periods of tension in Europe, by Soviet designs or hopes for the Nordic region as a whole.

SOVIET REGIONAL SECURITY AND THE RETURN OF THE PORKKALA BASE 1955–6

In the decade which followed the signing of the Finnish–Soviet armistice in 1944 the problem of Soviet regional security in the Gulf of Finland and the Baltic Sea changed fundamentally. In 1944 Molotov had stressed the strategic importance of the Porkkala base to close off access to Leningrad through the Gulf of Finland. In the years following the lease of Porkkala it became clear that Soviet control over the Baltic States and therefore over the south coast of the Gulf of Finland was unlikely to change. Technological developments made it possible for the USSR to close off the Gulf of Finland from its southern coast, and consequently the need for a base on both sides of the Gulf, which had arisen before the wars of 1939–44, ceased to exist. Porkkala could have been used not only as a naval base but also as an important military base. Soviet troops from Porkkala could have thrown a defence line across Finnish territory in order to repel a possible invasion from Sweden aimed at the Soviet Union. The Finnish–Soviet FCMA-Treaty provided against just such a contingency, however, so that this secondary function of the Porkkala base became largely redundant.

With the change in the balance of power in the Baltic Sea region since 1944 the problem of the defence of the Baltic Sea lanes had shifted from the Gulf of Finland to the Danish Straits. The military significance of the Åland Islands for control of the Baltic Sea region had also greatly decreased by the mid-1950s, and the Soviet canal network made it possible to transfer naval forces to the Arctic Sea through Soviet territory. All of these factors contributed to a change in Soviet strategic thinking about the importance of bases in the Baltic Sea region, which was reflected in the decision to move the headquarters of the Soviet Baltic fleet from Kronstadt to Kaliningrad-Baltisk in the mid-1950s.

In his memoirs Khrushchev observed that by 1955 there were no longer any military reasons for maintaining the Porkkala base, whereas for political reasons everything spoke in favour of relinquishing the base. The preservation of the base, he recognised:

> could only continue to damage our relations with the Finns. They were afraid the presence of our soldiers on their soil meant that we planned to deprive them of their independence and incorporate their country into the Soviet Union . . . It was high time to demonstrate that we had no territorial claims on Finland and no intention of forcing socialism on the Finns at bayonet point.

In discussions with Marshal Zhukov, Khrushchev also mentioned the effect of withdrawing Soviet troops from Porkkala on the rest of Scandinavia. This was pertinent since 'Sweden and Norway . . . [are] eying us apprehensively to see what we do with the Finns'. Zhukov affirmed that 'from the strategic point of view there is absolutely no point in keeping troops in Finland'. Khrushchev disclosed, however, that despite Molotov's claim in 1944 that he was merely conceding to pressure from the Soviet military in demanding Porkkala, in 1955 he 'stubbornly argued against' returning Porkkala, although his views did not prevail.[91]

The political argument for returning Porkkala was weighty. As Enckell had predicted in negotiations with Molotov in 1944, the Porkkala lease had been a heavy burden for Finland. Enckell had noted that the lease could be used to exert political pressure on Finland. In a speech in September 1955 Paasikivi described the Porkkala lease and the rights of Soviet access to Porkkala as 'having cast a shadow over Finland's neutrality and the entire international position of Finland'. He related that Marshal Mannerheim had been greatly distressed by the lease and had even suggested that, on account of the proximity of the base to Helsinki, the capital should be moved west to Turku. This suggestion, Paasikivi noted, could not be realised, but changed military and political circumstances by 1955 meant that 'the pen has mended what the sword has broken'. This, in his view, showed that 'friendly discussions and judicious settlements are the course which has to be taken in the arrangement of our affairs with the Soviet Union'.[92] The return of Porkkala to Finland in January 1956, twenty years before the lease was due to expire, was a vindication of the Eastern policy Paasikivi had conducted. It could be interpreted in particular as proof of his claim that the post-war Soviet interest in Finland was defensive. Above all it indicated that the

Soviet government could trust the Finns to follow a policy in conformity with the provisions of the 1948 FCMA-Treaty.

The Soviet offer to return Porkkala was undoubtedly related to the contemporary context of international relations, and in particular to the conclusion of the Austrian State Treaty and the removal of Soviet troops from Austria, which was part of the policy of *détente* exercised by the USSR in relation to the German issue. In his speech proposing the abrogation of the Soviet rights over Porkkala Prime Minister Bulganin referred to the relief of international tension towards which the Geneva heads of state conference had contributed. He argued that it was incontestable that 'the removal of military bases situated on foreign territory by other states also would significantly assist the further relief of international tension and would assist the creation of the conditions for the ending of the arms race'.[93] In the Nordic context one military base Bulganin must have had in mind was the Keflavik base on Iceland. In fact, when the USSR decided to evacuate Porkkala the Icelandic Althing resolved that the Americans had to leave Keflavik, a decision which was only reversed when Soviet troops marched into Hungary in 1956.

The Soviet government presented the elimination of foreign military bases as a matter of principle. Already before the issue of Porkkala arose, the USSR had returned the naval base of Port Arthur to the Chinese People's Republic. In an analysis of 'imperialist' military bases some years later, a Soviet scholar noted that such bases on foreign territories were an important instrument for the preservation of colonialism or the maintenance of neo-colonialism, for interference in the domestic affairs and foreign policy of the states on whose territory they are situated, and that they serve aggressive purposes. By an additional argument, such bases were alleged to be incompatible with the principles of the peaceful coexistence of states with different social systems, and to constitute an 'international crime'.[94]

It would have been difficult for the USSR to have maintained this line, which was directed largely for the consumption of Third World countries and the non-aligned movement, whilst maintaining the very well established bases of Porkkala and Port Arthur. In the Finnish case the withdrawal from Porkkala may well have been regarded as a precondition for the full expression of peaceful coexistence in bilateral Finnish–Soviet relations. The Soviet writer cited above was criticised by a Soviet reviewer, however, for failing to indicate that the former military bases at Port Arthur and Porkkala 'were of a different kind', since 'they were sanctioned by all the great powers of the anti-Hitler coalition and resulted directly from the Second World War as a means of preventing renewed aggression'.[95] This distinction may not be fully convincing but at least it betrays the Soviet feeling that the Porkkala base needed to be justified.

A further political influence behind the withdrawal from Porkkala can be found in the Soviet declaration at the beginning of 1955 that the USSR was willing to negotiate the extension of the period of validity of the 1948 FCMA-Treaty already at this stage, simultaneously with negotiations over the return of Porkkala. The Soviet abandonment of Port Arthur had been agreed upon at the same time as an FMCA-Treaty had been signed between the USSR and China. Since the Finnish–Soviet FCMA-Treaty was, indeed, extended for a further twenty years, the return of the Porkkala base may be interpreted partly as a trade-off for Finnish confirmation that the security principles enshrined in the FCMA-Treaty would continue to be observed in the future, as well as being a gesture of Soviet trust that the Finns would act according to those principles anyway.

The Soviet preparedness to relinquish Porkkala revitalised Finnish hopes set to rest by the peace treaty in 1947 that the Soviet government would be willing to part with that part of Karelia originally lost by the Finns in the 1940 peace treaty. The argument arose that if the development of military technology and changes in the strategic vulnerability of the Baltic Sea had meant that Porkkala had lost its significance as a base, then correspondingly the reasons given by Stalin in autumn 1939 for moving the Finnish–Soviet border further from Leningrad had lost their force. Mutual trust and the existence of the FCMA-Treaty, so the reasoning went, would ensure Soviet security in the Finnish quarter. In this vein a Finnish paper argued in 1955 that:

> the desire for an adjustment of the 1947 treaty is a general aspiration adopted by the whole nation and not merely by a few. If according to Russian broadcasts relinquishing Porkkala has strengthened the spirit of friendship and cordiality, in how much greater measure would this be achieved by returning the territory of Karelia.[96]

The issue of revising the territorial provisions of the 1947 peace treaty concerning Karelia was not brought up only in the Finnish press. Before the negotiations in Moscow for the Soviet withdrawal from

Porkkala the Finnish Defence Minister, Emil Skog, spoke privately with the Soviet Prime Minister, Bulganin, and suggested a revision of the border to a line extending half-way up the Karelian isthmus from the Gulf of Finland to Lake Ladoga. Bulganin rejected the idea out of hand, and according to Skog Defence Minister Zhukov was even firmer – for military reasons, he maintained, the borders could not be changed.[97] Kekkonen informed the Finnish parliament later that the issue of revising the border had been broached with the Russians but that the Finns views had not met Soviet approval.

Contemporary Soviet articles made no concessions to the Finnish view of the border issue, and Finnish analyses of the war period were severely criticised. Soviet territorial demands in 1939 were justified by the claim that 'British, French and United States imperialists helped to convert Finland into a springboard for attacking the USSR', so that 'everything was ready for a strike at Leningrad'. In these circumstances, the Finns were told, the Soviet Union 'only allowed the most minimal territorial changes in order to protect its north-west border'.[98] In August 1956 *Izvestiya* handled the border issue at length. 'Certain minor political groupings and newspapers in Finland', the paper observed, had 'swallowed the bait of the people across the Atlantic', who had 'spread the feeble lie that the 20th Party Congress allegedly recognises previous Soviet foreign policy "mistakes" which are therefore due for revision'. Such hopes about Soviet foreign policy, and in particular hopes for a revision of the 1947 treaty, were claimed, however, to be unrepresentative of the beliefs of the Finnish people and government. The Soviet government organ regarded wishful-thinking to be found in some Finnish newspapers about Finland receiving 'the Karelian islands and the Karelian isthmus along with Vyborg' as unfounded, since 'the question of the state boundaries between the Soviet Union and Finland was resolved finally by the 1947 peace treaty . . . and consequently is not open to any kind of revision'. *Izvestiya* detected the source of this 'artificially publicised campaign' in 'ill-disposed circles'.[99]

This article was the final blow against Finnish hopes for the recovery of Karelia, hopes which went beyond just 'ill-disposed circles'. Many years later the former Finnish diplomat Max Jakobson observed that 'in handling the territorial issue the difference in the viewpoints of Finland and the Soviet Union appeared, which so often had caused us false hopes as well as vain fears with respect to Soviet policy'. It well suited Soviet foreign policy at the time to give up the Porkkala base, but the revision of the border would instead have been a dangerous precedent, since a large part of the borders of the USSR were disputable and 'a concession in one direction could have created pressure for change in other strategically sensitive regions'.[100]

Many later discussions between Soviet and Finnish leaders confirmed the Soviet view that the borders which were formed by the settlement after the Second World War must be considered irrevocable. In a speech in honour of Kekkonen in Moscow in May 1958, for example, Khrushchev stressed that 'to prevent a new war breaking out it is necessary to recognise the status quo, the present situation as it has been formed'. 'Historical experience', he told his guest, 'reminds us that state borders have not changed without war'.[101] Finland has had to recognise that the security policy of the Soviet Union encompasses a far wider interest area than does that of Finland.

2 The 1961 Note Crisis

THE BACKGROUND: SOVIET CONCERNS IN SCANDINAVIA AND THE BALTIC REGION

In the mid-1950s Soviet–Scandinavian relations appeared to be developing in a positive direction. The Soviet Union was wont to stress that at the end of the Second World War Soviet troops had been withdrawn from northern Norway and had evacuated the Danish island of Bornholm, and Soviet spokesmen argued that during the war Soviet warnings had discouraged a German invasion of Sweden. These historical facts were emphasised to dispel anxieties about Soviet intentions in the North. By 1955 the Soviet press was arguing that 'the Soviet Union's whole post-war policy has been imbued with . . . a consistent desire to assist the Northern countries independent development', based on recognition of 'common interests'.[1] This kind of rhetoric reflected the more conciliatory tone adopted by the USSR in Europe while the 'Geneva spirit' prevailed, but it was also a response to the Norwegian and Danish decisions in 1953 to refuse the stationing of foreign troops on their territories. In November 1955 the Norwegian Prime Minister, Gerhardsen, reassured his hosts in Moscow that his government 'would not pursue a policy having aggressive aims and would not allow foreign armed forces to be based on Norwegian territory as long as Norway was not subject to attack or to the threat of attack'.[2] Conciliatory phrasing was used in the Soviet–Swedish communique drawn up after a corresponding visit by the Swedish Prime Minister to Moscow a few months later.[3]

Towards the end of the 1950s tensions were generated in Soviet–Scandinavian relations by the issue of the possible introduction of atomic arms into Scandinavia. In an interview for a Danish paper in January 1958 Khrushchev maintained that the location of atomic arms and missiles on Danish and Norwegian territory would materially damage the relations of these countries with the USSR. Khrushchev brought out clearly the regional significance the Soviet

43

government ascribed to such a course of action. The security and sovereignty of Finland and Sweden would be directly concerned, he argued, by any attempt to discharge atomic missiles against the USSR over the territory of these neutral countries from NATO bases in Denmark and Norway. In the event that the Danish and Norwegian governments were to 'yield to foreign pressure' and establish missile sites on their territory, Khrushchev declared, 'the Soviet Union will naturally be forced to begin corresponding measures'.[4] If this was more than just a case of Khrushchevian bluster it is likely that one such measure could have been some degree of military integration with Finland on the basis of the 1948 FCMA-Treaty. Nevertheless, Norway and Denmark had already decided in 1957 not to accept nuclear arms, and this decision had been a result of domestic pressures rather than a gesture of solidarity with Finland.

Sweden also came under strong Soviet criticism for permitting 'military circles' to campaign 'more and more actively for the atomic arming of Sweden', which allegedly 'would not only undermine her traditional neutrality' but would also greatly imperil her very survival'.[5] The debate in Sweden over the utility of tactical nuclear devices was viewed as a reflection of American atomic strategy. The USSR espoused the idea of converting the Scandinavian peninsula into an atom-free and missile-free zone which the Soviet government would be prepared to guarantee.[6]

Several further developments contributed to changes in the Soviet attitude to Scandinavia at the end of the 1950s. The entry of West Germany into NATO and the subsequent rearmament of the country was crucial in the formulation of Soviet strategic thinking. One practical consequence of West German NATO membership was a change in Norwegian military strategy, since the security of southern Norway was judged to have increased to such an extent that substantially more troops and armaments could be concentrated in the north of the country. In addition, the *Bundeswehr* took over the defence of Schleswig-Holstein from British and Danish forces in 1958, and already a year earlier a planning group had been set up to discuss cooperation between the West German and Danish navies in the Baltic Sea. The USSR took these as indications of the increasing power of the Federal Republic to determine NATO strategy.

Soviet leaders were particularly critical of the planned Danish–West German joint naval command to control the outlet to the Baltic, which was regarded as an attempt 'to establish German control over the Baltic Sea, to turn it into an "internal sea" of Federal

Germany to be used for aggressive purposes'.[7] Evidence of the rapid growth of the West German fleet and of Bonn's plans to construct a big submarine fleet for the Baltic equipped with Polaris missiles was used to support this claim. The Soviet armed forces in the Baltic Sea region were excused simple by the need 'to protect the interests of the USSR in the face of NATO's constantly intensifying military preparations in Northern Europe'.[8] Indications of the latter were discerned in the common military exercises of German, Danish and Norwegian troops, and in plans to establish a joint military command for West German and Danish troops. Close military cooperation between Denmark and the Federal Republic was alleged to amount to 'the virtual subordination of Denmark's armed forces' to those of West Germany.[9] By 1961 the Joint Baltic Command (COMBAL-TAP) had been established and the Soviet press pointed out that Norway had granted West Germany the right to use military bases in Norwegian territory and to build storage depots for the West German navy. The Norwegian government, the Soviet press declared, was being pushed into 'intensified military preparations in the North – the region of the USSR border' by 'fantasies' of the Soviet threat.[10] In September 1961 Brezhnev spoke forebodingly in Finnish Lapland: the end result of 'the rising militarism of West Germany', which was expanding into Northern Europe, would be 'familiar to the Finnish, Soviet and Scandinavian peoples'.[11]

Soviet leaders were primarily concerned about the increasing integration of the northern NATO members into the NATO command structure, which was regarded as ever more subordinated to West Germany. But the growth of NATO influence in Northern Europe and the Baltic Sea also aroused Soviet concern about the permanence of Finland's international position, which found expression in an emphasis on the principles which governed security relations with Finland. In this manner Deputy Prime Minister Mikoyan told the Finns in October 1959 that 'the Soviet Union and its military power are the guarantee of Finland's security', a relationship which arises from the Finnish–Soviet FCMA-Treaty.[12] Such Soviet emphasis on the 1948 treaty showed that the latitude of Finnish security policy would decrease in periods of international tensions, especially when these extended to Northern Europe.

By 1961 the Berlin crisis had greatly exacerbated the international situation. The chief of the Finnish general staff, Lt.-General Viljanen, warned the Finnish cabinet in August that the effects of the Berlin crisis could extend to Finland, and that the Soviet government at any moment could invoke the 1948 treaty and propose military consultations.[13]

The Finnish view of the Soviet obsession with West Germany and its military potential clearly emerges from talks between Kekkonen and President Kennedy in September 1961. Kekkonen told Kennedy that in his opinion Soviet leaders really feared the growth of West German military power and the dangers it caused to world peace on account of their historical experiences. Kekkonen observed that the Berlin issue was important for Finland since a crisis in Germany would at all times also influence the position of Finland. He recalled the wording of the Finnish–Soviet FCMA-Treaty, which refers to an attack carried out by Germany or its allies. Kennedy believed that the application of this part of the treaty could hardly befit the times, but Kekkonen was less sure. 'We do not wish to talk before events', he observed, 'but we are aware of the basis of our position'.[14] In the light of events later that year, and of the personal role Kekkonen played in them, this observation can scarcely be denied.

THE CRISIS DEFUSED

On 30 October 1961 the Soviet government presented the Finnish government a long note which outlined Soviet attitudes to the deteriorating international situation in Northern Europe and concluded with a proposal for Finnish–Soviet consultations as provided by the 1948 FCMA-Treaty. The Soviet note was above all an attack on the policy of West Germany and a warning to Norway and Denmark and to a lesser extent Sweden. The official policy of Finland was not criticised at all and Finland was only treated incidentally in the Soviet analysis of Northern Europe.[15]

The Soviet description in the note of increasing militarism in Northern Europe was familiar to earlier Soviet writings. The Baltic Sea was viewed as turning into a 'military springboard' for West Germany, with the West Germans dictating their will to the states of this region. Sweden was criticised for failing to speak out against West German penetration of Scandinavia and for having established contacts with the 'Bonn military junta'. The note referred to West German 'provocative actions in West Berlin and . . . military preparations on its own territory'. Directly after this reference to the tensions ensuing from the Berlin crisis the note proclaimed that: 'West German militarist and revanchist penetration into North

Europe and the region of the Baltic Sea as well as its attempts to use this region as a military base . . . for military adventures, directly concerns the security of the Soviet Union as well as the Finnish Republic.' The Soviet government correspondingly proposed consultations with Finland 'about measures to secure the defence of the borders of both countries on account of the threat of military attack which has arisen from West Germany and states allied with it'. Consultations with Finland were to be part of a broad range of security measures which were being implemented by the Soviet governments as tension mounted in central Europe and this tension spread to the more peripheral parts of Europe.

The Soviet claim that, in conformity with the requirement for consultations with Finland laid down in the FCMA-Treaty, a threat of attack had arisen in Northern Europe, was elaborated a week after the note had been sent to Finland. 'We in the Soviet Union believe that Norway and Denmark have no aggressive plans', a Soviet news commentator admitted, but by cultivating military and economic cooperation with West Germany 'ruling circles in Norway and Denmark help Bonn's military circles to realise the occupation of these countries, causing a threat on the Soviet–Finnish borders'.[16] It was the all-absorbing concern with West Germany which governed Soviet attitudes in Northern Europe, and which induced the Finnish government to regard the Soviet note seriously.

The Finnish Foreign Minister, Ahti Karjalainen, met his Soviet counterpart to sound out Soviet views in the middle of November. In discussions with Karjalainen, Gromyko argued that in the present international situation 'concrete conclusions about the security of our borders have to be made', and disclosed that Soviet military circles 'had already for a long time been demanding military consultations between Finland and the Soviet Union' in the framework of the 1948 treaty.[17] After this meeting the Finnish Prime Minister, M. Miettunen, felt assured that the Soviet note was a response to the general international situation rather than an indication of a change in Finnish–Soviet relations.[18] Further discussions a few days later between Finnish ambassador Eero Wuori and the Soviet First Deputy Foreign Minister Kuznetsov confirmed this view. Kuznetsov referred to recent events, including a visit to Oslo by Strauss, the West German Defence Minister, as proof that 'the situation in this region had been intensified and that an immediate threat to the security of the Soviet Union and Finland exists'.[19]

Kuznetsov's argument showed that Soviet perceptions were

influenced on a day-to-day basis by the military policies conducted in Scandinavia. Kekkonen was aware of this, and he spoke bitterly about Strauss's visit to Oslo when Finland was living 'under the shadow of the note'.[20] A few days later a Soviet broadcast confirmed the political character of the note. Northern Europe, Radio Moscow stated, 'can become a powder keg that can be the cause of a new universal conflagration', in light of which, 'the intent of the note delivered by the Soviet Union was to hinder the aims of West Germany'.[21] As a political instrument directed against West German military policies the note was designed to influence the present state or condition of international politics, which only in the very loosest sense posed a threat of armed attack in the North. Indeed, as the head of the Political Department of the Finnish Foreign Ministry, Max Jakobson, observed much later, 'in autumn 1961 there were no material grounds to claim the existence of a threat of armed attack'.[22] Kekkonen called, nevertheless, for a 'recognition of facts' and 'national realism'. Views about Nordic security so strongly expressed by the USSR, Finland's FCMA-Treaty partner, could not simply be ignored, although they appeared exaggerated or misplaced.

Kekkonen decided to play a high card. A personal meeting with Khrushchev to discuss the security of Finland and the USSR in the context of the mounting tension in Europe might succeed in convincing the Soviet leader of the harm which moves intended at closer military integration with Finland could cause. Khrushchev agreed to interrupt an agricultural tour to meet Kekkonen in the Siberian town of Novosibirsk. In a luncheon speech on 24 November Khrushchev admitted that the USSR did not fear an immediate threat of attack from the Scandinavian quarter. His concern was with the destabilisation of the Nordic region ensuing from Danish and Norwegian policies, which brought 'the danger threatened by the pursuers of German militarism and revanchism closer to the shores of Finland and the Soviet Union'.[23] Khrushchev commended the policy conducted by Finland as an essential and positive factor in the security system of the Nordic region, but stressed that during the present aggravated international tensions Soviet and Finnish interests demanded a 'firm assurance that Finland will still observe tomorrow its chosen foreign policy line, the Paasikivi–Kekkonen line'.[24] One of Kekkonen's tasks in Novosibirsk, therefore, was to try and convince Khrushchev that the Finnish policy was unwavering. Such an assurance could to some extent counteract Soviet concern about the regional situation in Northern Europe.

At Novosibirsk Kekkonen expressed his understanding of the security perspectives contained in the Soviet note and admitted that Soviet views about the possibility of war breaking out in Europe were 'quite weighty', but he suggested that the USSR withdraw its proposal for military consultations on two grounds.[25] Initially he pointed to Scandinavia, where the aggravated international situation had created' 'a state of nervous excitement and a war psychosis is spreading'. He argued that military circles and 'certain political circles' were taking advantage of this state of affairs to press for new appropriations for military equipment in various countries. If the USSR refrained from insisting on Finnish–Soviet consultations, this 'would be calculated to pacify public opinion in the whole of Scandinavia and would lead to a diminution of the need for military preparations'. Kekkonen assumed, therefore, an interrelation in the security policies of all the Nordic countries and appealed to regional Soviet security priorities in Northern Europe. Soviet security requirements with respect to Finland herself, Kekkonen reasoned, would be satisfied through Finnish observance of a policy of neutrality.

Kekkonen also appealed to the model of peaceful coexistence. If the Soviet Union were to withdraw its proposal for consultations, he argued, it would demonstrate to other Northern countries and to the whole world that even difficult issues could be resolved through a policy of peaceful coexistence in a manner satisfactory to both parties. This argument was again calculated to appeal to Soviet interests outside the purely bilateral context of Finnish–Soviet relations.

In reply to Kekkonen the Soviet leader affirmed that the increasing ascendancy of West Germany in NATO meant that the possibility of strikes from Norway against the Soviet Union through Finland could not be discounted. He claimed that the USSR had long ago given up directing military or political pressure against Finland. 'Were we to have aimed to put pressure on Finland', he reasoned, 'we would never have given up our Porkkala base – that would have been stupid'. Khrushchev agreed with Kekkonen that beginning military consultations would heighten the war psychosis and stimulate military preparations. Consequently, he regarded Kekkonen's advice to defer these consultations as 'sensible'. 'Let's agree', he suggested' 'that if the situation were to grow worse we would arrange to contact each other.' This informal arrangement was spelt out in the joint communique of the discussions, according to which the Finnish government would 'closely follow the development of the situation in Northern Europe and the Baltic Sea region', and in case of need 'transmit its view about carrying out required measures' to the Soviet government. This controversial statement once again disclosed the regional dimension of Soviet security policy concerns in Northern Europe.

In an interview some months later Kekkonen affirmed that the Soviet proposal for consultations had been prompted primarily by the desire 'to receive an assurance that it would trust in the continuation of the Finnish policy'. Soviet statesmen wished to be sure that Soviet security interests 'will not be disturbed in any circumstances through Finland'.[26] This implied that the Soviet leadership had real doubts about the continuity of Finnish foreign policy in autumn 1961, although Kekkonen claimed that these were 'in fact groundless',[27] and that but for these the Soviet note may never have been delivered regardless of the prevailing international situation. The internal political debate surrounding the Finnish presidential election campaign in 1961 becomes relevant here. This issue is dealt with later (see Chapter 6).

Although in retrospect Kekkonen interpreted the Soviet note as a problem in 'relations of confidence' with Finland, he also laid emphasis on the importance of the international context in which the note was sent. Already towards the end of 1957 and in the spring and summer of 1958 the Soviet government had addressed a series of notes to Finland pointing out the growing dangers of war and expressing particular concern about the growing military strength of West Germany. Kekkonen observed that 'we have no reason not to consider this anxiety as genuine, whatever we ourselves think about the situation',[28] He pointed out to the American Secretary of State, Dean Rusk, that the Soviet proposal for consultations with Finland had been just one of a series of military responses taken by the USSR in autumn 1961 to bolster its security as the threat of war over Berlin arose.[29] But Kekkonen believed that the timing of the Novosibirsk discussions was crucial since they took place at a stage when in many respects Soviet policy was moving in a more conciliatory direction. The favourable results of these discussions were not, therefore, exceptional to Soviet policy and did not demand a search for ulterior explanations.

There has been some speculation in Finland about the internal pressures in the USSR which may have influenced policy towards Finland in autumn 1961. The Finnish ex-diplomat Max Jakobson has argued that the Soviet note to Finland was a concession to a hard line group in the Soviet Party leadership, the Foreign Ministry and the defence forces, calculated to dissuade the West from believing that the Soviet Union had abandoned its campaign over Berlin out of weakness. Jakobson claims that Khrushchev's line, supported by those who gave priority to the need to calm international tensions through conciliatory gestures, had been reconfirmed by the time of the Novosibirsk meeting, which enabled the Soviet Party leader to accept Kekkonen's arguments to call off military consultations with Finland.[30] But Jakobson fails to produce any substantive evidence to support this analysis. He attempts to divert attention away from the numerous clear expression of Soviet concern over the deteriorating international situation and its implications for the Nordic region, and implicitly dismisses the notion that Soviet leaders could have harboured any feelings of increased insecurity on their north-west borders which led to the Soviet note of October 1961.

The outcome of the Novosibirsk meeting did not entail an abandonment of previous Soviet views about Nordic security. The *Pravda* account of this meeting on 25 November was relentless in its castigation of the 'revanchist and militarist' desires of West Germany to draw the Scandinavian countries into military conflict with the USSR. A couple of days later the Party organ specifically observed that the Soviet Union 'did not consent to postpone the military consultations because of a belief in the assurances by some leaders of the Scandinavian countries that the German militaristic wolf would have changed into a humble little lamb . . . no the wolf has not changed'. The Soviet government illustrated this in mid-December by warning the Danish government in a strongly worded official statement about Danish military complicity with West Germany.[31]

This continued Soviet preoccupation with the German question and the implications of West German involvement in Northern Europe shows precisely that although the timing of the Soviet proposal for consultations with Finland may partly have reflected fluctuating policy considerations within the USSR, the proposal in principle was in alignment with the broad priorities of Soviet security policy. Kekkonen's awareness of this is plain from a speech delivered in the aftermath of the Note Crisis in December 1961. He pointed out that the increased military preparations in West and East over Berlin and the German question in general had turned Finland into a 'focal point', since 'the military alliance involving West Germany mentioned in our 1948 treaty of cooperation extends to the Baltic Sea and our land borders in the North'.[32]

Since the Finnish–Soviet FCMA-Treaty was intended specifically to provide against 'the threat of armed attack' (Article 2), 'by Germany or any state allied with the latter' (Article 1), which could well be interpreted on the Soviet side as meaning West Germany and the NATO alliance, continued NATO military preparations in the North and the Baltic Sea region in close association with West Germany would be bound directly to concern the Finnish–Soviet security arrangement which had been enshrined in the 1948 treaty. Kekkonen had already drawn a clear connection between the German question and the 1948 treaty before the Soviet proposal for consultations, during discussions with Kennedy. It is only in light of these considerations that Khrushchev's suggestion at Novosibirsk – 'let's agree that if the situation for some reason were to grow worse we would arrange to contact each other' – can fully be understood. The final part of the communique of the Novosibirsk discussions followed naturally from these words, and presumed a greater activity in Finnish security policy which would be expressed in subsequent decades.

THE NORTHERN BALANCE THEORY

The course and resolution of the Finnish–Soviet Note Crisis have been referred to extensively as an illustration in practice of the 'Northern Balance' theory, which has come to dominate Western views about the strategic position of the Nordic countries. Western strategists have considered the stability of the Nordic region to derive from the existence of a 'low' Northern Balance, composed of a neutral Sweden resting between a Finland with a limited defensive agreement with the USSR in the form of the 1948 treaty, and a Norway and Denmark which have joined NATO but whose commitment is essentially defensive. Proof of the latter point is drawn from the refusal of both countries to have nuclear weapons or to permit the establishment of foreign bases on their soil in peacetime, and from Norway's self-denying ordinance against stationing troops in the Finnmark province which borders on Finland and the Soviet Union. The regional security-political system composed by the balance is believed to provide a buffer to deter the superpowers from increased political and military activity in the region. In Norway the balance has been conceived of as operating automatically: any Soviet attempt to upset the regional stability by, for example, increased military integration with Finland is judged to be deterred by the knowledge that the other Nordic countries would be liable to revoke the restraints they observe in their relations with NATO.[33]

Northern balance theorists have interpreted the Soviet note to Finland in autumn 1961 as just such an attempt to integrate the security and military policies of the two neighbouring countries. Emphasis has been laid on the Norwegian response to the note. After the contents of the note became public but before the Novosibirsk discussions the Norwegian Foreign Minister expressed the hope during a visit to Moscow that the balance which had been established in the North could continue without significant changes. In a public speech in Copenhagen the Defence Minister argued more strongly that continued pressure on Norway would not force Norway out of NATO, but on the contrary would drive Norway further into NATO. He stated that Norway understood the Soviet Union's concern for her own security, but he felt that Soviet leaders were sometimes uneasy without cause. He trusted Soviet realism to prevail and reminded Soviet leaders of the Norwegian attitude towards stationing nuclear weapons on Norwegian territory.[34] Supporters of the Northern Balance theory argue that these Norwegian statements, which in the case of the Defence Minister took the form of a clear warning, provided a basis for Kekkonen's arguments at Novosibirsk concerning the growth of military preparations and a 'war psychosis' in Scandinavia, and that this ultimately persuaded Khrushchev to defer military consultations with Finland out of consideration of possible counteracting measures by the other Scandinavian countries.

In the years following the Note Crisis this chain of reasoning became officially accepted in Norway. The commander of the Norwegian defence forces, F. Johannessen, recalling the Note Crisis observed in 1964 that while 'it is true we do not know why the Soviet Union withdrew its pressure . . . it may have been influenced by the possibility that Norway could change its attitude towards bases of foreign powers or nuclear arms'. The Norwegian admiral continued to draw a lesson that encapsulates Northern Balance thinking:

If Norway or Denmark were to let foreign military forces or nuclear arms on their territory in peacetime, as counter-pressure the Soviet Union could transfer troops and facilities to Finland . . .

If again the Soviet Union were to attempt to change the prevailing situation in the North by certain measures, Norway would respond to this by threatening to change its base and nuclear arms policy. This knowledge that any measure of this kind will cause a chain reaction will certainly make the Soviet Union think again before it begins anything in the Northern region.[35]

This argument was confirmed by the Norwegian Foreign Minister, John Lyng, in a parliamentary statement in 1966, when he said that 'if the Soviet Union discloses intentions about a base on Finnish soil, we will reconsider the base policy we observe with respect to our allies'.[36] It may well be that Norwegian warnings of this kind have been one factor serving to restrain Soviet leaders from seeking closer military integration with Finland, but the course and resolution of the 1961 Note Crisis did not bear out the theory of the Northern Balance which has so strongly influenced subsequent Norwegian and Danish policy.

The point that has largely been ignored is that the original imbalance introduced into the Nordic region was the markedly increased military integration of Norway and Denmark into the NATO command structure, which at the time corresponded to no move on the Soviet part in the direction of Finland. It is true that NATO involvement in Denmark and Norway did not lead to an abandonment of one of the major structural 'restraints' these countries had accepted, but the definition of what previously had been such a restraint surely in part had to lie with the Soviet Union, since it was this country which may previously have felt itself deterred by a perceived level of restraint in Danish and Norwegian policy. The USSR was dubious about the Norwegian base policy, since it observed that West Germany had been granted the right to use military bases on Norwegian territory. The definition of a base was to become a bone of contention in the Nordic region in later years. Considering these points, the Soviet proposal for military consultations with Finland could be regarded as a counter-move to the acceptance of Norway and Denmark to participate in NATO's Baltic Sea Command structure.

The Soviet counter-move failed. COMBALTAP was established in 1961 and Soviet leaders never succeeded in redressing the imbalance through pressures upon the Nordic states. Kekkonen's reference to a Scandinavian 'war psychosis' was certainly an indication of some degree of interrelation in the security policies of the Nordic states, but the results of Novosibirsk were no vindication of the Northern Balance concept, since by that time the balance had already swung into an imbalance as a result of the original NATO move with regard to Norway and Denmark.[37]

The USSR has managed to compensate for increased NATO involvement in the North through the continued development of the Murmansk base, which lies outside the strictly Northern European area. If NATO is to be matched by the expansion of the Murmansk base rather than by increase Soviet pressure upon Finland or Sweden this may be an important factor in the Finnish ability to avoid a repetition of the political-military pressures that they were subject to in 1961 from the Soviet Union.

The Norwegian conception of the Northern Balance as an automatic counteraction to Soviet attempts to change regional conditions in the North has been rejected in Finland. The most that Finnish officials have conceded is that a balance exists in the North as a static regional condition between the spheres of interest of the superpowers.[38] The Finns are aware that the original restraints which Norway and Denmark imposed on their security policies in 1953 and 1957 were simply responses to domestic pressures and were not aimed at assisting Finland. The Finns realise that the Norwegian variant of Northern Balance thinking is not reconcilable with the central premise of the Paasikivi–Kekkonen foreign and security policy line, namely that Finnish–Soviet relations operate primarily on a bilateral basis and function well without third party pressures. The Northern Balance theory presumes that in its relations with the Soviet Union Finland relies on NATO, through the agency of Norway and Denmark, to avert measures which the USSR may propose by invoking the 1948 FCMA-Treaty. The Finnish authorities do not accept this, and they foresee a further problem arising if the principles behind the Norwegian view of the Balance became generally accepted: if Norway and Denmark were to regard it in their interest to revise their relations with NATO in the direction of increased integration, perhaps as a consequence of developments in arms technology, pressure would follow correspondingly to activate the military provisions of Finland's FCMA-Treaty, regardless of whether the issue directly concerned bilateral Finnish–Soviet relations. It has been in the Finnish interests to emphasise the compelling character of this bilateral link.[39]

In practical terms the Norwegians in particular have employed the idea of a Northern Balance as a tactic to hold off participation in a nuclear-free zone, which would deprive them of their nuclear 'option', namely the threat to escalate in a situation of crisis in Northern Europe. The Finns naturally have been concerned about the possibility of such escalation since it implies the operation of the military articles of the 1948 treaty.

Soviet commentators have referred in the past to the existence of a relatively peaceful 'Northern sheltered corner', but deny that this is the product of a Northern Balance. They believe that the principles behind the Balance theory increase tensions in the North through their assumption that the military confrontation between the Eastern and Western blocs in Central Europe necessarily is reflected in the alignment of forces in the North. Soviet writers have consistently claimed also that this theory has been used as a justification for the NATO presence in Northern Europe. Norwegian and Danish membership in NATO is alleged to restrict the independence and freedom of choice of these states and to create unnecessary tensions in the Nordic region. In the Soviet view it is precisely NATO measures 'which conceal a potential threat of upsetting the "Northern Balance" which certain Western and Scandinavian statesmen eulogise'.[40] These views contradict the assumption in the Northern Balance hypothesis that Soviet designs in the Nordic region, and closer military and political integration with Finland in particular, are only held in check by Norwegian and Danish NATO membership and by their option, if need arises, of further integration into the NATO system, or by the possibility that Sweden might reconsider her policy of neutrality.

The Soviet Scandinavian specialist Lev Voronkov argued in 1982 that the increasing involvement of Norway and Denmark in NATO military planning meant that no balance or status quo could prevail between the Nordic countries. He underlined that joint Finnish–Soviet military exercises can only take place once a threat of attack has been jointly established and concluded that in these circumstances 'there is no balance, rather their prevails an imbalance when we consider these real [NATO] military preparations'.[41]

Arguments in favour of or against the theory of a Northern Balance have always been based on an appraisal of Soviet motivations in the North, above all towards Finland. An examination of post-war Finnish–Soviet security relations does confirm that on many occasions the USSR has considered its policy towards Finland as part of a Nordic policy, and that the character of these relations has been influenced by Soviet security relations in the Nordic region as a whole. But to say that there have been contingent interrelationships in the security policies observed by the Nordic countries is quite different to claiming that relations of interdependence have arisen which are both mechanical in operation and predictive in character. The dynamic element in the Northern Balance theory has worked more on the level of policy proclamation – and unilaterally from the West – than on the level of the actual implementation and interaction of security policies in the Nordic region.

3 The Scope of Finnish Security Policy 1961–84

The Note Crisis had profound implications for Finland's security policy. In 1961 the Soviet government had felt itself compelled to resort to the military provisions of the Finnish–Soviet FCMA-Treaty to bolster the security of its north-west borders and as a parallel aim to influence the development of the northern flank of NATO. The basic line of Finnish security policy required the preservation of Soviet trust in the Finnish preparedness to carry out the military provision of the 1948 treaty when the need arises. It followed that both during the Note Crisis and in subsequent years Finnish leaders had to avoid creating the impression that Finland would be disinclined to activate Articles 1 and 2 of the treaty as such. As a consequence, Finnish foreign policy in the 1960s was calculated to serve the interests of the country best through working to prevent a situation arising in the Nordic region in which the military provisions of the 1948 treaty would have to be invoked.

The final part of the communique of the Novosibirsk meeting foretold the direction of Finland's future security policy. According to one Soviet interpretation, during the course of the Novosibirsk discussions Finland accepted the responsibility to take initiatives to safeguard the security of Finland and the USSR in Northern Europe. This role was described as 'an important factor of foreign policy activity and initiative-making' for Finland, which acted as 'a stimulus for her deep and continuing interest in the foreign policy problems arising in the Baltic and Scandinavia'. By this Soviet argument Finland's role in the international system underwent a change through an extension of the territorial scope of the country's security policy; Finland became 'an active subject of international relations with its own responsibility for the fortune of peace in the area of Northern Europe'. The activation of Finnish policy was recognised to be related to Finland's commitments undertaken in the FCMA-Treaty, but these were described as no more than 'a natural juridical strengthening of the national line in foreign policy'.[1]

The informal agreement undertaken by Kekkonen at Novosibirsk, which broadened the perceived range of competence of Finnish security policy, inspired disparaging remarks about Finland's 'watch-dog role' in the West, and in particular in Norway. A common assumption was that Finnish concern about security matters in the Nordic region in the 1960s was prompted by a need to placate the Soviet Union. Finland was even accused of acting as a vehicle for sponsoring or promoting Soviet policy in this region. Finnish officials responded by claiming that while individual Finnish initiatives in the Nordic region may have corresponded with Soviet *démarches*, they have been contrived independently to conform with the national security interests of Finland. This controversy, which was later incorporated into the Finlandisation debate, requires a careful scrutiny of the security proposals made by Finland.

The logic which encouraged an extension of Finnish security policy in the 1960s to cover developments in the Nordic region also heightened Finnish concern about bipolar international issues. In Kekkonen's view the Soviet note in 1961 had shown how tensions in Central Europe could spread to the Nordic region, and it had been related to West Germany's position in NATO. Throughout the 1960s Kekkonen continued to believe in the interrelationship of bipolar confrontation in Central Europe and tensions in the North. In 1966 he observed:

> The security policy problems of the Baltic Sea are closely connected to the situation of Central Europe and above all to the German question. Increasing tension in Central Europe is easily reflected in the Baltic Sea region. In the course of history its effects have even reached the shores of our country.[2]

Kekkonen recognised that the means at Finland's disposal to alleviate tension in Central Europe were limited, but Finnish security policy increasingly sought to decrease the likelihood of conflict between the alliance systems in Europe through reducing both psychological tensions and military levels.

FINNISH SECURITY, NORDIC NEUTRALITY AND A NUCLEAR-FREE NORTH

Almost a decade before the Note Crisis Finnish leaders displayed an interest in regional, Nordic security arrangements quite independent of Soviet prompting. In a statement in January 1952 Prime Minister Kekkonen, with the approval of President Paasikivi, claimed that a 'neutral alliance between the Scandinavian countries could have been thought of as a logical continuation' of the 1948 treaty. The advantage of such a plan would have lain in the fact that even 'the theoretical threat of attack against the Soviet Unon through Finnish territory would have been removed', and it would have led to increased cooperation between the neutral Nordic countries.[3] Kekkonen's scheme would have given Finland the greatest possible legal security against attack, but as a practical possibility it had already been eliminated by Danish and Norwegian entrance into NATO. Kekkonen envisaged some kind of neutral bond between Sweden and Finland which would enhance the security of both countries. But his speech was more a reaction to Cold War tension and a comment on plans for Nordic security initiated at the beginning of the 1950s than a programme for the future.

The retrospective element in Kekkonen's statement was not fully understood at the time. The Soviet response in *Pravda* cited Finnish Communist claims that 'Kekkonen's speech contains a direct appeal to Denmark and Norway to leave the Atlantic Pact', which 'from the point of view of Finnish interests . . . would be desirable'.[4] This interpretation, which partly explains Soviet praise of Finland's 'non-participation in military blocs' by the mid-1950s, was an expression of wishful thinking on the Soviet side. The Soviet promotion of Scandinavian neutrality was a calculated political act. It served the purpose of ensuring that Swedish territory was denied to NATO and it brought pressure on Norway and Denmark to disengage from or limit their commitment to the Alliance. This campaign appealed to the 'tradition' of Nordic neutrality which had been a unifying factor between the Nordic countries in the 1930s. The Soviet view, expressed for example by Khrushchev in 1964, was that 'the most dependable guarantee of security for countries such as Norway, Denmark, Sweden and Finland is a policy of neutrality that would be recognised by both sides'.[5]

The idea of a Northern defence and neutrality league was mooted in Finland in the 1960s.[6] In 1965 Kekkonen accepted that at the current stage of arms technology neutrality 'seems to offer small states in a favourable geographical position a better chance of survival than does an alliance with one of the great nuclear powers'.[7] But he rejected the idea of a Northern defence league as unrealistic since it presumed the abrogation of the 1948 treaty, which was out of the question. Kekkonen reformulated an idea which had first arisen during the debate at the end of the 1940s over the Northern defence league, namely the possibility of the Scandinavian countries receiving security guarantees from the Western states. He publicised a scheme originally proposed by the Finnish army officer Aimo Pajunen. A neutral Fenno-Scandia could be formed if Norway were to withdraw from NATO and conclude a treaty similar to the Finnish–Soviet FCMA-Treaty with the United States or Great Britain. Kekkonen did not consider this to be a very likely possibility, but he believed that if realised this arrangement would contribute to Finnish security by reducing military tensions in the North through diminishing the likelihood of international tensions automatically being reflected in this region.[8] The plan would create a balanced security arrangement in the Nordic region based on guarantees from the two great power alliances.

Kekkonen went on to propose 'a treaty arrangement with Norway' to 'protect the border area between Finland and Norway from possible warfare'. In peacetime a neutralisation of the Finnish–Norwegian border would be calculated to ensure a low level of military tension in the North, while in a real armed conflict between the great powers such a treaty would assist the parties to remain outside belligerencies. Kekkonen's offer was intended to uphold Finland's neutrality by freeing Finnish Lapland from the threat of becoming contested territory between the armies of the two blocs. A statement from the NATO side – by Norway in practice – that it does not harbour aggressive designs on this frontier, given in the form of a neutralisation of the frontier, would have reduced the vulnerability of the weakest area of Finland and created a kind of balanced security system between the 1948 treaty and Norwegian frontier neutralisation that would indirectly bind NATO.[9] Furthermore, although the Norwegian–Soviet border would have been left outside this security arrangement, in reality it would certainly have been influenced by the latter.

The Norwegians turned down Kekkonen's schemes, since, they argued, the security of their country partly depends on the option to receive nuclear weapons if necessary, which they would be denied if they were to withdraw from NATO or agree to a neutralisation of the frontier. This view has also turned Norway into the major stumbling block for Finnish attempts to turn Norway into a nuclear-free zone. Since Finnish support for a Nordic nuclear-free zone has frequently been interpreted in the West as evidence of Finland's preparedness to sponsor Soviet policies in the Nordic region a careful examination of Finnish motives is required to understand this important proposal.

In a series of notes addressed to Finland towards the end of 1957 and in the spring and summer of 1958 the Soviet government pointed out the growing danger of war stemming from the activities of NATO, and requested Finnish support for the cause of prohibiting nuclear tests.[10] The USSR received Finnish agreement in principle, but it was not until a joint Finnish–Soviet communique in May 1958 that the Finns gave their support for the creation of a nuclear-free zone in Central Europe, based on the 1957 Rapacki plan,[11] which would also run through the North. In a speech in June 1959 Khrushchev proposed the formation of a 'rocket and atomic-free zone in the Scandinavian peninsula and the Baltic Sea region',[12] but the harsh tones of the speech, which included an attack on NATO and German militarism, discouraged any positive response from Finland.

International conditions at the beginning of the 1960s left their imprint on the outlook of Finnish policy-makers. The 1961 Note Crisis was taken as an indication of the vulnerability of Northern Europe to external pressures in the international arena, while the dangers perceived in the Cuban missiles crisis emphasised that geographical isolation could not ensure security in a nuclear world. In February 1962, the Swedish Foreign Minister, Östen Undén, proposed a non-nuclear club in Northern Europe as part of a wider scheme. Undén's idea, which was not official Swedish policy, acquired broader legitimacy through a statement by United Nations Secretary General U Thant in 1963 that nuclear-free zones should be created throughout the world. The widespread international interest in these schemes finally encouraged Kekkonen to present a Finnish proposal for a nuclear-free North on 28 May 1963, which he suggested was necessary to prevent the unrest and tension which the location of nuclear arms in this area would cause. Kekkonen argued that such a zone would stabilise the *de facto* position of all the Northern countries and ensure that this area would remain outside any speculations associated with the development of nuclear arms. Kekkonen was clearly referring to debate over nuclear strategy within NATO and to the possibility of Denmark and Norway participating in a multilateral nuclear force or of nuclear arms being located on their territory.

Despite the international background to Kekkonen's proposal, it was received with a considerable degree of scepticism throughout the rest of the Nordic region, since it was alleged by many to serve Soviet rather than Nordic interests. Since 1958 the Soviet press had been strongly pushing for the formation of a guaranteed rocket and nuclear-free zone in Northern Europe, which 'could lead to the emergence of a wide belt of peace in Europe', and 'might also mark the first stage of a shift by all the Northern countries to positions of neutrality'.[13] The association of a nuclear-free North with a withdrawal of Denmark and Norway from NATO in the long term was one cause of Scandinavian suspicions about Kekkonen's initiative. Furthermore, the Scandinavian NATO states have argued that the Kekkonen scheme would deny them the right to summon nuclear forces in an emergency, that is to say to revoke their self-imposed restraints over nuclear arms. In their view, therefore, it would not only restrict the room for manoeuvre in their foreign policy, but would facilitate Soviet operations from the Murmansk area in the event of conflict between NATO and the Warsaw Pact states.

The Danish and Norwegian stand was reinforced by the Soviet attitude to the proposal that Soviet territory in Northern Europe – the Kola peninsula, and therefore Murmansk – should be included in the nuclear-free zone. Already in 1960 Mikoyan replied testily to a question in Oslo on this point: 'It is known that Soviet territory is not a part of Scandinavia and it is not expected to be included in it'. 'Do you want to expand Scandinavia at the expense of the Soviet Union?', he queried.[14] In reply to a similar question in Denmark some years later, Khrushchev observed that Soviet territory could only be considered under the terms of a comprehensive denuclearisation scheme between the great powers.[15]

The Soviet response to Kekkonen's initiative in 1963 predictably was positive. In the Soviet view the realisation of his proposal would erect a 'formidable obstacle . . . to NATO plans to militarise Northern Europe and involve it in the arms drive'.[16] Foreign Minister Gromyko described the proposal as one 'of great value', and affirmed that the USSR on its part was ready to guarantee such a zone.[17] The Western suspicion that Finland had come under pressure from the USSR to sponsor a nuclear-free Scandinavia was dismissed by later Soviet commentators as a total misunderstanding of Finnish–Soviet relations and of Finnish foreign policy.[18]

Kekkonen himself, however, felt constrained to account for his initiative more fully. He explained at the end of 1963 that before making the proposal he had neither solicited Soviet opinions nor informed the USSR about his intentions. While he recognised that many steps taken by Finland have had a favourable reception in the USSR because they have not conflicted with Soviet policy, Kekkonen emphasised that 'the fact that some political measure may be in agreement with Soviet policy has not prevented and will not in future prevent Finland from supporting it or from directly proposing it when it concurs with the interests of the Finnish people'.[19] In fact, Kekkonen finally became convinced of the idea of a nuclear-free North during a visit to Yugoslavia in the early 1960s, where the interest in nuclear-free zones had arisen independent of Soviet attitudes.

Kekkonen aimed at isolating the Nordic region from international tensions elsewhere, a requirement for Finnish security which directly reflected the thinking behind the final part of the Novosibirsk communique. Contemporary developments in NATO nuclear strategy, which could involve the Scandinavian NATO members, could be viewed as an extension of those military preparations among the NATO states to which the Soviet government had referred to justify the need for consultations with Finland in 1961. In these circumstances, Kekkonen's initiative in 1963 should be understood partly as a warning to neighbouring Nordic countries, against the background of the Cuban missiles crisis, that the existence of plans to introduce nuclear arms into Scandinavia could lead to a situation in which Finland would be obliged to honour the promise given by Kekkonen at Novosibirsk and suggest consultations with the USSR, either informally or on the basis of Article 2 of the 1948 treaty.[20]

The formation of a nuclear-free zone in the North would be equivalent to this region 'contracting out' from the area of potential conflict by a prior decision of policy. This would not only reduce Soviet incentives to resort to the military provisions of the 1948 treaty, it would also to some degree reduce the likelihood of missile strikes and land-based attacks from or against Murmansk, which, through infringing Finnish territory in Lapland, could engage the whole country in the conflict. In this respect Kekkonen's proposal was closely related to his subsequent initiative for the neutralisation of the Norwegian–Finnish frontier. Both initiatives derived from Finland's position as a neutral state in the vicinity of a region torn between the competing interests of the great power alliance systems.

In November 1965 Kekkonen went so far as to criticise openly West German plans for participation in a multilateral nuclear force on the grounds that it would be regarded by the USSR and other Warsaw Pact countries as a threat to peace. The Soviet press interpreted this as an expression of Finnish understanding of how Northern European security 'will be reduced if the *Bundeswehr* makes its way to the nuclear control panel'.[21] Yet Kekkonen was not merely echoing Soviet views, he was once again voicing concern about Finnish security if tensions generated in Central Europe over the German issue and West German involvement in NATO were to spread to Northern Europe.

Kekkonen's criticism of the nuclear arming of West Germany was regarded by some in Finland as well as abroad as an abandonment of the principle Finland had adopted not to become a party in issues between the great powers. Soviet spokesmen argued that this misrepresented the issue, since it created a problem for the security of all the European countries, including the neutral ones.[22] The Finnish authorities tended to agree that the neutral states in Europe could also benefit from attempts to forestall the development of further military threats between East and West, and that they could even contribute to such 'peace-seeking' moves. But in 1965, as in later years, they were careful to discern the threat to peace as lying in the effect of German (or NATO) policy on Soviet perceptions or of Soviet policy on Western perceptions, rather than in the policy concerned itself. But the practice of Finland's instrumental view of neutrality, which developed in the 1960s, was little understood in the West and it created an ambiguity about Finland's views and proposals on Nordic security which for many could only be explained by Finland's alleged need to defer to Soviet pressures. This interpretation was encouraged by Western strategists who did not fully understand the implications of Finland's post-war treaties with the Soviet Union.

FINLAND'S POSITION AS A SOVIET BORDER STATE

In Western eyes Finland's strategic significance in the 1950s was assessed in regional terms. Dominant Cold War patterns of thought demanded a clear division between Eastern and Western political alignments. As previously indicated, the American State Department had considered Finland a special case in the late 1940s, but Marshall had denied that Finland had been relegated to the Soviet sphere of influence at Teheran. In July 1950, soon after the formation of NATO, an understanding had been reached between the United States and Britain such that 'it was not anticipated that in the case of an attack by the Soviets action would be taken to assist Finland'.[23] Finnish ministers were told clearly in September that no United States 'guarantees' existed for Finland in the event of such an attack.[24] Thus the argument that 'military and moral considerations suggest that Finland's eastern border be recognised as the northernmost segment of the Western defence frontier in Europe'[25] had already decisively been rejected. But the question of how much political support Finland could expect from the West in the event of Soviet military pressure was left open.

In the 1950s and 1960s there was occasional speculation about the areas in Europe outside NATO which would be supported by the United States in a crisis and those which would be abandoned to the Soviet 'sphere'. In the East, however, the post-Stalin Soviet leadership openly rejected the division of countries into spheres of influence, which Khrushchev branded as 'the policy of imperialism . . . a most inveterate colonial policy'. In Khrushchev's view, 'if you reason that Cuba is a small country and therefore, because of its geographical location, should be included in the sphere of influence of the United States of America, what then should we do with respect to our neighbours, which are also small countries?'[26] Khrushchev stressed the good-neighbourly relations which existed between the USSR and its border countries Finland and Afghanistan.[27] In his report to the Twenty-third Party Congress in 1966 Brezhnev similarly maintained that 'our relations with Finland and Afghanistan are characterised by trust, friendship and cooperation'.[28]

Until the end of the 1960s Finland still occupied a rather vague area in Western strategic planning. But the Soviet invasion of Czechoslovakia in 1968 was felt to have created a need in NATO to specify the countries within its own sphere of influence so that the Alliance could lay down the principles of action for a possible future contingency of a similar type and signal to Soviet leaders where the West would draw the line. Finland was regarded as one of the borderline countries falling into a so-called 'grey zone'. According to press reports, after the NATO Council meeting in November 1968 the West German Foreign Minister, Willy Brandt, intimated that the NATO command had included Finland among those countries an attack on which would cause a serious international crisis, and even that NATO guarantees applied to Finland. The West German Foreign Minister later rebutted the charge of having extended NATO's security zone to include Finland, but acknowledged 'the fact that NATO's security interests would be violated by an attack on Finland'.[29]

The Soviet press responded initially by citing a West German claim in *Die Welt* that the security of NATO depended on the security of the small neutral countries of Europe and by stating that the American Secretary of State, Dean Rusk, has indeed included Finland in the grey zone.[30] A Soviet article later claimed that attempts by NATO 'to intensify its activity in Northern Europe' were expressed in its 'urge to extend its influence to the neutral countries of the area and include them in its sphere of interests, the so-called "grey zone" '.[31] But a Soviet APN commentator had excluded Finland from those states believed to have come under discussion at the NATO meeting.[32] The Soviet Union clearly was uncertain about the outcome of the crucial NATO Council meeting; in this situation Finnish attitudes would carefully be followed.

Writing under a pseudonym Kekkonen argued that if Finland had been placed in the grey zone of states under NATO military protection it would mean that the NATO states had discarded their recognition of Finland's position of neutrality. He maintained that such a NATO guarantee could not in fact be accepted by Finland, since it would denote 'a unilateral repudiation of the cooperation and assistance treaty [of 1948], which Finland is not even legally entitled to do'. A NATO guarantee, he wrote, would represent an attempt by NATO to act as 'some kind of guardian with respect to Finland in international politics', which 'would directly influence our country's policy of neutrality in a fateful way'. The Soviet reaction to a statement of NATO military guarantees for Finland, as Kekkonen recognised, could be to demand consultations on the basis of the Finnish–Soviet FCMA-Treaty.[33]

Despite these apprehensions, it appeared that henceforth Finland would be left out of the contingency planning of NATO, and some circles in Finland claimed that Finland's chances of conducting a self-reliant policy of neutrality correspondingly had improved. One consequence of Finland's changing role in Western strategy at the end of the 1960s was the emergence of talk of Finlandisation, which was used to intimidate recalcitrant NATO members in Europe. But in the aftermath of the grey zones debate there were no visible Soviet attempts to press for closer military integration with Finland in response to the withdrawal of any residual Western military or political commitments to Finland.

A full decade later, rumours were aired in Scandinavia, however, that during a visit to Finland in July 1968 by the Soviet Minister of Defence, Marshal Ustinov, accompanied by seven generals, a Soviet proposal for joint Finnish-Soviet military exercises had been made.

Well before this visit the organ of the minority faction of the Finnish Communist Party had invoked the idea of combined exercises to counteract plans by NATO in Northern Europe.

In response to a parliamentary question put on 5 October the Finnish Minister of Defence, Taisto Tähkämaa, did not directly deny that a Soviet proposal for combined exercises had been made. He observed that the 1948 FCMA-Treaty renders Finnish–Soviet military cooperation possible 'in a crisis situation precisely defined by the Treaty', but that 'peacetime joint military exercises or other similar cooperation in the military sphere would . . . be incompatible with Finland's international status'. In this context Tähkämaa stated that the Finnish government 'knows that the government of the Soviet Union is not endeavouring to alter the stable situation in the North, nor have any proposals that would indicate this been presented by the Soviet Union'.[34] This official view was confirmed by Minister of Defence Lasse Äikäs after a meeting with Marshal Ustinov in July 1980. The Soviet Scandinavian specialist Lev Voronkov later admitted that such military measures would only be possible after 'a threat of attack is jointly established in discussions' as referred to in the 1948 treaty.[35]

In an interview in Norway Kekkonen interpreted the rumour about the Soviet proposal as an attempt to disturb Finnish–Soviet relations.[36] Unofficial sources indicate that the whole affair was more complicated than appears from the evasive responses of the Finnish authorities. The importance of the episode, however, lies in its outcome: the Finnish government stuck to the principles of its policy of neutrality, which would have been challenged by joint Finnish–Soviet military exercises equally well as by the acceptance of a NATO security guarantee of the kind presumed in the grey zones debate a decade earlier. But the Finnish policy of neutrality would not exclude 'good relations between the defence forces of Finland and the armed forces of the Soviet Union', nor contacts between these forces in the form of 'customary exchanges of visits in addition to procurements of material and training'. After pointing this out in response to the parliamentary question about Finnish–Soviet military exercises, the Finnish Minister of Defence stated that the intention was to continue and develop these contacts[37] (see Chapter 4). The limited character of such contacts has not always been appreciated in the West, where allegations have even been made – and correctly rebutted by Finnish officials – that the Soviet Union had helped the Finns to build military roads from east and west in Finnish Lapland.[38]

The relations of the Finnish and Soviet defence forces came under further scrutiny after the Soviet military intervention in Afghanistan in December 1979. The Norwegian press reported on Soviet military manoeuvres near the Finnish border and in the Gulf of Finland, while Swiss and Swedish papers published articles on 'anxiety in Finland' because of Afghanistan.[39] Some observers may have recalled that Finland had been categorised alongside Afghanistan in Brezhnev's report to the Twenty Third Party Congress in 1966. But Finnish–Soviet relations were placed in a separate European category apart from those of Afghanistan and the USSR in the reports of both the Twenty-fifth and Twenty-sixth Party Congresses. In early 1980 speculation arose in Finland about the comparability of the 1948 Finnish–Soviet FCMA-Treaty and the 1978 Soviet–Afghan Treaty of Friendship, Good-Neighbourliness and Cooperation. But the latter treaty, in fact, does not contain particular provisions for Soviet military assistance,[40] and the Finnish Foreign Minister assessed such parallels to be 'entirely without foundation'.[41] Some in Scandinavia interpreted Soviet statements justifying military intervention in Afghanistan as general points with general validity, which reserved Soviet leaders the right to pass judgements on the nature of each state on the Soviet periphery and to take corresponding action. The Finnish authorities did not accept such views; they portrayed their relations with the USSR as *sui generis*. The Finnish Under-Secretary of State, Keijo Korhonen, stated in September 1980 that the Afghanistan crisis did not affect Finland's neighbouring geopolitical areas, nor in his opinion did it affect Finland's relations with any other country.[42]

From the Finnish point of view the security implications of the intensifying crisis in Poland, which became critical once martial law was imposed in December 1981, were far more serious than the distant clashes in Afghanistan. It was out of an awareness of this, no doubt, that the Foreign Affairs Committee of the Finnish government convened in mid-December to deliberate the Polish situation. From the perspective of the stability of the Nordic region the military takeover in Poland clearly was much preferable to the possible alternative of open Soviet military intervention. But although President Koivisto denied that the events in Poland affected Finnish–Soviet relations,[43] it was a fact that this military-political crisis involved a Baltic Sea state bordering on the USSR, a situation which, according to Soviet writers in the 1970s, would influence directly the security of both the Finnish and Soviet states.

In 1977 the Soviet writers Bartenev and Komissarov had described the 1948 treaty as a 'mutual security and military assistance pact', and argued that despite the reference to Germany in Article 1 the treaty created an obligation to repel an attack, as described in this article, from whatever quarter it may come. They considered the problem in the North to be one of 'the security of Finland and the security of the Soviet north-west border in a wider sense, of security which is directly linked to, and is dependent on, the kind of military-political situation which arises in Northern Europe and the Baltic Sea'. In their view it was clear that 'if the danger of this area changing into a military bridgehead against the Soviet Union arises, then the security of Finland and its territory is also endangered, in other words the situation arises for which the military-political articles of the 1948 treaty provide.'[44]

Once the debate these Soviet writers had initiated had run its course, Finnish diplomats uneasily acknowledged the 'service' Bartenev and Komissarov had performed 'by showing how these matters may be thought about in official circles in the Soviet Union'.[45] Many Finns were anxious because these Soviet views spelt out the Soviet claim, which had been implicit in Soviet behaviour during the Note Crisis, but which had been recognised by few Finns, that Soviet military consultations may be initiated on the basis of the 1948 treaty during a certain state of political-military relations in the Nordic region and not only when an attack or threat of attack as laid down by the treaty is present (see interpretation of the treaty in Chapter 1, and the course of the Note Crisis in Chapter 2).

It appeared that influential figures in the USSR had concluded by the 1970s that since Soviet security arrangements with Finland existed as one component in the Nordic policy of the USSR they should be operated accordingly. For Finland this underlined that the destiny and security of the nation were still inextricably bound to the constellation of forces in the Nordic region as a whole. The Finns rest their hopes in the belief that the interests of the great powers in the Nordic region lie mainly in preventive not intrusive measures. This summarises the Finnish view of the strategic wrangles between the Soviet Union and the Nordic NATO states over the past two decades.

FINLAND AND THE NORDIC REGION IN SOVIET STRATEGY AFTER THE NOTE CRISIS

The most significant strategic development in the Nordic region since the Note Crisis has been the increasing concentration of the great power alliance systems on the Arctic Sea and the Northern Cap region. The introduction of missile carrying submarines and the shift in the centre of gravity of the Soviet fleet to the open seas led to a build-up of the naval and auxiliary resources of the Soviet Northern fleet on the Kola peninsula, and transformed the ice-free port of Murmansk from a regional security problem for the Soviet Union into part of the global balance of power. Murmansk, which is located only sixty miles from the Norwegian border, was developed into the world's largest naval base. Soviet 'bridgehead' anxieties have shifted largely from Finland to Norway, since Norwegian territory could pose a threat to Soviet vessels plying the northern seas. So long as the Soviet Union considers Norway to be only a local or regional security problem there appears to be little need for the USSR to be greatly concerned about the question of who controls the Norwegian coast. But once this territory is considered to be part of the global balance between the alliance systems then the possibility of military operations on land or by air in the Northern Cap area, which could involve Finland, has to be taken into account.[46]

In the West, and in particular in Norway, strategists have concluded that during a crisis the Soviet Union would be tempted to take control of the Norwegian fjord system to assist the operations of its Northern fleet against vital Western sea links on the North Atlantic. The assumption is, therefore, that Finnish Lapland would be valuable to the Soviet Union for the purposes of military transit, and attention has been drawn to the strategic implications of the development of the communications infrastructure of this region since the early 1960s. Finnish defence specialists have argued, however, that in any event the USSR possesses good ice-free ports on the Murmansk coast and that the long transport route overland would only increase unnecessary costs.[47] In the Finnish view, formulated in the 1960s, the functions of the Soviet Northern fleet are primarily defensive, and the classic submarine and crusier battle in the Atlantic of past wars has lost its former significance.[48]

The First Finnish Parliamentary Defence Committee, which submitted its report in 1971, nevertheless recognised the existence of 'anxiety on both [NATO and Soviet] sides about the use of Finnish territory as an attack route'. NATO sources, the committee noted, had discussed Soviet desires to make use of the Finnish road network, while the USSR had considered it possible that NATO would wish to gain control of Finnish Lapland to increase the depth of its own defence.[49] The report of the second Defence Committee, submitted five years later, stressed that it was important that Finland 'cannot be used militarily for transit or as a base area', and acknowledged that 'the air space and road system of Finnish Lapland adjacent to the strategically important northern seas could, during a conflict between military alliances, offer a possibility of outflanking the other side's positions'.[50] This view was confirmed by the latest Defence Committee in 1981, which also disclosed the Finnish view that NATO and Soviet policy in the North was one of territorial denial to the other side. According to the specialists on the committee:

> In the present situation both leading great powers possess an effective capability to protect their vital interests in Northern Europe . . . [and] without significant troop transfers neither power will be able seriously to threaten the vital interests of the other by means of conventional arms.[51]

But the Finns have remained dubious about Soviet expressions of concern over the possibility of hostile land operations against Soviet territory from Norway, since they are aware of the very considerable logistical problems which would be involved. It appears that the idea of a rapid strike overland against Murmansk, which may have been included in NATO military planning in the 1960s, has long been abandoned on these logistical grounds. Finnish appreciation of this influenced the Finnish reaction to plans for the creation of a rapid deployment force in Norway at the end of the 1970s.

Even before the Note Crisis, however, Finnish leaders, out of consideration of the requirements of the Finnish policy of neutrality, took seriously the anxieties of the great power blocs about the possible hostile use of Finnish air space. Finnish policy has presumed in particular the need to prevent the violation of Finnish air space in Lapland.[52] As a consequence, both the Soviet Union and Britain were prepared to accept the Finnish argument in the early 1960s about the defence requirements of a neutral state, and to revoke the ban on guided missiles which had been imposed on Finland by the peace treaty of 1947.

In 1971 the Parliamentary Defence Committee (PDC) pointed out that Norway had constructed many airfields, and recognised that in the Soviet view the territory of Finland creates pressure on the air defence system of the Soviet north-east regions. The committee also remarked on the build-up of Soviet air forces in the Kola and

Leningrad region and noted that both great power blocs could strengthen their air forces in Fennoscandia very rapidly.[53] The second PDC laid down plans for moving one-third of the Finnish air forces to northern Finland by 1985, while the report of the third PDC in 1981 emphasised that it is in the interests of both alliances that Finnish air space remains under Finnish control and that 'Finland is able to make an intrusive use of her air space prohibitively costly'. Although the existence of the Finnish air defence in Lapland creates a potential for use in crisis or war, this statement may also be interpreted as one about the political function of the Finnish air forces in peacetime in Northern Europe. The Finnish planes in Lapland are more than symbolic, since it is understood that they will intercept foreign planes that venture into Finnish air space during the great power military exercises in this buffer region.

Soviet security sensitivity over the Murmansk base region in peacetime was illustrated by an incident in April 1978 when a commercial airliner belonging to South Korea Air Lines intruded deep into Soviet territory north-east of Murmansk, apparently intending to make a short cut, and was forced to make an emergency landing by Soviet fighters in Soviet Karelia.[54] Soviet officials recalled this incident in trying to justify the notorious decision to shoot down an aircraft of the same company which intruded over another strategically sensitive region of the USSR, the vicinity of Sakhalin, in September 1983.[55] Despite their dramatic impact, both incidents made Soviet air defences appear clumsy. In the light of this, the Finnish determination to defend her air space could also act as an important early warning system for the USSR of a strike from Norway.

The issue of controlling Finnish air space involves not only the threat perceived by the USSR in the possible use of Norwegian air fields against Kola and the Murmansk base, but also the possibility, not officially acknowledged in Finland, that during a crisis or war the Soviet Union may wish to make use of the existing airfields in Norway to extend Soviet air cover for the operations of the Soviet Northern fleet further into the Atlantic. It is unclear whether the Finnish general staff expect the Finnish air force to act against such Soviet activity via Finnish Lapland, or to provide facilities for the USSR to assist Soviet operations and to strengthen Soviet defences against a possible Western air strike on the Murmansk base area. If the latter objective is in mind, and perhaps it should be noted without drawing any firm conclusions from the fact that the Finnish air defence is situated predominantly in north-east Lapland, technological advances will create increasing pressure to integrate the Finnish and Soviet air defence systems through military consultations at an early stage in any crisis developing in the Nordic region. Even in peacetime, as the reception in Finland of the commander-in-chief of the Soviet air force, Marshal Kutakhov, in autumn 1982 illustrates, contacts exist between the Soviet and Finnish air forces.

The official Finnish defence doctrine does not introduce specific threat scenarios, since by doing so, a Finnish diplomat explained, Finland 'would intentionally single out one of our neighbours as a potential aggressor', which 'would run counter to the basic tenets of Finnish foreign policy thinking'.[56] But the Finns admit that the air space problem constitutes a 'special issue', since according to the 1981 PDC 'its inviolability would apparently be threatened first in a crisis situation, and attempts to exploit it could be made without violating our land and seas areas'.[57] This seems to be just the situation in which the USSR may call for military consultations with Finland leading to military assistance on the basis of the 1948 treaty.

If Finnish defence policy were to be determined solely by Soviet security desiderata then Finland would be compelled to concentrate nearly all of its resources on maintaining air control in Finnish Lapland. This would imply an abandonment of Finland as a territorial entity as well as of the principles behind a policy of neutrality. The Lapland issue has in fact drawn attention away from the air defence of Finland's most populated and industrially developed areas further south. It would be a naive presumption that in major European conventional hostilities, which would in all likelihood rapidly involve the Nordic region on account of the strategic significance of the Murmansk base, these regions of Finland would necessarily be left inviolate. Such naivety is certainly not to be found in the latest Swedish PDC report, although the report considers Sweden's (like Finland's) northern parts to be strategically significant. NATO plans acknowledge that in a conflict of this order the USSR probably would be in a position to benefit from strategic facilities in southern Finland.

All three Finnish parliamentary defence committees have stressed, however, that Finland forms a territorial whole, to be defended in all parts. On these grounds considerable Finnish resources have been put into the defence of Helsinki. The committees have also upheld the necessity of Finland's own independent defence capability to be available in time of crisis so that Finland need not rely purely on the opportunities for military assistance provided by the FCMA-Treaty with the USSR. Finland's Lapland defence plan, therefore, is not directed purely at air defence. The Finns have transferred appreciable infantry forces to these remote regions under the prompting of the report of the second PDC. They have developed the infrastructure for the regional defence of Lapland, although Finnish officers do not anticipate a NATO ground strike through Lapland in any future East–West conflict. The rationale for these forces may be that they act as a political assurance to both East and West that Lapland should not be conceived of as an area of problem-free military transit. But the Finnish policy creates military expectations within both NATO and the USSR of Finnish action on their behalf in a crisis or conflict.

The USSR is reassured by the existence of the 1948 treaty but Soviet spokesmen are uncertain about the Finnish interest in guerilla warfare tactics and critical of studies of Finnish defence which emphasise self-reliance at the expense of the military provisions of the treaty. The Finns have tried to allay such Soviet concern by admitting that the main determinant of their position 'from a military-political standpoint' remains the question of 'how the Soviet Union will assess the military threat potentially directed against Soviet targets through Finnish territory'.[58] But in NATO circles this simple reality continues to cast doubt on the Finnish resolve to defend their entire territory, including Lapland, against allcomers.

In an interview in January 1983, the commander of NATO forces in Western Europe, General Bernard Rogers, informed that he was disturbed lest 'the Finnish and Soviet governments might decide that the Finns would not fight with the determination we should hope for' in the event of a Soviet strike at NATO bases in Norway through a Scandinavian corridor.[59] Rogers believed that Soviet ground forces plan to cross Finnish Lapland during a crisis in the Nordic region and that the Finns may be prepared, after a token resistance, to concede to Soviet demands for military transit. This would statisfy both the minimal requirements of neutrality and the spirit of the 1948 treaty. While Rogers' interview was assailed in the USSR as a provocation intended to scare Finland with the Soviet military threat and to 'hamstring its friendly relations with the Soviet Union',[60] the Finnish foreign and defence ministers expressed their 'astonishment' and attributed the general's views to faulty information.

The Finns argue that Murmansk is part of the global strategy of the superpower blocs and that the Soviet military build-up on the Kola peninsula 'makes all military arrangements . . . [in the North] strategic in character'.[61] But they recognise that the two Soviet motorised infantry divisions, a marine infantry regiment, and numerous Soviet ground-attack aircraft, all currently based in this area, are evidence of a potential Nordic dimension in Soviet policy. The Soviet infantry on the Kola peninsula may also be intended for rapid defence deployment. The Finnish general staff may consider the chances of a NATO ground strike at Kola slight, but it recognises that Soviet military leaders may judge otherwise. Despite this defence rationale for these Soviet forces, Finnish defence specialists are aware that since the early 1960s Soviet military thinking has changed. Defensive plans are now conceived in offensive, preventive terms. The Nordic dimension of Soviet policy, which the Kola land forces in theory permit, could involve military action against the NATO communications infrastructure on Norwegian territory and the occupation of the Norwegian airfields.

Contrary to General Rogers, however, Finnish specialists assert that a Soviet offensive thrust against NATO installations in northern Norway would not require the use of Finnish territory, since it could more easily be accomplished by air and sea power. By employing airborne and amphibious troops in a putative offensive, the USSR could perhaps bypass the main Norwegian line of defence in the southern part of Troms province. Geography would not permit this if Soviet troops were to try a short cut through Finland, or probably even through Sweden.[62] Furthermore, the East–West transport infrastructure in Lapland remains poorly developed; it is not well developed even on the Soviet side of the border.[63] All of this induces scepticism among Finns about the Rogers type military scenario in the North, although they have been by no means indifferent to the Soviet military build-up on Kola. As a matter of politics Finnish officials have been more vocal, however, in their opinions about developments in Norwegian–NATO relations and the practice of Swedish neutrality which could affect the stability of the North.

Despite its independent national objectives, Finland's Nordic policy shares some common ground with Soviet policy in the North, but there are crucial differences. The Finns acknowledge that Soviet policy 'attempts to restrict the operations which the NATO presence in Norway and Denmark give rise to, and in particular to prevent the growth of West German influence in the North'.[64] But since the primary Finnish concern is to maintain the status quo in the North, the Finnish government does not object to the NATO involvement in the Nordic region in principle, although there are those to be found on the Finnish political spectrum who do. The Soviet view, as expressed by Khrushchev in 1964, is that 'peace in Northern Europe would be facilitated if Norway and Denmark did not have military obligations linking them with states that have no relation with this region'.[65] This is not how Finnish officials would state the case. Since the early 1960s their concern has been rather than once Nordic–NATO and in particular Norwegian–NATO relations become more strongly pronounced the result will be a stronger extra-regionalisation of Norwegian security policy and a greater likelihood that a conflict in the North would have serious security implications for Finland.

During the 1960s the Soviet press focused attention on West German control of 'so-called "supply bases" ' in Norway, and on the 'complete subordination of the Norwegian air force' to the West German military.[66] It noted plans to build 'a major military installation to serve NATO submarines' in the border region of Norway and the USSR, and the entrance of Norway into the permanent NATO naval force in the Atlantic.[67] A NATO Council decision in 1968 on strengthening its northern flank was interpreted as proof of attempts to 'step up the bloc's military effort in this area'.[68] In conformity with the Finnish policy of neutrality Kekkonen reacted cautiously to such Soviet observations. He considered it to be 'difficult to say' whether NATO activity in Northern Europe 'has increased or remained the same', although he felt that it was 'clear that the Soviet Union has the view that the activity of NATO has increased'.[69] But when a qualitative tightening of Norwegian–West German military relations seemed to be pending in the mid-1970s Kekkonen felt constrained to express his views more forcefully.

Since the beginning of the 1960s West German air and naval forces had taken part in NATO military exercises in Norwegian air space and territorial waters. But it was only in June 1976 that the Norwegian government decided to permit West German army troops to take part in military exercises on Norwegian territory. During a visit to Oslo in September 1976 Kekkonen strongly emphasised the significance for Finland of the restraints on Norwegian policy concerning bases and the storing of nuclear arms. He referred to the traditional policy of Norway which had excluded certain allies from NATO military exercises in Norway. On its part the Soviet press assailed the Norwegian decision as one quite contrary to previous Norwegian assurances of the country's desire 'to stave off any situations that might increase tensions' in the Norwegian–Soviet border region, and speculated about plans to change the Norwegian policy towards military bases.[70] This was a continuation of earlier speculation about the existence of sounding out talks within NATO for the possible creation of a NATO military base in northern Norway to replace the Keflavik base in Iceland.[71]

In an unofficial speech in March 1977 Kekkonen went so far as to maintain that the Norwegian government had recently come under pressure from 'military persons, NATO devotees' and from 'right wing papers, which had whipped up hostility to the Soviet Union and in this respect have now also set to work on the relations of Finland and Norway'.[72] Soviet concern about the implications of a visit by the West German Defence Minister to Norway at this time apparently was taken seriously in Finland, although some Western observers interpreted Kekkonen's heated words as an attempt to appease the Soviet Union with an eye to a visit to Finland by Prime Minister Kosygin, which took place a few days later. The Norwegians proved to be responsive, moreover, since no West German combat troops thus far have in fact taken part in NATO exercises on Norwegian soil, although West German auxiliary troops have been included.

One Norwegian interpretation of this affair has been that the Norwegian government's response was intended to avert the possibility that the USSR might react to the presence of German combat troops in Norway by invoking Article 2 of the FCMA-Treaty with Finland. According to this argument, Kekkonen's speeches were an indirect warning of this possibility.[73] Yet Kekkonen may have over-reacted to the West German presence in Norway towards the end of the 1970s. Although Soviet leaders have retained a political obsession with Germany, which was fuelled throughout the 1960s by real concern about the possible maverick intentions of West Germany within NATO, their declamatory statements against West German involvement in the Nordic region in the 1970s were intended primarily as propaganda to limit the NATO presence in general in this area. Soviet concern about NATO activities in Norway was transferred increasingly from the West German to the American presence. Since the late 1970s Soviet leaders have played upon divergent views between the two NATO allies, West Germany and the United States, so it has no longer been politically expedient to continue to attack West Germany in the Nordic context. These political priorities have much reduced such Soviet criticism, which now is directed at the strategic implications of the American military infrastructure in the North.

Soviet attacks on Norwegian policy became more strident at the end of the 1970s. The operation of the airborne warning and control system in Norwegian airspace, the use of Norwegian air bases for servicing NATO aircraft, and the establishment of foreign communications monitoring stations on Norwegian territory were branded as attempts by NATO to turn Norway 'into a base of operations for the bloc in Northern Europe'.[74] A critical Norwegian survey of the country's nuclear arms and base policy concluded in 1978 that 'Norway renders the United States some strategic services that are of even greater service to it than the mere deployment of its troops and nuclear weapons in peacetime'. The writers argued that 'these services also seem to be more provocative in relation to the USSR than are ordinary military bases'. A Soviet reviewer of this work observed that NATO nuclear submarines and aircraft carrying such weapons were enabled to operate in the Atlantic 'largely thanks to the system of bases and other facilities on Norwegian territory'.[75]

A *Pravda* article criticising Norwegian–American talks in 1980 for the creation in Norway of permanent weapons depots to outfit an American brigade for emergency landings near the Soviet border went so far as to conjecture that 'these dangerous storehouses may conceal components . . . of tactical nuclear weapons'. The Norwegian government denied that the prepositioning of heavy equipment for American troops on Norwegian soil contradicted Norway's basing policy, but the Soviet contention was that from a military viewpoint 'every foreign military strongpoint is in effect a base, regardless of how many foreign servicemen are stationed there at any given time'.[76] These developments in Norwegian policy were proclaimed to be jeopardising the security of all of Northern Europe, which 'cannot fail to reflect on the development of interstate relations in that region'.[77] The interrelation of the security policies of the Nordic countries compelled some response from Finland.

Prime Minister Koivisto admitted in June 1980 that the interpretation of the restrictions set by Norway on its security policy was the Norwegians own affair, but affirmed that Finland 'wished to believe that Norway has not changed its security policy and that the country does not want to change it in the long term'.[78] Three months later Kekkonen asserted less hesitantly that American arms depots in Norway would not change the security balance in the Nordic region in any way,[79] and this was interpreted in Norway as an official statement that the arms depots conformed with Norway's NATO base policy. In fact, Norway arrived at a political decision in the same year not to prestock heavy material for an American marine amphibious brigade in northern Norway at Tromsö, but in Troendlag in central Norway.

Despite their independent responses, both Finnish and Soviet statesmen in common have consistently been concerned about any extra-regional implications of developments in Norwegian policy. For the Finns such changes could undermine their own position. One Finnish foreign policy specialist drew disturbing parallels in 1979 between the current Soviet reaction to NATO developments in Northern Europe and the character of Nordic relations at the time of the Note Crisis.[80] In the light of the foregoing the prospect of a large NATO airlift to northern Norway cannot be viewed with equanimity among Finnish politicians and defence specialists. This new strategy was anticipated already in 1974, when Norway signed a confidential memorandum of understanding for the use of eight airfields by American reinforcements during a crisis, but it was signalled publicly in general terms by American statesmen only at the beginning of the 1980s. It is intended to offset delays caused by slower reinforcements by sea, hindered by hidden Soviet submarines, in the event that Norway were to be attacked by the USSR across its Arctic border. A Norwegian minister admitted, however, that an attempt at such an airlift 'could be construed as provocative', and that as a strategic countermeasure the USSR could well invoke the military provisions of the 1948 treaty with Finland.[81] This kind of Northern Balance thinking is likely to increase Finnish anxiety and uncertainty about great power designs on Finnish Lapland.

In addition to the Arctic Sea, the Baltic Sea will continue to be a primary strategic importance in the operational planning of the USSR in the 1980s. This is indicated by the violation of Swedish territorial waters by a Soviet submarine in October to November 1981,[82] and the presence of submarines engaged in coordinated operations tracked in Swedish waters in autumn 1982, which were an open challenge to Swedish neutrality. The Finnish Foreign Office considered the former incident not to impinge on Finland,[83] although some Swedish defence specialists speculated that Soviet strategists might be thinking of 'hiding' their submarines in neutral waters in the event of war, which clearly would involve the Finnish Baltic archipelago. In fact, in June 1982 a Finnish coastguard vessel dropped warning charges on a submerged submarine in the demilitarised Finnish waters around the Åland Islands, which was probably part of a broader operation directed against the northern parts of Sweden. The Finnish government's concern, expressed by the publicising of this act, has not been allayed by the conclusion of the Swedish Submarine Defence Commission, which published its report in April 1983, that the recent submarine intrusions must have been of a military operational kind in the form of preparations for actual missions to be undertaken in case of war.[84]

At the same time the Swedes rejected a Soviet allegation that they had been cooperating with NATO in military intelligence activities directed against the USSR,[85] and brushed off strong Soviet criticisms in February 1982 that an agreement on arms sales and on cooperation over military technology with the United States would undermine confidence in Sweden's neutrality.[86] Soviet claims that the growing defence budget of Sweden exceeds the requirements of neutrality reflect the Soviet concern that Sweden is becoming increasingly integrated into the Western defence system.[87] The American Defence Minister, Weinberger, had expressed his expectations of such a course for Sweden already before the major submarine incident, during an official visit to Sweden in October 1981.[88]

The primary Finnish concern is that the clumsy and provocative behaviour of Soviet submarines may propel the Swedes to enter into relations of military dependence on the United States or NATO, to the detriment of Swedish neutrality. Such an adjustment in Sweden's policy would certainly lower the 'threshold' of Finnish–Soviet military consultations if not directly lead to attempts at some degree of military integration between the two states.

NUCLEAR WEAPONS AND SECURITY DILEMMAS IN THE 1980s

In an important speech in Stockholm in May 1978 Kekkonen argued that technological developments were working towards the possibility of a limited nuclear war in Europe and that Northern Europe would be by no means immune from the effects of such nuclear strategies. To avert this danger he urged the Nordic countries to begin negotiations to establish a Nordic arms control arrangement founded on the basic security policies adopted by the states in the region, which would be intended to insulate them as completely as possible from the effects of nuclear strategies in general and new weapons in particular. To ensure the nuclear-free status of the area the states party to the arrangement could receive superpower guarantees that nuclear weapons would not be used against their territories under any circumstances.[89]

Kekkonen's proposal renewed and updated his earlier plans for a Northern nuclear-free zone. Finland had failed to initiate a dialogue between the Nordic countries on this subject in the 1960s. Their attention had been focused more on the global problem of nuclear proliferation, which had led to the Non-Proliferation Treaty in 1968. Despite Soviet support for Finnish interest in nuclear-free zones in the 1970s[90] Finland also failed to have this issue included in the CSCE Final Act.

The Swedish government responded favourably to Kekkonen's initiative in 1978, but made the reservation that 'such a plan has to take into account the tactical nuclear weapons which are in our proximity and which can be directed at objects located in the North'.[91] Swedish diplomats pointed out that the USSR has nuclear weapons installed from the Kola peninsula down to the Baltic states. They were probably most anxious over the presence of Soviet SS5 intermediate-range missiles on Kola, which cast a shadow over the whole of Scandinavia. Sweden was also worried about the redeployment of Soviet submarines equipped with nuclear warheads into the Baltic Sea, which became public knowledge in February 1978. Following reports that the USSR had installed nuclear weapons on surface vessels as well the Swedes became even more concerned about the limits of any proposed nuclear-free zone. Kekkonen insisted that the issue of widening the proposed zone to include international waters 'can be settled only with the cooperation of the nuclear armed states'.[92] The Finns similarly were disinclined to try to include the Kola peninsula in the territorial scope of the zone, partly because they believed that the USSR is needed not as a participant in but as a guarantor of a Northern nuclear-free zone.[93]

Soviet commentators were quite explicit that any nuclear-free zone in the North could not be extended into international air space without contravening international law. Since the USSR is a nuclear power, a Soviet spokesman argued:

> neither its territory nor any part thereof can be included in a nuclear-free zone or in a so-called 'security belt' adjacent to the nuclear-free zone . . . it would be wrong to raise the question of the limitation of the military activity of a single nuclear weapon power merely because it borders on a nuclear weapon-free zone.[94]

Calls to include Soviet territory in the nuclear-free zone were interpreted as attempts to take advantage of a natural Soviet interest in the creation of such a zone 'to obtain one-sided strategic interests for NATO in the name of "regional security" '.[95] There was some substance to these Soviet views since the nuclear neutralisation of Kola would constitute an abandonment of a major element of the Soviet strategic force, which rests with the Soviet missile carrying submarines in the warm water port of Murmansk.

Despite all previous Soviet objections, during an interview for a Finnish paper in June 1981 Brezhnev disclosed that the USSR 'does not preclude the possibility of considering some other measures applicable to our own territory in the region adjoining the nuclear-free zone in the North of Europe'.[96] He conceded that the Soviet Union was prepared 'to discuss this question with the countries concerned'. But some months later Foreign Minister Gromyko told his Swedish counterpart, O. Ullsten, that the Northern countries should not expect a more exact response from the USSR before they themselves has jointly agreed to begin consultations.[97] The Finns were told that the Soviet party did not wish to set prior conditions which later, during possible negotiations, may cause difficulties. All the details of a proposed nuclear-free zone were considered to be subject to negotiation.[98] The most the Finns could be expected to do in these circumstances was to try to keep channels open for negotiation between the other more hesitant Nordic countries and the nuclear power to the east. In this context the Finnish and Swedish foreign ministers had turned down a proposal at the end of 1980 for a nuclear-free zone including only Sweden and Finland.

Finland reacted cautiously to Swedish Prime Minister Fälldin's view that the Soviet–Swedish submarine incident in November 1981 compelled the Swedes more strongly to emphasise the need to include nuclear arms in the Baltic Sea within any nuclear-free zone in the North.[99] The Soviet foreign policy adviser to Brezhnev, G. Arbatov, stated in April 1982 that the presence of Soviet strategic devices in the North meant that the North could not become a complete nuclear-free zone. He pointed out the strategic value of the Arctic and Baltic Seas for the USSR.[100] But in the exacerbated international situation both the USSR and Finland were agreed in December that the realisation of a Northern nuclear-free zone had assumed 'even greater urgency'.[101]

In June 1983 once again the Finns were the first to hear a Soviet offer to inject new life into the scheme for a nuclear-free North, this time from the new Soviet leader, Andropov. During an official visit to the USSR when Koivisto promised that the Finns would continue their efforts towards such a zone, he was informed by Andropov that 'the Soviet Union could also discuss the issue of making the Baltic Sea region nuclear-free with the relevant parties'.[102] This Soviet concession was, no doubt, primarily intended to allay Swedish anxieties about the Baltic Sea. The Swedish Prime Minister, Olof Palme, called it 'a positive step forward', and even the NATO states Norway and Denmark described Andropov's proposal as 'interesting', although Norway pointed out that he had said nothing about the Kola peninsula or nuclear arms in the Arctic Sea region.[103]

In November 1983 a Soviet Central Committee official clarified the Soviet stand by informing that the USSR was prepared to remove its Baltic complement of nuclear-armed submarines, a reference to the six Soviet 'Golf'-class submarines equipped with SS-N-5 missiles. He made no mention of missile stocks on the Baltic shore.[104] But by 1984 the essential difficulty for the creation of a Northern nuclear-free zone was less its territorial scope than Norwegian and Danish (but not Swedish[105]) insistence that such issues should be brought forward in the broader European context of arms discussions between the great powers, since by November 1983 the negotiations on medium-range missiles had been broken off at Geneva. Nevertheless, at the opening of the Stockholm Conference on confidence building measures the Finnish Foreign Minister tentatively brought up the question of 'formal arrangements' to guarantee the preservation of the Nordic region outside nuclear strategic speculations, especially those linked with new arms technology.[106] It appears that Finland may try to keep the issue alive in the mid-1980s during the exchanges at Stockholm.

In his speech in the same city in May 1978 proposing a Nordic arms arrangement, Kekkonen had already underlined the gravity of the political problems created by the proposed introduction of cruise missiles into Europe. He pointed out that according to the information available the technical properties of these missiles, unlike those of the intercontinental missiles maintained by the nuclear powers hitherto, 'may make the use of third country and neutral air space a routine matter'. In a controversial article written in November 1979 the Soviet specialist on Finland, Yuri Komissarov, used Kekkonen's words to support his contention that the NATO Eurostrategic missiles decision would endanger the position of Finland and the whole of Northern Europe. He considered the new NATO missiles to be aimed specifically against the north-western regions of the Soviet Union, so that the paths the missiles presumably would follow on the way to their targets would impinge on Finnish air space. Any such flight, in Komissarov's view, 'would very urgently prompt the question' of Finland's and Sweden's 'right and obligation to defend their territorial integrity'. Komissarov recalled in this connection that 'there exist certain obligations which bind Finland and the Soviet Union [under the terms of the FCMA-Treaty] . . . in the event of Finland or the Soviet Union through Finnish territory, becoming the object of a military attack'.[107]

On the political level Komissarov may have been attempting to remind Norway and Denmark through Finland and Sweden that cruise missiles would create difficulties for the security policies of the latter states. In response to Kekkonen's speech in Stockholm the Swedish Foreign Minister, K. Söder, had already expressed Swedish anxieties about the consequences of the development of tactical nuclear arms.[108] Komissarov's article, and an equivalent article published in Sweden, may also have been intended to persuade Finland and Sweden to try to bring the question of cruise missiles to a joint negotiation table with the Warsaw Pact countries.

The Finnish view had been that security problems created by developments in military technology should be resolved through political means. But a few days before the NATO decision to deploy cruise missiles in Europe the Finnish Foreign Minister replied to Komissarov through an assurance that even in altered circumstances the obligations enshrined in the 1948 FCMA-Treaty retained their importance, and Finland had to be able to be capable of defending her territorial integrity.[109] The report of the Finnish defence committee in 1981 recognised that the deployment of cruise missiles would pose 'additional challenges to the air defence systems of neutral countries', and promised that 'with the development of new methods of intercepting cruise missiles our surveillance and interception systems will be supplemented as deemed necessary and possible within the constraints of our resources'.[110] The need for technological developments of this kind may reduce the 'threshold' of Finnish–Soviet consultations (see Chapter 4 on military defence), but this excerpt indicates that Finland still expects to maintain an independent defence stand, even in the area of these new defence demands, rather than to rely automatically on Soviet military assistance.

A member of the defence committee, Raimo Väyrynen (not Foreign Minister Paavo Väyrynen) sparked off a rather worried debate in Finland, however when he pointed out later that although the provisions of Finland's 1947 peace treaty prohibit the deployment of nuclear weapons on Finland's territory, theoretically it would be possible for the USSR to transfer nuclear weapons to Finland as part of the military collaboration that could be initiated, by mutual consent, through applying Articles 1 and 2 of the 1948 FCMA-Treaty.[111] President Koivisto tried to still such speculations by affirming that 'we will not allow nuclear weapons to be brought into our country'. 'The idea that the Soviet Union might force them on us' he regarded as 'insulting to our neighbouring country'.[112] This was interpreted as a broad commitment to exclude the stationing of nuclear weapons on Finnish territory even in the event of war.

Speculation also arose in Finland that the deployment of any foreign troops or military installations on Finnish territory might, in the worst case, invite limited nuclear strikes by other nuclear-weapon powers. It was in the Soviet interest to try and induce the Finns to believe that they were already exposed to a potential Western nuclear strike. This could encourage Finland to seek shelter through recourse to military collaboration with the USSR. The latest Finnish defence committee judged that Finland was unlikely to become a target for a nuclear attack in itself. But a Soviet writer refered to NATO contingency plans which were leaked to the press and published in Finland in 1980,[113] and which mentioned twenty Finnish towns as objects for nuclear strikes, to try and persuade Finnish readers that American military strategy 'is directed not only against the USSR and other socialist countries but also against many other regions and countries'.[114] In this context Soviet spokesmen could also point to a Western report in spring 1981 revealing that the planned flight paths of NATO nuclear bombers operating against Murmansk, Leningrad and Archangel, and based in Great Britain, presume the violation of Swedish and Finnish air space.[115]

The Finnish Foreign Office must have been aware that the potential threat from cruise missiles could generate increased Soviet interest in forward based radars, which could result in pressure on Finland among other Nordic countries. The implications for Finland of the imminent deployment of Americans cruise missiles in Europe, in light of the existence of the 1948 treaty, finally led to a decision in November 1983 to announce that Finland (independent of the USSR) is building up the surveillance and interception technology required to shoot down low-flying missiles, including twenty new radar stations.[116] This decision followed the lead of the Swedes, whose military planning programme for 1984–9 reveals that new mobile radars are being brought into service and that Sweden is developing its own early warning system to search for cruise missiles.[117] These military perceptions show that both neutral Finland and Sweden share the perception that cruise missiles have created a threat to their security of a new type from the West.

Yet despite this perception, the current Finnish view appears to be that land-based cruise missiles will have no direct effect on Finland. This was repeated by Foreign Minister Väyrynen in November 1983. Finnish Foreign Ministry officials believe that these cruise missiles will not be targeted at Murmansk, and therefore will not infringe Finnish air space. The real Soviet security problem, which may directly concern the issue of the territorial integrity of neutral Sweden and Finland is considered to lie with the nuclear missiles deployed in submarines and surface vessels, and from bombers, which may be projected at Soviet targets off or across the coastal waters of Norway.[118] This view is not totally convincing, however, since the effectiveness of at least the NATO submarines depends on vulnerable navigation systems operating on Norwegian territory, and the overwhelming importance of Murmansk during an extensive nuclear exchange may therefore encourage the use of central European NATO cruise missiles alongside larger strategic missiles, via Finnish air space, against this target. NATO planning could be very different if nuclear missiles were actually sited on Norwegian territory.

The Finnish Under-Secretary of State, Keijo Korhonen, was inclined to believe in autumn 1980 that Komissarov's statements about cruise missiles were concerned primarily with current discussions about Norwegian policy on bases.[119] As previously mentioned, there have been some Soviet speculations about the possibility of American arms depots in Norway containing components for tactical nuclear weapons. A Soviet commentator stated quite plainly late in 1980 that he considered the new missiles in Europe and arms depots in the Nordic area as two links in the same chain.[120] In early 1982 a Soviet specialist on Scandinavia asserted that Norway and Denmark had not rejected the possibility of their territories being used in the near future as sites for a nuclear attack against the USSR. He argued that the heavy equipment being stored in Norway would enable nuclear missiles to be projected in this way.[121] Soviet onlookers are suspicious that the creation of a rapid deployment force in Norway implies that during a crisis in the North tactical nuclear missiles would also rapidly be deployed in Norway. This scenario may involve logistical difficulties, but in 1982 the Norwegian Foreign Ministry under the new Conservative government admitted that Norway's self-imposed restriction on receiving nuclear arms in peacetime does not 'prevent the Norwegian defence in the event of war from being supported by external forces which have at their disposal nuclear weapons for tactical use by their own units'.[122]

The strategic problems confronting Soviet leaders in the Nordic region in the 1980s appear more intractable with each passing year, since they believe that American and NATO involvement in this area has qualitatively changed in recent years through the gradual introduction into Norway of the essential communications and surveillance infrastructure for conducting a nuclear war with the Soviet Union. In so far as this perception is accurate, this tendency responded to the increasing strategic significance of Murmansk and the Kola peninsula. But in so doing it undermined Finnish hopes that the territory of the Nordic states could be preserved as an area of regional rather than strategic interests in the calculation of forces and planning of the great power alliances.

The direction of NATO policy in the Nordic region may induce a flexible-minded Soviet leadership to make material concessions by offering to include certain weapons systems in contiguous Soviet territory in a regional arms arrangement in the North. Soviet spokesmen will continue to press for the creation of such an arrangement, even if the benefits it offers to Soviet security in the North become more difficult to identify, since, as one Soviet specialist argued in 1983, the realisation of a North European nuclear-free zone 'would serve as an illustrative example for the formation of analogous zones in other regions of the continent, or even beyond its borders'.[123] In this sense, and on this issue, Finnish interests coincide with those of Soviet policy towards Europe in general (see Chapter 5, and Finnish–Soviet foreign policy cooperation). But if the prospects of a Northern nuclear arms arrangement satisfactory to both the Nordic states and the USSR is at all attainable, then the Finnish preparedness to keep the issue alive, as declared by Koivisto in Moscow in June 1983, serves not merely a Soviet, but a Nordic and ultimately a general European interest, that of arms control and mutual restraint over nuclear weapons. After discussions on the issue in Helsinki in summer 1983 even the United States Vice-President, Bush, affirmed that 'we have a better feeling for the idealistic and genuine peaceful motivation that lies behind those who advocate such a zone'.[124]

4 Finnish Neutrality: the Touchstone of Relations with the East

Within Finland the concept of neutrality has served to create a consensus over Finnish foreign policy, although there remains some ambiguity about what neutrality requires of or implies for Finland. A process of development in Finnish attitudes towards neutrality has taken place, which has resulted in increasing mutual understanding about the content of neutral policy among the major political forces in Finland. Even official Finnish spokesmen have not conceived of neutrality as a static or absolute state or institution; since the mid-1950s the character of Finnish neutrality has reflected the changing international environment in which it has operated. If at times Finnish neutrality appears to have been formulated ambiguously, this has reflected attempts to fulfil divergent expectations of neutrality in East and West, in particular with respect to the conduct of neutral policy during peace.

The legal basis of Finnish neutrality has been a Western rather than a Soviet concern. Finnish arguments aimed at reconciling Finnish treaty commitments and neutrality have been intended to bolster the credibility of Finnish neutrality in the West, where neutrality has usually been considered as a status and norm in international relations with a standardised legal content. The credibility of Finnish neutrality in the eyes of Western statesmen, and therefore their political relations with Finland, are strongly influenced by certain minimal legal criteria related to the application of neutrality during hostilities. But since Soviet statesmen also resort to legal explanations of their international behaviour, the Finns have been able to employ legal arguments arising out of neutrality as a political instrument to maintain distance between Finland and the USSR.

The relation between a policy of neutrality and the neutrality of international law is that with the aid of the former attempts can be

89

made to create the realistic preconditions for a state of neutrality, as defined by international law, in time of war. The Finnish policy has aimed, therefore, at keeping the state outside political conflicts, in particular between the great powers. But the policy adopted has been highly flexible, since the Finnish view has remained that 'no handbook, still less a code of laws, of a policy of neutrality exists, which contains a generally recognised programme of behaviour for neutral states'.[1]

THE RECOGNITION OF THE FINNISH POLICY OF NEUTRALITY

Finland had little opportunity to exercise a real policy of neutrality or to claim a neutral status during the period of Paasikivi's presidency. Until the 1947 peace treaty Finland was an enemy state in relation to the Allied powers. Neutrality in the classical sense was also proscribed by the Finnish–Soviet armistice of 1944, through which Finland entered a state of war with Hitler's Germany. It was not until 1954 that the Finnish government made a declaration of protocol ending the state of war with the states previously allied with the German Reich, despite the problem of their recognition. In addition, Finland had leased Porkkala to the USSR for fifty years as a military base and, more decisively, was obliged by the 1947 treaty to permit Soviet rights of military passage to the base by land, sea and air.

The Porkkala lease was a crucial handicap. In autumn 1939 the Finnish government's refusal to cede 'Hanko or any islands in the immediate proximity of the Finnish mainland' as military bases to the USSR was justified by Finland's 'policy of absolute neutrality' and 'firm resolve to remain outside any group of great powers and to hold aloof from any wars and conflicts between them'.[2] Already before the negotiations for the 1948 FCMA-Treaty, Foreign Minister Enckell bemoaned the fact that 'Article 4 of the peace treaty [concerning Porkkala] in any event prevented Finnish neutrality in the case of war'.[3] A legal case can be made that the Porkkala lease did not necessarily constitute an overriding obstacle for Finnish neutrality. The lease of such a base to a belligerent power before a given war, it has been argued, does not in itself proscribe the neutrality of the state which has relinquished that area, since the area leased may be regarded as outside the territorial scope of its neutrality.[4] In the event of an attempt to establish the neutrality of Finland after the 1947 peace treaty, Porkkala çould perhaps have been considered a non-neutral enclave. But despite these legal considerations, upon the outbreak of a war a belligerent power in conflict with the USSR would in all likelihood have attempted to prevent access to the leased area by military means, in which case Finland may very well also have become an object of hostilities.

In the late 1940s Finnish statesmen were concerned also with the implications of the 1948 FCMA-Treaty for Finland's long term neutral aspirations. In 1950 United States diplomats considered that while

> it is believed that Finland would prefer to remain neutral in any general war . . . the Soviet interpretation of the Finnish–Russian freindship pact might be pressed to require Finland to engage on the Soviet side even though the circumstances might not coincide with the conditions set forth in the pact.[5]

Before the Finnish delegation was sent to negotiate the 1948 treaty Paasikivi already admitted that 'we do not hope for neutrality in the meaning of international law'.[6] The view that, by virtue of its geographical position, Finland already had the chance to remain outside military operations was, none the less, accepted by many among the Finnish delegation.[7] But even after favourable negotiations, Paasikivi was aware that the Finnish press equated the signing of the treaty with 'the abandonment of traditional impartiality, of neutrality'.[8]

Paasikivi argued that formal legal principles of neutrality were not decisive. He referred to a clause inserted into the preamble of the FCMA-Treaty which expressed Finland's 'desire to remain outside the conflicting interests of the great powers'. This clause had met no objections from the Soviet delegation.[9] Paasikivi had foreseen the psychologically beneficial impact of this clause on the Finnish people, and the Finnish delegation had pointed out to Molotov that certain phrases should be included in the preamble of the treaty for psychological reasons.[10] But Paasikivi never claimed that this clause endowed Finland with a legal status of neutrality. Regardless of its phrasing, the clause, placed as it was in the preamble of the treaty, lacked the binding character of the treaty articles proper. It acted as an expression of intent, similar to that contained in Paasikivi's reply to Stalin's original proposal for the FCMA-Treaty in 1948: 'especially after the hard experiences of the last war the Finnish people wish to remain outside international disputes'.[11] The public statements of neither the Finnish Parliamentary Foreign Affairs Committee, Prime Minister Pekkala, nor Foreign Minister Enckell, expressed the preamble desire in terms of the legal notion of neutrality in 1948.[12]

Any chance of Finland acquiring a position of neutrality ultimately depended on the outlook of the great powers, and in particular the Soviet Union, since their recognition of such a stand would be essential. During the height of the Cold War the USSR and the United States could only conceive of neutrality as a political expedient to promote or hinder their strategic plans. Paasikivi aimed at keeping Finland outside great power disputes, but he recognised that Finland's pre-war brand of 'neutrality' had become suspect in Soviet eyes. It had been Paasikivi who, as the delegate for the Finnish government during negotiations in Moscow in October 1939, had informed the Soviet government that the Finnish status as a neutral state presumed an 'uncompromising effort to keep out of every dispute' and that the Finnish policy of neutrality led to an 'uncompromising decision to defend . . . neutrality even by force of arms'.[13] In fact, even at that time Finland had had close connections with Germany, and these had been tightened later in the form of military collaboration against the USSR.

To the Soviet Union the conclusion of the 1948 FCMA-Treaty gave the notion of Finnish neutrality a pronounced pre-war stamp. In October 1939 Paasikivi had been instructed to tell the Soviet delegation that the conclusion of a Finnish–Soviet mutual assistance treaty would be incompatible with Finland's policy of neutrality.[14] The Soviet government had withdrawn its proposal for such a treaty 'to enable Finland to maintain her strict neutrality'.[15] Once the 1948 treaty was signed the Soviet press assailed Finnish 'ruling circles and official organs of the right-wing parties' for their stress on Finland's 'neutrality', which was described as tantamount to a policy of 'restoring the extremely sombre past'. To *Pravda* the 'concept of neutrality' was being 'confused with that of "double-dealing" in Finland'.[16] The late 1940s were years during which influential Soviet figures still anticipated a more or less clearly pronounced pro-Soviet orientation to emerge in Finnish foreign policy. In an address to the Cominform in 1947 Zdhanov had even classified Finland among those countries believed to form a progressive front with the USSR and the People's Democracies against 'imperialist' countries.[17]

American diplomats had not lost hopes for Finnish neutrality during a conflict. In a paper drawn up in 1950 it was suggested that

Finland's neutrality 'would be desirable from the United States point of view', and that this could be accomplished if upon the outbreak of war or when it was 'obviously imminent' the United States were to inform Finland that it hoped the country would remain neutral and that the United States was prepared to give assurances to respect such neutrality. But American strategic policy remained paramount, since the report expressed uncertainty about whether United States military plans 'call for military action which would necessitate our infringing Finnish neutrality'.[18] The Americans identified strategic benefits in Finland's nascent policy of neutrality in the mid-1950s since, as one contemporary observer wrote, this policy 'played a part in denying to the Soviet Union a key area' and thus 'served the same aims as the American policy of containment'.[19]

In the early 1950s a fundamental reorientation of the entire conduct of Soviet foreign affairs was initiated. By 1955 the example of the 'third position' taken by many former colonies of Europe, the emergence of neutrality as an issue in European politics, and the reduction in great power strife had led Soviet leaders to conclude that neutrality could be conceived of as a form of peaceful coexistence, as an institution in which the principles of this new Soviet doctrine could be expressed, and that neutral states could perform a political function by constructing 'peace zones'. The evacuation of the Porkkala base and the abrogation of the Soviet rights associated with it, and the example of Austria, finally resulted in a novel reference at the Twentieth Congress of the Soviet Communist Party by Khrushchev to the Soviet intention to 'develop and strengthen friendly relations with Finland, Austria and other neutral countries'.[20] In Finland this statement was interpreted as a formal recognition of the neutral standing of the country in international affairs in a legal sense, although in the USSR Finland's neutrality was already conceived in an 'active' political sense.

In 1952 Prime Minister Kekkonen had already spoken about the 'certain kind of neutrality' which the FCMA-Treaty presumed, and after Khrushchev's statement the connection between neutrality and this treaty became established on the Finnish side. In a speech during a visit to Finland by Bulganin and Khrushchev in summer 1957 Kekkonen declared the 1948 treaty to be 'the first document of international law in which Finland's neutrality is expressed'.[21] He alluded to the phrase in the preamble which expressed Finland's desire to remain outside the conflicts of interest of the great powers. Finnish authorities referred to Soviet legal scholars who described a relationship between the 1948 treaty and Finnish neutrality to try and derive a legal substantiation for that neutrality. Such comments by Soviet scholars formed the second level of encouragement for Finnish neutrality. They did not necessarily represent official Soviet views but they were derived from authoritative Soviet sources and were considered to hold semi-official status (see below on the legal basis of Finnish neutrality).

Over several visits by Finnish and Soviet statesmen to each other's countries the preamble clause in the 1948 treaty came to be regarded as an expression of Finland's neutral foreign policy. The term 'neutrality' was first used in the joint communique of a Soviet visit to Finland in 1957: 'It was recognised on the Soviet side that the peaceful and neutral foreign policy followed by Finland . . . promotes the security of international peace'.[22] Four months later Khrushchev described Finland's policy as a 'neutral and independent policy, a policy supporting peace'.[23] Such recognition by the USSR of the Finnish policy or course of neutrality on a political level also influenced the legal status of Finnish neutrality. But this recognition accorded by Soviet statesmen was intended less as an acceptance of certain international legal norms on which neutrality has traditionally been based than as an indication of Soviet trust in Finland's foreign policy course.

In the 1950s Finnish government programmes referred quite often to Finland's desire to remain outside the conflicts of interest of the great powers, but it was not until 1958 that the Finnish government affirmed that it would follow 'a set line of neutrality' in its foreign policy. It became important for Finland to acquire Western acknowledgement of Finnish neutrality to balance Soviet acknowledgement. Kekkonen considered that without the trust of both East and West Finnish neutrality would be worthless. In the ritual language of Finnish foreign policy Kekkonen stressed that it would be futile to expect good Finnish relations with the West to take place at the expense of those with the East, and he encouraged references to Finland's 'special relations' with the East. But in the early 1960s this hid the fact that Kekkonen was in fact much more Western oriented than Paasikivi previously had been.

In a series of foreign visits over 1960–2 Kekkonen received acknowledgements for the Finnish policy of neutrality from the major Western states. After discussions in London with Macmillan in 1961 the British government expressed its 'understanding of the Finnish neutrality policy'. At the end of 1961 President Kennedy assured

Kekkonen that 'in America the grounds for the neutrality policy Finland follows are understood'.[24] A similar 'understanding' for the Finnish policy was expressed by President de Gaulle after a state visit by Kekkonen to France in 1962.[25] The 'understanding' or 'respect' of Western states for Finnish 'endeavours' or 'intentions' to conduct a neutral policy, which Kekkonen received during these and later visits, followed the rather indirect phrasing of the preamble clause of the Finnish FCMA-Treaty, which at most only alludes to Finland's neutrality.

THE LEGAL BASIS OF FINNISH NEUTRALITY

A West German legal specialist has argued that since the Finnish obligation to defend the territorial integrity of the state 'with all of its available forces', in accordance with the Hague Conventions of 1907 concerning neutrality, is expressed in an international treaty (the 1948 FCMA-Treaty), this may create a legal relation of permanent neutrality.[26] Although the 1948 treaty was concluded with only one state the Finnish obligation in this treaty alludes to neutral relations with a group of states, namely the great powers. But on the basis of the treaty these powers cannot also be regarded as guarantors of Finnish neutrality. One Finnish scholar has claimed, however, that the document of 1948 amounts to a unilateral treaty of neutralisation in the military sense. A Soviet military guarantee of Finnish neutrality can be inferred from the contents of the treaty, he argues, since according to the treaty the USSR will not permit an enemy to penetrate Finnish territory, although there are no grounds for Soviet military presence if such an attack or its immediate threat is absent.[27]

Both Finnish spokesmen and foreign scholars have laid more emphasis, however, on Finland being honour-bound to follow consistently a policy corresponding to the basic criteria of permanent neutrality than on the fixed and binding nature of that neutrality in international legal terms in the manner of Swiss or Austrian neutrality.[28] The speaker of the Finnish parliament admitted in the late 1960s that 'Finland's neutrality cannot be defined according to international law as permanent neutrality', since 'it would not suite our position'.[29] The unwillingness of Finnish governments to refer to the foreign policy course of the country as one of permanent neutrality has reflected a reluctance to fix that course rigidly to conform to a model of the permanently neutral state. This model would ultimately need to be derived from the practice and proclamation of Switzerland, which at times would ill suite the subtle and flexible requirements of Finland's security position between East and West.

The Austrian legal specialist S. Verosta has argued, nevertheless, that Sweden and Finland can be described as practising a '*de facto* [or effective] permanent neutrality'.[30] Verosta notes that Finnish statesmen themselves feel their policy to be bound by the basic provisions of permanent neutrality, although these provisions may be fairly loosely defined. Despite any legal uncertainty, Finnish neutrality is also generally acknowledged and in principle recognised abroad on both bilateral and multilateral levels in interstate transactions. A unilateral proclamation of neutrality by a state, the neutrality of which is then officially recognised by other states, is quite capable of creating a legal relationship whether a contractual arrangement or treaty commitment between the states concerned exists or not. The state which has made such a proclamation is then honour-bound to maintain this permanent or '*de facto* permanent' neutrality.

'*De facto*' neutrality, or the term adopted by Sweden, 'freedom from alliances', refers to a policy conducted in time of peace through which the conditions can be created to enable the country concerned to maintain a status of neutrality in the event of war. In a lengthy analysis of the character of contemporary neutrality the Finnish Foreign Minister, V. Merikoski, explained in 1963 that 'a peacetime policy of neutrality and neutrality in time of war . . . are tightly linked to each other: the consistent application of the former is in general the precondition of the latter'.[31] But difficulties may arise in interpreting the peacetime requirements of such a neutral state. The Swiss view appears to be that such a policy requires the neutral state to avoid airing its opinions in conflicts between third states, although neutral states clearly have the right to offer 'good services' or mediation even during hostilities. But Kekkonen went beyond this to claim that the neutral country can use a policy of neutrality to resolve conflicts between third states. He believed that active work for international reconciliation, based on the principles of the United Nations charter, would help to confirm Finland's neutral status, for with common acknowledgement of the Finnish policy of neutrality in the United Nations the major powers would feel a stronger obligation to respect the country's neutral status in the event of conflict in the future.[32] Another disputed area has been the relationship between 'armed neutrality' and the Finnish policy in peacetime, which became an object of protracted debate in Finland.

The Norwegian scholar Nils Ørvik has cast doubt on Finland's neutrality by asserting that in effect the Soviet Union has reserved for itself the right – even if, to be more exact, not the sole right – to determine when the military provisions of the 1948 FCMA-Treaty should be implemented. Since this treaty, in his view, is 'by form and content a potential alliance', any Finnish aspirations for neutrality would have to be abandoned during a conflict or threat of conflict in Northern Europe, as determined by the USSR, and replaced by Finnish–Soviet military cooperation.[33]

Despite Ørvik's contention, the existence of the 1948 treaty does not in itself act as a legal impediment to Finnish neutrality as many in the West have believed. The first article of the treaty obliges Finland to fight, within its own borders, to repel attacks and defend its own territory. Since Paasikivi's assessment of this commitment in 1948, it has been observed generally in Finland that this only recognises what Finland should do in any case 'faithful to its obligations as an independent state'. Article 1 obliges Finland not to permit the use of her territory as a base or for passage in an attack made against the USSR. This seems to imply an unconditional state of wartime neutrality. The notion of neutrality is still applicable in the event of a military attack as envisaged in Article 1, since the traditional right of neutrality is expressly founded on the principle that neutrality can be violated without that violation necessarily leading to the end of neutrality. But if particularly extensive conflict breaks out on the territory of a neutral state, as illustrated by the history of Belgian neutrality, there arises a considerable probability of war between that state and the attacker.[34]

There remains the question of whether an application of the cooperation mechanism in the circumstances described in Article 1 of the 1948 treaty would create an absolute obstacle to Finland's wartime neutrality. Finland's neutral status would obviously not be contravened by receiving arms, supplies and other material aid, since international law does not forbid military assistance from a belligerent to a neutral – in contrast, of course, to assistance given the other way round.[35] Although the arrival of Soviet troops on Finnish territory would be in conflict with traditional neutrality, it would not necessarily or automatically mean the end of it. It is true that while the conditions and contents of the consultations referred to in Article 2 of the 1948 treaty are not specified, they can indisputably begin already during conditions of peace. But in this case the notion of wartime neutrality does not really arise. If a war were to begin in the fashion circumscribed by Articles 1 and 2, and the USSR becomes a participant in it but Finland remains outside it, then Finland could still practice her neutrality. If the Soviet Union were not to be a belligerent but itself to remain neutral, or if in consultations it is agreed that Soviet troops will be sent to Finland only when an armed attack is directed against Finland, then there would still be no theoretical obstacles to Finland's neutrality.

Although no contradiction necessarily arises between the application of the FCMA-Treaty and Finnish neutrality in the circumstances conceived of above, it is obvious that in many circumstances the letter and spirit of the treaty would preclude a continuation of neutrality. Moreover, since neutrality ultimately lies in the eye of the beholder, the conduct of Finnish military consultations with the USSR while peace still prevails, which the 1948 treaty provides for, would render the chances of Finnish neutrality being preserved much dimmer and its credibility abroad much weaker than may appear from the foregoing analysis.[36] Yet much effort has been expended in Finland in attempts to equate Finnish neutrality with the 1948 treaty,[37] and part of the initial encouragement for these arguments came from the Soviet Union.

When Kekkonen first claimed that Finland's neutrality was expressed in the international legal document of the FCMA-Treaty his view was supported by an authoritative contemporary study of international law written by two Soviet specialists. The authors, S. Krylov and V. Durdenevski, the latter of whom was a legal adviser to the Soviet Foreign Ministry, considered that since the Finnish–Soviet treaty of 1948 had been concluded expressly to prevent a renewed German attack it held a special position among the bilateral treaties which the USSR had concluded. In their view an assessment of the Finnish obligations assumed under the treaty suggested that it was 'more a treaty guaranteeing neutrality than a treaty of mutual assistance in the real sense'.[38] On the twelfth anniversary of the treaty *Pravda* described it as 'an international juridical document which confirms Finland's neutrality'.[39] In 1963 a Soviet journal determined that the obligations undertaken by Finland in the treaty were 'in no way in conflict with Finland's international obligations as a neutral country', since 'neutral states have the full right to defend themselves against attack and thus to secure assistance from those who are prepared to give it'.[40] The Finnish Foreign Minister used these sources in 1963 to support his view that the 1948 treaty hindered neither Finland's neutral status nor the Finnish desire to observe a policy of neutrality in peacetime.[41] Soviet academics interpreted the treaty in a fashion favourable to Finnish neutrality also later in the 1960s.[42]

As Finnish views of the 1948 treaty derived from statements by such Soviet writers were not disputed in the USSR, Finnish spokesmen assumed that they were responding to the official Soviet view. Yet references to the neutrality component of the treaty were nowhere to be found in Soviet government statements in either the 1950s or the 1960s. The Finns should, therefore, have acted with greater caution, and considered these references less as expressions of political significance about policy attitudes and more as definitions, incidentally favourable to a legal characterisation of Finnish neutrality, formulated in the Soviet academic establishment. These unofficial Soviet views were put to mistaken use in Finland later in the 1960s to bolster legal conceptions of Finnish neutrality and to reinterpret the intentions of the FCMA-Treaty as a whole. This created doubts in the USSR about Finland's military commitments and contributed to a period of Soviet reluctance to refer to Finnish neutrality at the end of the decade. The Finnish inclination to exaggerate the implications of unofficial Soviet interpretations of the 1948 treaty was criticised later in the USSR.[43]

If it still seems necessary to place Finnish neutrality in a legal framework, then the provisos contained in the 1948 treaty could perhaps be taken account of by using the term 'qualified neutrality'. Such neutrality has been defined as follows:

> The neutrality of a state was qualified if it remained neutral on the whole, but actively or passively, directly or indirectly, gave some kind of assistance to one of the belligerents in consequence of an obligation entered into by treaty previous to the war, and not for that particular war exclusively.[44]

This definition would emphasise Finland's general desire to remain neutral as long as possible, even during a crisis, through a policy of neutrality. In addition, it would recognise the nature of Finland's military-political commitments with the USSR, which may tighten when such a crisis escalates. Unfortunately, despite its appropriateness for Finland, the notion of 'qualified neutrality' has fallen into disuse and is no longer recognised in classical international law.

NEUTRALITY AND MILITARY DEFENCE

Finnish statesmen have accepted that Finland should prevent any part of her territory from forming a military vacuum which could encourage an infringement of the territorial integrity of the state. The principles behind Finland's neutrality and sovereign independence share this presumption. The size and equipment of the Finnish defence forces were restricted, however, by the provisions of the 1947 peace treaty (see Appendix 1), which can only be revoked with the consent of both signatories, the Soviet Union and Great Britain. This set a ceiling on the Finnish defence capability, which was particularly frustrating because of the restrictions set on modern armaments systems. Similar restrictions on the Austrian armed forces inspired protests in the 1960s that Austrian neutrality was being compromised. But until 1961 the defence forces played little part in promoting Finland's neutral image.

In August 1961 the chief of the Finnish general staff, Lt.-General Viljanen, emphasised how essential it was for Finland to be able to show the Soviet military leadership that it could itself, through its independent defence capability, take care of the military duties described in the 1948 treaty.[45] He argued that attention should be paid in particular to an effective air defence, which required that the restrictions on missiles in Article 17 of the peace treaty be lifted. A small working group was set up to assess Viljanen's proposals and the practical significance of the 1948 FCMA-Treaty. This group, which began its work before the Note Crisis that autumn, proved to be the antecedent of the parliamentary defence committees and the beginning of the defence component in Finnish neutrality.

As previously described, at the peace conference in 1946–7 the Soviet delegation had opposed the limitations on the size and scope of the Finnish defence forces. In 1962 Finland found it more difficult to persuade Britain than the USSR to concede 'defensive' guided missiles to Finland. This was eventually managed, although Austria has never achieved a similar concession. The Finns proclaimed this as 'concrete proof of the fact that trust is felt in Finland's desire for neutrality on both sides'.[46] It is also true that since the 1950s the USSR has sold Finland armaments far exceeding the immediate needs of a conscript standing army of 34 400 men (the limits of the 1947 treaty), and the peace treaty limitations on manpower and equipment have never been interpreted by either main signatory power as a ban against training and arming a large reserve force.

Most recently, the stipulations of the peace treaty (Article 17) were not permitted to form an obstacle to the Finnish purchase of modern mines in 1983 from the USSR and Britain.[47] All of this indicates that, contrary to the beliefs of those inclined to generalise about Finlandisation, the Soviet Union has not attempted to impede the development of the Finnish defence forces.

There exist well established contacts between the Soviet and Finnish armed forces, and channels for discussion between Finnish and Soviet statesmen and military leaders through bilateral exchange agreements as part of the Finnish 'good-neighbour' policy in normal peacetime conditions.[48] These contacts arise quite independently of the framework of the military provisions of the FCMA-Treaty, although, at least since the Note Crisis, Soviet writers have urged on the strengthening and further development of the Finnish and Soviet armed forces and the training of their personnel 'faithful to the spirit of the FCMA-Treaty'.[49] Despite the apparently unsuccessful advances by Ustinov in July 1978, in recent years Soviet observers have been keen to acknowledge that such military contacts 'have greatly expanded, having assumed some new forms'. Proof of this is drawn from 'the exchange of visits by high military commanders, combat ships, air squadrons, and military sports delegations', which in the Soviet view have 'become traditional'.[50] No doubt Soviet leaders would like incrementally to increase these contacts to lay the groundwork for possible future military consultations or cooperation under the terms of the 1948 treaty. But Finnish military leaders have shown no inclination to encourage such a process; they have observed strict limits in their military relations with the USSR. Lest these relations appear unfitting for a neutral state, it should be realised that military contacts have long existed also between Finnish and Western military officials, despite Soviet suspicions in this respect.[51]

The Finnish government has tried to balance the purchase of military equipment from East and West in order to avert foreign doubts over the sincerity or durability of the Finnish policy of neutrality. It was recognised in 1964 that, even in the absence of political conditions attached to agreements for procuring military supplies, a tendency for procurements to be made one-sidedly from one of the two great powers 'would give the other side reason to suspect that the fact of one-sided procurements results from political dependence, which in certain situations could limit decisively Finland's opportunities to maintain her policy of neutrality'.[52] The Finnish Minister of Defence stressed at the end of 1969 that Finland would be strictly neutral in the acquisition of military supplies from abroad and would take steps to avoid relations of dependence.

In fact, Finland has not managed to balance its purchases from East and West, but has acquired simply from both sides. Since 1960 the procurement from East and West was nearly in balance only once, in 1963, and the highest expenditure continues to be on defence purchases from the USSR.[53] The funds earmarked for arms acquisitions in the Finnish budget in June 1983 increased substantially in an attempt to rectify a temporary imbalance in Finnish–Soviet trade. In recent years the notion of a procurements balance may have been used by the Finnish military to justify increases in military expenditure rather than to safeguard Finnish neutrality. Neverthe-less, some attempts have also been made in Finland to construct an independent arms industry.[54]

Some in Finland have argued that strengthening the Finnish defence capability would assist Finland to maintain her neutrality, since this would raise the 'threshold' beyond which Soviet leaders would feel the need to invoke the military articles of the 1948 FCMA-Treaty during a crisis in the Nordic region.[55] But towards the end of the 1960s worries were expressed that the Soviet veto over programmes for the modernisation of the Finnish defence forces (through the 1947 peace treaty), if exercised, could enable the USSR to exploit international crises to its advantage through resorting to the assistance mechanism in the 1948 treaty.[56] A counter-argument in Finland maintained that increasing Finland's defence readiness increases the Soviet need for political-military coordination with Finland, that is to say the need to consult with Finland, and therefore lowers the 'consultations threshold'.[57] These were rather academic arguments, but they were important since by the late 1960s the only real difference which remained between the security policy views of the major Finnish political parties was over the level of the Finnish defence budget and the degree of reliance to be placed on Finland's independent defence forces *vis-à-vis* the military provisions of the 1948 treaty.

Thus far, however, the Finnish authorities have resolved not to rely on constructing the Finnish national defence by means of peacetime assistance from the USSR. The independent neutral defence priori-ties of Finland also mean that the character of the Finnish defence forces is not merely adapted to the attack scenario described in the FCMA-Treaty, nor even during such an attack would Finnish defence depend purely on Soviet assistance as provided by the treaty.[58] But

Soviet writers have criticised the Finnish tendency to self-reliance in defence matters once it has led to assertions that Finland should fulfil the obligation to repel attack 'with only its own forces and without beginning military cooperation with the Soviet Union'.[59] Soviet observers have been aware that those who incline to the right politically in Finland are wont to stress the significance of neutrality, even permitting it to overshadow the 1948 treaty, while those on the left in fact regard this treaty as the safeguard for Finland's security in a crisis or conflict which may develop in the Nordic region.

The importance attached by Finnish leaders to the image of Finnish neutrality in the West as well as the East emerges from correspondence between Kekkonen and the commander of the Finnish defence forces, General Yrjö Keinonen, in January 1969. Keinonen had stated publicly that Finland's minimal defence capability should be that required during a surprise attack to ensure sufficient time for the conduct of consultations with the USSR as provided by the FCMA-Treaty.[60] But Kekkonen believed that this description would render a mistaken picture of the position and function of the Finnish defence forces, 'as in some way "alongside" the Soviet defence forces'. Kekkonen was worried about such an impression 'in particular on outsiders', since it could enable claims to be made that 'the security strategy of our country is constructed to depend on the military assistance of the Soviet Union, and in a situation of crisis ultimately to attend the Soviet Union'.[61] Finnish statesmen do not disregard the latent military potential of the FCMA-Treaty. But the official and majority view in Finland has always been that in principle the function of the Finnish defence forces is the defence of the country by its own means. This conforms with the basic principle behind the Western notion of 'armed neutrality'.

5 External Affairs

THE LIMITS OF FINNISH–SOVIET COOPERATION ON INTERNATIONAL ISSUES

The thesis of the peaceful coexistence of states with different social systems, which has underlain the Soviet foreign policy outlook since the mid-1950s, was well adapted to the development of Finnish–Soviet relations within the framework of the non-military articles of the 1948 FCMA-Treaty. Steps intended to promote the coexistence of states could be undertaken on both bilateral and multilateral levels.

On the bilateral level Soviet statesmen in the 1950s were quick to see the importance of relations with their small European non-socialist neighbour as an advertisement for their new foreign policy line. As early as November 1954 Deputy Prime Minister Mikoyan presented Finnish–Soviet relations as an example for other states of the operation of the principles of peaceful coexistence.[1] The Soviet press described these relations as having formed 'a unique laboratory' for the 'real equality of nations, large and small'.[2] The Finnish Prime Minister, Fagerholm, admitted to Bulganin in 1957 that 'nothing comparable to these relations can be found in the whole of Europe'.[3] The death of Stalin in March 1953 had opened the way for a broad reappraisal of Soviet relations with the West, and the case of Finland could be used to reassure the West of Soviet intentions.

In addition to bilateral trade and economic relations, Soviet leaders could point to the Finnish–Soviet treaty of 1948, which Brezhnev later proclaimed to have served as 'a great signpost for the beginning of peaceful coexistence between the nations of post-war Europe'.[4] The Finns were to concur that this treaty had illustrated the Soviet doctrine 'when even the idea of peaceful coexistence was hardly at all expressed in Europe'.[5] The evacuation of the Porkkala base could also be explained as a practical expression of these principles.[6] The nature of Soviet relations with Finland could be used to relieve Western anxieties during the negotiations leading to the

Austrian State Treaty and to agreement over Austrian neutrality. These events improved the Soviet image in the West and contributed to hopes for *détente* in great power relations – the 'Geneva spirit' – in the mid-1950s.

Soviet spokesmen claimed that peaceful coexistence could also operate multilaterally. They termed such multilateral activity 'peace-promoting', 'peace-seeking', or simply 'peace policy' and measured its success by the geographical extension of 'zones of peace'. In 1954 Mikoyan tentatively acknowledged that Finland 'like the Soviet Union', considers 'the relief of international tension an important task . . . as [it is] necessary for all states to struggle to unite to secure peace'.[7] But it was not until a United Nations seat was finally made available to Finland in 1956 that Finnish statesmen had a forum in which to express their broader foreign policy outlook. The Paris peace treaty of 1947 anticipated Finnish participation in the UN organisation but the refusal of the West to accept the admission of certain East European states into the UN had led to the Soviet Union retaliating by opposing the admission of other states, including Finland. The deadlock was only broken through a 'package deal' in autumn 1955 which reflected a toning down of Cold War antipathies.

Finland had already made a declaration of intent to work for international peace and security according to the aims and principles of the UN in Article 3 of the 1948 FCMA-Treaty. A clause in the preamble of the treaty expressed the parties 'firm endeavour to collaborate' in this cause (see Appendix 2). In the late 1950s Soviet leaders were probing to find how far the Finns would permit such 'collaboration' to go. In February 1957 Finland received a Soviet note requesting Finnish support as a United Nations member in the cause of working against the growing threat of war in the world.[8] The following May Voroshilov affirmed that 'we attach great value to the struggle of the Finnish people and their government for the easing of the international situation, struggles for the forbidding of atomic and hydrogen arms'.[9] But this characterised a general Soviet attempt to mobilise the European neutrals against Western nuclear arms policies and extend 'zones of peace'. Khrushchev himself stressed the regional dimension of Finland's 'peace-supporting' policy aimed at 'the creation of firm peace in North Europe . . . preserving the Baltic Sea as a perpetual zone of peace'.[10]

During the 1960s Soviet statesmen began to observe that a policy of neutrality, as practised by Finland, should necessarily include a 'peace policy' component. The Finnish policy began to be described as a 'peace-seeking policy of neutrality' in joint Finnish–Soviet communiques. For the Finns this reflected the greater activity to be found in their security policy, but on the Soviet side it also reflected an increasing emphasis on the desirability of Finland working for the coexistence of states in cooperation with the USSR.

In 1964 Foreign Minister Gromyko identified 'another broad area' for cooperation with Finland 'formed by those as yet unresolved international problems, the settling of which . . . deeply interests the Soviet Union as well as Finland'. To Gromyko these issues included 'ensuring European security in all its aspects as well as general and complete disarmament'. He urged the development of Finnish–Soviet cooperation for 'the settlement of those international questions which are not adapted to the framework of bilateral relations'.[11] Two years later Kosygin declared that Finnish–Soviet cooperation was 'moving to a new stage, which gives opportunities to settle those kinds of questions which perhaps were not even considered earlier'.[12] These Soviet statements were largely declaratory in the 1960s, they were reflected in no substantive measures. The Finns were active in their proposals for the Nordic region and Kekkonen was critical of some aspects of German policy (see Finland and Nordic neutrality in Chapter 3), but the Finnish voting pattern and general activity in the United Nations placed the country in a fairly cohesive Nordic group (except during East–West disputes, when the Finnish tendency to abstain reflected the habits of the non-aligned countries).

A Finnish–Soviet communique issued in June 1966 expressed both parties' agreement on the usefulness of a European Security Conference, but it was not until 1969 that Finland decided to take action over this proposal which had long been favoured by the USSR. Soviet leaders praised Finland's initiative to sponsor and host the conference; to Podgorny in July 1970 it was a step of 'great value'.[13] Initially the Finns practised their responsibilities as hosts for part of the SALT talks, which were held in Helsinki from 1969 to 1972. Finland went on to host the first and third (final) sessions of the European Security Conference in the summers of 1973 and 1975. The consolidation of a stable security system in Europe would offer mutual benefits to Finland and the USSR.

For Finland the hosting of the SALT talks and the Security Conference were not intended as a means to draw closer to the USSR internationally, nor were they the reluctant expressions of a 'Finlandised' foreign policy, rather they were designed to broaden the scope of Finland's international activity and were part of a

Finnish attempt to build up multilateral structures for cooperation through international organisations.[14] Finland's promotion of these measures for great power dialogue coincided with her presence on the UN Security Council during 1969–70. For some in Finland this diplomatic drive could be regarded as an attempt to create a greater 'freedom of movement' for Finland, even to return to the pre-war Finnish framework of relations, which had relied on the possibility of appealing to international organisations in the event of problems with the USSR rather than on the resolution of these problems bilaterally.[15] This may explain the Soviet decision to veto the candidature of the Finnish diplomat, Max Jakobson, for the post of UN Secretary General in 1971, although Kekkonen denied that this candidature had been a Finnish attempt 'to join the West and disengage itself from the East'.[16]

Whatever hopes Finland's active involvement in the UN at the turn of the decade may have inspired among Finnish diplomats, Soviet statesmen were loath to criticise Finnish policy at a time when multilateralism was also encouraging strong Finnish support for the CSCE process. The Finnish concern for the development of *détente* between the great powers in the European context meant that Finnish activity in the UN system in the 1970s has corresponded with core interests of the Soviet Union in many areas. In 1974 a Soviet writer observed that 'European problems are an important element in the international affairs of the Soviet Union and Finland at the present stage' and identified a 'mutual orientation of the two countries in international affairs', which 'springs directly from the obligations undertaken by the USSR and Finland under that part of the 1948 treaty which bears on the strengthening of peace and security'.[17] This revealed a Soviet attempt to argue that Finland was contractually obliged to continue working for *détente* alongside the USSR. But this view has never been expressed in official Finnish–Soviet communiques in the 1970s, although they have indicated Finland's willingness to engage in broad discussions about European security with the USSR. These discussions exhibit a form of interstate behaviour by no means peculiar to Soviet relations with Finland. A Soviet–Danish protocol was signed in 1976, for example, which instituted regular consultations in the spirit of peaceful coexistence. The USSR and Denmark agreed to hold consultations on issues promoting 'international *détente* and strengthening international security', problems 'of mutual interest or the subject of multilateral international talks'.[18]

The Helsinki Final Act of 1975 achieved an important Soviet goal by ratifying the post-war territorial boundaries in Europe. It called for an expansion of cultural and scientific ties, but it failed to create a new pattern of European East–West relations as had been hoped in the USSR. In subsequent years this goal appeared ever more remote, but Finland tried to sustain the *détente* process in the follow-up meetings in Belgrade (1977–8) and Madrid (1980–3), not out of a compulsion to collaborate with the USSR but in conformity with the aims of the increasingly coherent body of European neutral and non-aligned states. One tangible benefit of the Security Conference for Finland had been the confirmation of the right of a country to neutrality, which was included in the declaration of principles of participant states.

Kekkonen believed that the role of the neutral and non-aligned states was to offer compromise solutions. In 1981 he told a Yugoslav paper that the presence of states outside the military alliances 'has often been calculated to balance the political atmosphere in Europe'.[19] Soviet leaders, despite their disillusion with many aspects of the 1975 agreement, valued this mediating, 'bridge-building' role which Finland, among others, could still perform. At the Twenty-sixth Congress of the CPSU in spring 1981 Brezhnev paid a particular tribute to Finland and to Kekkonen personally for their contribution to 'the consolidation of European security'.[20]

The new Soviet leader, Andropov, was conscious of Finland's role in the *détente* process. Speaking already in 1978 in the Karelian city of Petrozavodsk, which had been occupied by the Finns during the Continuation War and in which he had worked after the war, Andropov described contemporary Soviet–Finnish relations as 'an integral and stable system of cooperation on a basis of equality in various political, economic and cultural fields'. Here, in his view, was 'an example of *détente* embodied in daily contacts, *détente* which makes peace stronger'.[21] In December 1982, soon after assuming the post of General Secretary, Androprov portrayed relations with Finland as a 'vivid example of the vital power of peaceful coexistence'. 'In our troublesome age', he stated, they 'show mankind a reliable path towards a peaceful future'.[22] These eulogies revealed the value Andropov accorded to Finland's model of bilateral relations with the East.

The severe and progressive deterioration of great power relations and the breakdown of international dialogue in the early 1980s led also to further Soviet emphasis on the importance of Finland's multilateral diplomacy in Europe. 'Now when cold winds blow from across the ocean and the United States administration strives . . . to destroy the system of international cooperation', a Soviet writer declaimed in 1983, Finland 'clearly shows its belief . . . in *détente* and a policy of disarmament as well as in the resolutions of the CSCE final document'.[23] When the Soviet Prime Minister, N. A. Tikhonov, visited Finland in December 1982 President Koivisto told him that since 'so much of a positive nature' had been achieved in Europe through the CSCE process, 'it cannot be in any party's interest to attempt to place obstacles in the path of *détente*'.[24] Already in April, after meeting a CPSU delegation headed by Andropov, Prime Minister Kalevi Sorsa (in his capacity as Social Democrat Party chairman) had declared that 'our ideas . . . concerning the need for joint efforts to safeguard peace coincide'.[25] Next year Andropov and Koivisto agreed on the importance of strenghtening and increasing the effectiveness of the United Nations.[26]

Andropov hoped, no doubt, that Finland, among the European neutral and non-aligned states, could help to retrieve something from the stalled talks at the Madrid Review Conference.[27] Throughout the Madrid meeting Finland had worked to facilitate the emergence of a consensus on a substantive and balanced final document, and Finland became a co-sponsor of the compromise proposal which finally broke the deadlock. In June 1983 Andropov praised Finland's active participation in Europe and in particular 'the struggles of Finnish diplomats in the Madrid Conference'.[28] Helsinki was chosen as the site of a preparatory meeting for the Stockholm Conference on European disarmament, which hoped to develop the notion of confidence building measures as agreed in Madrid. The acrimony in East–West exchanges had increased over autumn 1983, but at Stockholm early in 1984 the Finnish Foreign Minister reaffirmed Finland's 'vital interest' in the continuation of the CSCE process.[29] As a CSCE state Finland could participate in negotiations on military security at Stockholm, and it is likely that the USSR will continue to exhort Finland to offer her services as a mediator as the channels for normal East–West dialogue are narrowed.

It is probable that during this decade the Soviet leadership will make further attempts at political coordination with Finland in the international arena, despite Finland's commitment to the image of an impartial 'bridge-builder'. Within Europe the Finns were commended by Soviet spokesmen for being among the first to condemn the preparation of neutron weapons and the proposal to site them in

Europe.[30] The Finns appealed to the CSCE countries to prevent new mass destruction weapons from being sited in Europe. Finland, like the Soviet Union, endorsed the Swedish government's proposal in January 1983 to create a zone in Europe free from battlefield nuclear weapons. Finland agreed with the USSR on the importance of concluding an international agreement banning the deployment of all types of weapons in outer space. In harmony with the USSR, but also alongside many non-aligned states, in 1983 Finland voted in the United Nations against the first use of a nuclear strike. Finland had already been the first of the Western states to support the Soviet proposal presented at the Twenty-sixth Congress of the CPSU in 1981 for a global treaty to prohibit the use of force in international relations.

It may appear from these examples that Finnish leaders are permitting themselves to become a party to one-sided campaigns orchestrated by the USSR and aimed against American or NATO nuclear strategy. A Soviet author recently tried to argue that Finnish support for many of the general proposals and initiatives announced by the USSR during and after the 1981 CPSU Congress shows the conviction of the Finnish people and leaders in 'the nobleness and constructiveness of the foreign policy line of the Soviet Union in the present world'.[31] But Finland's activity at all levels in the structure of relations set up by the United Nations and its specialist committees has provided the country with an arena in which to express its independent foreign policy outlook, albeit one shared in many essential respects by the European neutral and non-aligned states. Thus, Finland's opposition to the first use of a nuclear strike was a stand which had already been adopted by Sweden, and it was intended as a declaration of principle rather than as a statement in the controversy between the Warsaw Pact and NATO. Since Finland has supported all *démarches* aimed at limiting the use of nuclear weapons this has led to Finland voting for resolutions in the UN which the USSR has refused to support. These have included the proposals in 1977 for a Latin American nuclear-free zone, for the creation of a nuclear-free zone for Southern Asia and for a reduction of military budgets.[32]

In 1983 a Soviet writer praised the 'desire for peace, the state of health and realism characteristic of Finland's foreign policy'; he referred to Finland's 'reasonable attitude' to the Middle East situation and Afghanistan, and the unity or closeness of Finnish and Soviet views in joint communiques 'over issues related to the national liberation struggle of people's and the elimination of colonial rule'.[33] In fact, this description reflected little new in Finnish policy. In the latter case, since the early 1970s Finland had more openly been supporting the general formulae of the non-aligned states over colonial issues, which had much common ground with Soviet statements but were also widely supported in the UN General Assembly. The Soviet bloc and the non-aligned group of states tended to agree on the colonial character of certain specific crises. In August 1982 Finland voted for the resolution in the United Nations sponsored by the non-aligned countries which censured Israel strongly for her attack on Lebanon. Already earlier Finland like her neutral neighbour Sweden had occasionally criticised American involvement in Vietnam,[34] and in October 1983 both countries, together with most of the rest of the world, voted to censure the American invasion of Grenada. Finland's stand on these issues was again a question of principle. From her past history Finland tended naturally to identify with small states resisting attempts by powerful states to encroach on their self-determination, and in the case of Grenada the American position appeared untenable even to most Western states. But in general Finland has exercised a strong degree of neutral restraint in the major disputes between East and West, and this determined her public statements over Afghanistan.

Since joining the United Nations Finland has kept to one principle of conduct in particular in disputes between the great powers: while Finnish statesmen may not have approved let alone supported Soviet actions in such crises they have refrained from joining campaigns led by the Western states against the USSR in international forums in situations in which the USSR has proclaimed its vital security interests to be at issue. Finland abstained, accordingly, during the vital votes in the UN condemning Soviet military intervention in Hungary in autumn 1956.[35] Since Finland also remained outside any Soviet sponsored campaigns against the Western states, she abstained over a Soviet resolution in February 1957 calling on the UN to end American 'interference' in the 'internal affairs of the Soviet Union and the People's Republics'.[36] Finland showed similar restraint during the Czechoslovak crisis in August 1968. Foreign Minister Karjalainen eventually expressed the Finnish hope in the UN 'that foreign forces will be withdrawn from the country and that all external restraints will be removed as soon as possible in accordance with the wishes of the people of Czechoslovakia'.[37] The Finns went no further since they argued that if no states were to exercise a measure of neutral restraint in the crisis then all attempts at conciliation would be doomed to failure.

The Finnish response to Soviet military intervention in Afghanistan at the end of 1979 was even more non-committal. A Foreign Ministry communique looked forward to a normalisation of the situation in Afghanistan corresponding to 'the hopes of the parties involved and of the international community'.[38] Contrary to the great majority of non-aligned states Finland abstained in the crucial UN vote in mid-January 1980 calling for an immediate, total withdrawal of 'the foreign troops' from Afghanistan.[39] But this was probably determined less by the factual content of the resolution than by the Finnish belief that in the current situation voting meant adopting a stand 'for or against' the Soviet Union, although the Finns have continued to abstain on votes over the Afghanistan issue. In a similar vein Finnish diplomats have refrained from taking sides over the destruction of the South Korean airliner by the USSR in September 1983. At a joint meeting the Nordic foreign ministers 'deplored' the 'tragic incident' and stressed the importance of adopting 'necessary measures . . . to prevent similar tragedies in the future', but used no stronger language.[40]

The Finns gave absolute priority to ensuring that the East–West dispute which the assumption of power by the military in Poland in December 1981 gave rise to would not be reflected in Finland's relations with the USSR. In the absence of conclusive evidence to the contrary, President-elect Koivisto was inclined to regard the Polish situation as an internal affair of Poland. In his view the army had taken power once the Polish government and Party had lost control of events since 'perhaps it was the only Polish organisation which could still influence events'.[41] In the case of Poland, both Finland's security (through the existence of the 1948 treaty) and her established neutral stand induced her once again to retire and wait for conditions of reduced international tension.

FINNISH–SOVIET TRADE

From the early post-war years Finnish–Soviet trade assumed political connotations. Under Paasikivi trade became an instrument in Finland's Eastern policy. He believed that the Finnish will to develop mutual trade with the USSR would be interpreted by the Soviet leaders as a further indication of Finland's readiness to maintain good political relations with the eastern trading partner.

The war reparations imposed on Finland in the post-war settlement compelled a rapid expansion of the Finnish shipbuilding and machine industry, since the Finns had to deliver reparations in the form of goods desired by the Soviet Union. Although this laid a heavy burden on the Finnish economy, it encouraged considerable diversification in Finnish industry, and once reparations came to an end in 1952 the basis for continued trade with the Soviet Union had been created. In fact, already in June 1950 Finland signed a trade treaty and a framework treaty for 1951–2 in Moscow, which secured the continued development of the metal industry through increased exports to the USSR.

A further encouragement to Finnish–Soviet trade lay in a commercial agreement concluded in 1947, which followed the guidelines of the Paris Peace Treaty. This agreement contained an unqualified most favoured nation clause, basically similar to a previous trade agreement of 1940. The USSR seems to have attached considerable importance to the most favoured nation principle, since although in practice this clause had little influence on trade at the time, the Finnish government had shown its willingness to take Soviet interests into consideration by placing trade with the USSR on an equal footing with all other trade conducted by Finland.[42]

The thesis of peaceful coexistence, which underpinned the foreign policy strategy of the Soviet Union under Khrushchev, did not change the economic preconditions of Finnish–Soviet trade relations, but it strengthened their political content. Peaceful coexistence presumed the objective necessity of trade between socialist and capitalist countries. In 1959 Deputy Prime Minister A. Mikoyan pointed out that Finland had acted as a pioneer in signing long-term trade treaties with the Soviet Union. He acknowledged that 'of the West European states Finland is our largest trade partner', which he considered 'understandable' as 'a habit between good neighbours'.[43]

Since relations with Finland were given a positive role in Soviet policy as an example to Western states, and since trade acted for Soviet leaders as an indicator of the overall state of relations between countries, Finnish statesmen paid close attention to the volume of trade with the USSR. There is some evidence of Soviet sensitivity towards the growth of Finnish–West German trade at the expense of the USSR,[44] and it has been shown that before all three periods of crisis in Finnish–Soviet relations, 1948–9, 1958–9, and 1961–2 (see following chapter), Finland's trade with the Soviet Union had decreased, and increased proportionally with the Western countries.[45] In 1973 Kekkonen observed that the Soviet share of Finland's foreign trade had fallen by over 5 per cent since 1954 (in fact the figures are 19·7 per cent in 1954 and 11·9 per cent in 1973). After the reparations years the Soviet share of Finnish trade peaked at 23·5 per cent in 1953, but had remained fairly steady (except for a dip to 12·9 per cent in 1961) between 1955 and 1968, averaging at almost 16 per cent. The real decline in this share took place between 1969 and 1973. Nevertheless, Kekkonen interpreted this as a 'negative trend' against Finnish interests, and declared that 'a change must be brought about through our instrumentality'.[46] There followed an abrupt increase in Finnish imports from the USSR in 1974, and the Soviet share of Finland's total foreign trade rose rapidly over the next few years until it approached 20 per cent of this total figure. In 1975 Kekkonen criticised an expression attributed to Paasikivi in the immediate post-war years, according to which Finland should take care that trade with the Soviet Union never exceeds 20 or 25 per cent of the total Finnish trade.[47] The two presidents differed in their views since Kekkonen believed not only in the political benefits but also strongly in the economic benefits of trade with the Soviet Union. Although Kekkonen realised that the long run political and economic interests of Finland and the USSR were incompatible, in acknowledgement of the principles of peaceful coexistence he recognised that the shorter term promotion of welfare goals through mutual exchange was a common interest of both countries.[48]

The strong political colouring of Finnish–Soviet trade in the Soviet frame of reference has led to Soviet leaders using trade relations to demonstrate the Soviet comprehension of an unsatisfactory state of political relations between the neighbour states. The USSR unilaterally broke off trade relations and negotiations with Finland in this manner in 1949 and 1958. A Finnish initiative in May 1958 to open up the Saimaa Canal in Soviet Karelia for traffic, if the USSR were to concede rights of passage for Finland, was received favourably in Moscow, but negotiations about the project were suspended by the political crisis which arose in Finnish–Soviet relations in autumn 1958 (see following chapter). But the political obstacles for trade and economic cooperation were not to be found solely on the Soviet side. An earlier Soviet initiative to develop the Saimaa Canal in 1953 had already in fact been shelved in response to doubts about its economic benefits expressed on a Finnish committee.[49] Yet Kekkonen regarded the economic advantages of using the canal as 'incontestable', which left him with the impression that 'the negative stand was influenced by unexplained political motives'.[50]

The canal issue was eventually resolved. After a visit by Kekkonen to Moscow in November 1960 the USSR announced its willingness to lease that part of the Saimaa Canal situated on Soviet territory to Finland for fifty years. Although negotiations were interrupted once again during the Note Crisis a treaty was signed in August 1962 and approved by the Finnish parliament the following year. Soviet commentators praised this achievement as a practical expression of peaceful coexistence and pointed out the economic benefits that would accrue to eastern Finland.[51] It is worth noting that the Soviet concession had security conditions; under terms of the Saimaa treaty the Soviet authorities can, if they find it necessary for security reasons, enforce special regulations applying to all ships in the leased part of the canal.

Throughout the 1960s and 1970s Finnish–Soviet economic relations continued to pioneer methods of trade and forms of cooperation between East and West. In 1955 the two countries had concluded a special treaty on scientific-technical cooperation, which was reinforced by a treaty in 1966. The following year Finland was the first Western state to establish a permanent commission for economic cooperation with the USSR. The commission set up work groups to clarify the possibilities for cooperation in various areas, and carried out preparatory work from 1970 to arrange a treaty of economic, technical and scientific cooperation, which was formally signed in 1971. At the same time projects on the concrete economic level, like selling gas to Finland, were agreed upon.

By the mid-1970s various joint Finnish–Soviet projects had been completed besides the Saimaa Canal, and new ones were under construction or preparation. Finland had built power plants on the Soviet side of her eastern border, contracted to modernise a pulp and paper mill a few miles from the Finnish border at Svetogorsk, and agreed to construct a forest industry centre at Pääjärvi. The Soviet Union also assisted in the construction of atomic power stations on Finnish territory at Loviisa. In November 1973 the framework treaty was signed for a joint project to build a mining town and develop mining facilities in Soviet Karelia at Kostamus.[52] This more than any other comparable project, has had the effect of combating the traditionally high level of unemployment and underemployment in the northern and eastern border regions of Finland. More recently Finland has contracted to build industrial centres in the Leningrad area (Tosno), in Siberia (Norilsk), and at the end of 1983 a Finnish consortium finally concluded a deal to construct a grain harbour in Estonia at Muuga. Since the late 1970s, moreover, there has been a spectacular increase in the volume of cooperation between Soviet organisations and Finnish firms in the joint construction of industrial projects in third countries.[53] As in the case of the Saimaa Canal, it seems that many of these joint projects, despite their economic profitability, would have been far more difficult to realise without a strong mutual political input. It has become quite usual for the neighbour states first to conclude a framework treaty for a large project at the political level, and thereafter to conclude a commercial agreement between purchaser and deliverer. In this way the intertwining of politics and economics has become institutionalised.[54]

It has been claimed in fact that the Soviet authorities have used their political position for economic ends, in particular in gaining the contract for constructing the Loviisa power stations and for the provision of new locomotives for Finland in the early 1970s. The Finnish authorities have pointed out, however, that by doing business with the USSR Finland saves on foreign currency and can adjust its balance of payments more satisfactorily. This occurs because Finnish–Soviet trade is undertaken in barter terms in trade agreements planned for a five year period, so that a deficit in one year can be adjusted in the next. Since at the end of the 1960s the Finns had difficulties in securing sufficient imports from the USSR to match the volume of goods they were willing to export, large Soviet contracts at the time may have been more adventageous than Western or even Finnish ones to ease this import problem.[55]

The economic benefits of trade with the Soviet Union have won broad recognition in Finland. The methods of agreement by which trade with the USSR is carried out have provided greater stability than trade with the market economies. The Finnish metal and machine tools industry, which is still largely based on the Soviet market, has in addition been provided with a certain amount of stability and shelter from the vagaries of Western industrial competition. The Soviet market has provided a margin of safety for the development of sophistication, and thereby competition in the Western markets. Furthermore, through the import of Soviet goods on a long term basis Finland has been assured of adequate deliveries at fixed prices of cereals, petroleum products, coal, coke, and synthetic fertilisers, all of which have fluctuated widely in availability and price on Western markets.[56] Indeed, the latest plans and agreements for Finnish–Soviet trade extend up to the year 2000.

Finnish economists have recognised that trade with the USSR has had the effect of counteracting the development of inflation in Finland. In recent years Soviet commentators have also argued that for Finland economic relations with the USSR have acted to some extent to reduce the pressure of the recession in the West and to secure a more favourable GNP growth rate. It is true that in 1979 and 1980 Finland's GNP grew by 7·5 per cent, but then the delayed recession hit the economy hard, despite trade with the East. Nevertheless, border trade with the USSR, such as the Kostamus project, continued to stimulate the Finnish economy. This employment issue induced the Confederation of Finnish Industries to issue a statement during the 1981–2 presidential election campaign in support of 'those parties and persons' who had been most active in developing and diversifying Finnish trade with the Soviet Union on the basis of the Finnish market economy.

It could be argued that the worse East–West relations in general become, the better the Finnish position will be on the Soviet markets. Finland has refrained from participating in politically motivated economic boycotts against the USSR by Western states. A Soviet writer even claimed in 1983 that 'the economic and technical development of Finland is inseparably linked with cooperation with the Soviet Union'.[57] To Western ears this may sound uncomfortably close to a relationship of dependence, and Western observers have been particularly concerned about Finland's high level of Soviet oil imports. They have pointed to the strain imposed on the Finnish economy when in autumn 1973, at a time when the Finns were importing 74 per cent of their oil requirements from the Soviet Union, the USSR raised the price of its oil exports to Finland to the Rotterdam notation level. The Finnish Foreign Minister, Karjalainen, explained that Finland and the USSR had already agreed in the 1950s that world market prices would be followed in trade agreements between the two countries. He argued that Finland would not lose in the long run so long as the Finns kept their own exports to the USSR up to the world price level. In fact, Finnish prices may have been a source of previous Soviet grievances. In 1974 Kekkonen pointed out that if the USSR were to wish to criticise Finland's economic policy, 'an incomparable and legitimate opportunity would be offered by describing how Finland's continuing level of costs, often by an unrestrained rise, influences trade between Finland and the Soviet Union'.[58] Finnish officials hoped that since oil imported from the USSR is paid by Finnish exports, the increase in oil prices would lead to growth in Finnish production and therefore improve employment prospects.

By the beginning of the 1980s the Finns had coped so successfully with the oil price increases that a huge imbalance in Finland's favour had developed in the barter trade with the USSR. Many in Finland and abroad anticipated that the problem of finding new products for import from the USSR would force a considerable compensatory reduction in Finnish exports to the Soviet Union.[59] But the Finns resolved to increase imports of Soviet arms, and in April 1982 Finland signed a scientific-technological cooperation programme for the exploitation of Soviet oil and gas resources with the USSR in the Northern waters. The following June Koivisto and Andropov agreed to begin negotiations to investigate the possibilities 'to considerably increase deliveries of Soviet natural gas to Finland'.[60]

Finland's imports of Soviet gas may simply replace Soviet oil which the USSR may be less willing or able to export to Finland later in the 1980s. These new deliveries can also be interpreted as an expression of the value attached by Soviet leaders to the high quality and technical level of imports from Finland. There is a sense in which the USSR relies on Finland technologically as a window to the West. The Finns themselves have sought to reduce a sense of dependence on Eastern energy sources by building up and becoming engaged in international, multilateral structures for cooperation. They do not believe that their neutrality is compromised by their import structure more than that of Sweden is, which is highly dependent on high technology imports from Western states.

FINLAND, THE USSR AND ECONOMIC INTEGRATION WITH WESTERN EUROPE

The interests of both politics and trade have induced Soviet leaders to resist overly close Finnish participation in the post-war political-economic integration of Western Europe. To exercise influence on Finland Soviet spokesmen have employed arguments derived in the first place from the political requirements of friendly and non-discriminatory relations between the Finnish and Soviet states, and secondly they have referred to the requirements of neutral policy. All Finnish treaty relationships with Western states have also been concluded under the shadow of the 1948 FCMA-Treaty. Soviet leaders have relied ultimately, however, on the restraint exercised by their Finnish counterparts, and they have been willing to listen to reasoned Finnish arguments aimed at the protection of Finnish economic interests in the West.

In July 1947 the Finnish government was faced with the decision whether or not to accept the offer of Marshall Aid. Romania and Hungary were opposed to participation in the plan, and despite initial interest Czechoslovakia followed suit after having provoked a negative Soviet reaction. The Soviet Union regarded the Marshall Plan as an attempt to construct an anti-Soviet bloc and warned Europe against becoming 'enslaved' to the United States. It was an open secret in Helsinki that the deputy chairman of the Allied Control Commission, Savonenkov, had informed the Finnish Prime Minister, Pekkala, that the USSR expected a negative response from Finland toward Marshall Aid. Otherwise there existed no clearly formulated Soviet threat against Finnish participation. The Finnish Parliamentary Foreign Affairs Committee and all the Finnish political parties besides the SKDL were in favour of accepting the plan.[61] But the Finnish government decided to issue a declaration that Finland would be unable to take part in the Marshall Plan, since 'the political position of Finland has not yet been stabilised through a permanent peace treaty, and as the Marshall Plan has given rise to strong differences of opinion between the great powers'.[62] This note made it clear that the Finns had reacted not so much against the plan itself as against the international situation it had given rise to.

The Finnish government recognised that to accept Marshall Aid would be to entail the risk of confronting the USSR contrary to the premises of Finland's new Eastern policy even before its foundations had firmly been laid through the ratification of the peace treaty. The Finns had reason to be cautious during this delicate period. The Finnish decision meant that Finland alone of the Northern states remained outside measures for Western integration, opting to develop her economic life autonomously, although her metal industry gravitated Eastwards.

The course of the Finnish negotiations for a special agreement with EFTA in 1960–1 demonstrated the means by which Finland could preserve relations of confidence with the USSR while edging towards the institutions of Western economic integration in pursuit of Finnish trade interests. This may have strengthened the credibility of Finland's policy of neutrality in the West, but Finland did not aim at full membership of EFTA since Finnish statesmen recognised that such a status clearly would not correspond with the Soviet view of the commitments of neutral policy.

In general the Soviet Union tried to dissuade neutral countries from joining EFTA. If Finland were to join the association, Soviet commentators argued, the attempts of the NATO member states in EFTA to achieve their own economic and political goals would be bound to influence Finland's neutrality and international position. The Finns tried to overcome such political misgivings through working towards the eventual creation of a special institutional framework for entering into EFTA so that there would be no question of Finnish policy being influenced by the stronger member states of a supra-national power.

Soviet leaders were particularly concerned about the possibility of Finnish–Soviet trade suffering from Finland's entry into EFTA. In October 1959 Deputy Prime Minister Mikoyan acknowledged that it would be the Finnish government's decision whether or not to join EFTA, but he presumed that Finland would consider 'taking account of trade conducted with the Soviet Union to be important in all its arrangements'.[63] Some 15 per cent of Finnish exports were going to the USSR and the 1947 most favoured nation concession was still in force. After Finland had engaged in probing talks with the EFTA countries she received a memorandum from the Soviet government in May 1960, which in all probability asked Finland for an unqualified most favoured nation clause with respect to the (EFTA) Seven, just as the USSR had demanded from the Seven unsuccessfully earlier that year.[64]

The Soviet Union was not openly opposed to Finland's discussions with the Seven but warned her against undertakings which would weaken the conditions for the development of Finnish–Soviet trade. In summer 1960 Kekkonen gave a personal guarantee to the USSR that a Finnish arrangement with EFTA would not change Finland's chosen foreign policy course, which may have influenced Soviet leaders. During a visit to Finland in September 1960 Khrushchev expressed Soviet aversion to 'separate Western economic groupings which have a more clearly expressed political character'. But Kekkonen's promise may have underlain Khrushchev's stated 'understanding [of] the Finnish desire to preserve its competitiveness in Western markets'. He disclosed that the USSR was ready to enter into negotiations with Finland about how 'to preserve and further develop the exchange of goods between Finland and the USSR' if Finland were to wish to conclude a separate trade agreement with EFTA.[65] The Finnish–Soviet discussions which followed in November confirmed that Soviet leaders were primarily concerned with the continuity of Finland's trade with the USSR.[66] An Agreement on Customs Matters was concluded, which in practice granted the USSR the same duty reductions as were scheduled in the Finnish–EFTA (FINEFTA) agreement. Once an understanding had been reached with the Soviet Union Finland advanced to a new round of discussions with the EFTA countries, which led to the eventual conclusion of the FINEFTA agreement in spring 1961.

One motive behind the conciliatory Soviet attitude towards the Finnish EFTA issue in autumn 1960 may have been the desire to bolster Kekkonen's chances in the pending presidential elections, although Kekkonen's EFTA diplomacy failed to prevent the formation of an electoral front against him. The balanced course of negotiations between East and West which Kekkonen presided over, and the ensuing conclusion of an agreement with EFTA which Soviet leaders had originally in principle been opposed to, may have had a stronger influence outside Finland on Western opinion. Western confidence in the Finnish policy of neutrality increased, and even in the USSR the Finnish EFTA negotiations may have confirmed Finland's neutral course, since Finland had remained outside the political arrangements of the West and had agreed to acknowledge the Soviet interest in Finnish trade on the basis of the 1947 most favoured nation principle.[67]

In 1955 Finland had managed to enter the Nordic Council, despite the initial Soviet criticisms of this organisation. For Finland this acted as a first step towards closer Nordic economic cooperation, although the Soviet press was strongly critical of plans for a Nordic customs union in 1958–9. These plans were revived in Denmark in early 1968, when the idea of a Nordic customs union together with some common institutions to facilitate Nordic economic cooperation was aired. Soviet criticism of the political character of the EEC had sharpened by winter 1968, and Soviet commentators argued that the so-called Nordek plan could not be considered an independent undertaking of the Nordic countries, since it was a transitional phase to dependence on the EEC.

Finnish leaders were fully aware of the Soviet opposition in principle to closed economic communities, and after a visit to

Leningrad in May 1969 Kekkonen claimed that this also applied to Nordek. In his view the Nordek issue was related to Finland's commitment to a policy of neutrality, which among other matters required Finland to 'maintain trade as widely as possible with the Soviet Union'.[68] It was true that Finnish neutrality had been referred to rather sparingly in Moscow over the previous few years. If this had ensued from Finland's trade and economic policy it meant either that the USSR had begun to emphasise that neutrality covered commitments undertaken in the sphere of economic relations, or that the USSR did not regard Finland's integration plans as purely economic in character. The former view may have been intended to forestall further reductions in the Soviet share of Finnish trade; this decline had followed the FINEFTA agreement. Since the East European socialist countries had not received most favoured nation status in this agreement, a perceptible decline had also taken place in their trade with Finland.

In March 1970 the Finnish cabinet took the decision to remain outside Nordek. In a speech the following month explaining this decision Kekkonen made an overture to the EEC. Indeed, it has been argued on the Finnish Left that the real explanation for this decision lay neither in the fear of tarnished neutrality nor in the fear of adverse Soviet reactions, but in the recognition by Finnish industrial and commercial circles that the interest of the EEC in Northern Europe meant that Finland had a chance of getting a free-trade agreement of its own with the EEC.[69]

The political problems arising out of the Finnish intention to negotiate a trade agreement with the EEC in the early 1970s strained to the utmost Finland's ability to harmonise the perceived requirements of neutral policy with the economic demands imposed by the integration of Western Europe, while retaining Soviet confidence in the continuity of Finland's policy. The groundwork for the EEC venture was laid by the prolongation of the 1948 FCMA-Treaty, five years before its formal expiry date, consequent on a Soviet initiative in July 1970. In Washington Kekkonen explained that this had been intended 'to remove any possible doubt about the consistency of our policy', which was of particular importance 'in view of Finland's vital interest in maintaining her trading position in all markets'. Any arrangements the Finns may have to enter into, he added, 'must of course be in accord with our policy of neutrality'.[70]

The Finns began negotiations with the EEC in April 1970, and agreed to initial a free-trade agreement in July 1972. During this period Soviet observations about Finnish policy towards the EEC were restrained. Soviet articles concerning the subject were allusive and used various indirect arguments, despite their outspoken assessments of the EEC policy of other European neutrals. In November 1971 *Pravda* claimed that 'any form of cooperation with the closed grouping of the EEC, which is in fact the economic backbone of NATO, may create a threat to the present peace-seeking foreign policy course [of Finland]'.[71] Next month Finnish right-wing circles who were laying hopes on Finland conducting negotiations with the EEC were accused of counting on being able to weaken Finnish–Soviet relations 'with the aid of this Western political grouping'.[72] Such rather general allegations left the Soviet stand towards the Finnish free-trade agreement unclear. In March 1972 Brezhnev indicated the readiness of the USSR to live with the EEC, although Soviet attacks on its nature and objectives continued.

About a month after Finland's free-trade agreement was initialled in Brussels, in August 1972, Kekkonen discussed the topic with Kosygin and Brezhnev at the latter's *dacha* at Zavidovo. Thanks to a press leak the content of these discussions became well known,[73] although the EEC topic was not even mentioned in the official communique of the meeting. The Soviet leaders expressed their concern about the political effects of the EEC agreement within Finland. They feared that 'certain forces' in Finland would acquire the means to engage in activities against the FCMA-Treaty. They suspected also that the EEC countries intended to disturb the prevailing friendly relations between Finland and the Soviet Union through imposing further economic conditions. In these circumstances, while the Soviet leaders stressed that they did not wish to infringe Finnish sovereignty, they warned Finland against acting in such a way that what had been built between the neighbour states would be lost. In the Soviet view a further danger arose from the effects of the EEC agreement on Finnish–Soviet trade, since it could lead to Finland losing its markets in the USSR. Brezhnev and Kosygin interpreted the EEC agreement as a political issue in so far as the EEC represented a closed economic organisation. While the Soviet leaders appeared to understand Finland's wish to conclude a trade agreement with the EEC, they felt that it would have a general political significance: 'when trade begins it goes together with politics'. They admitted, however, that ultimately the decision whether to conclude the agreement rested with Finland herself.[74]

Kekkonen responded to the Soviet arguments at Zavidovo with a personal assurance to the Soviet leaders that Finland's EEC agreement would not influence the favourable development of Finnish–Soviet relations. Since the topic inspired a strong critical debate in Finland, Finnish leaders were compelled to argue the case for the EEC agreement carefully with the intention of allaying Soviet suspicions and winning as much domestic support as possible.

Some in Finland were concerned that an expansion of free-trade with the EEC countries could be expected to lead to a clear increase in and dependence on Finnish–West German trade, which would influence balanced relations with the DDR and engender future disputes with West Germany. This could create difficulties for the conduct of Finland's neutral policy.[75] But Foreign Minister Karjalainen asserted that no trade arrangement could affect Finland's 'political relations presumed by the [1948] FCMA-Treaty',[76] and in October 1973 the Finnish government formally announced that this applied to the EEC agreement. Kekkonen went further to provide his 'own opinion' that if it became evident that the conclusion of the EEC agreement was retarding 'the increase in Soviet and Finnish trade as it continually should increase', Finland would give notice of her intention to cancel the agreement.[77]

In their opposition to the free-trade agreement the Finnish Left referred to Article 4 of the 1948 FCMA-Treaty and Article 3 of the Paris Peace Treaty, which enjoin Finland not to participate in any international alliances or coalitions directed against the USSR. Although from a juridical perspective the EEC agreement clearly would not lead to an alliance in the sense intended in the wording of the 1948 treaty, many believed that were Finland to conclude the agreement this could well be construed by Soviet leaders as participation in a coalition directed against the USSR. Kekkonen himself drew the line before formal association with the EEC. 'This is something we would never do', he observed, 'since the EEC is a political agreement it is impossible for us to be engaged'.[78] But he underlined that the USSR had set no conditions for any Finnish agreement with the EEC, although he admitted that 'were we to have had an assurance that the Soviet Union considered the free-trade agreement to breach the FCMA-Treaty, the free-trade agreement would have been left unconcluded'.[79] Foreign Minister Karjalainen denied that the FCMA-Treaty 'had ever, formally any more than factually, limited our rights to look after our economic interests in changing conditions of trade policy and economics'.[80] During the ratification of the EEC agreement in 1973, all three actors, President,

Cabinet, and Parliament, issued separate resolutions intended to bolster Soviet confidence in the Finnish policy, which stressed that the agreement would not affect Finland's previous international obligations.

In Kekkonen's view the objective of the Finnish EEC agreement had been a trade arrangement 'which would suit our policy of neutrality and would be economically balanced'.[81] The two components of this statement complemented each other, and it seems that the Finnish policy presumed that an increase in trade links with the West should be compensated by a corresponding increase with the East. Already during the course of the EEC negotiations in 1971 talks had commenced in Moscow to enable Finland to become the first non-socialist country to sign a treaty with the Council for Mutual Economic Assistance (Comecon). An agreement was signed in May 1973 and ratified the following June. Finland simultaneously activated and renewed her economic, technical and scientific cooperation with the USSR through a foundation treaty, which paved the way for subsequent large joint Finnish–Soviet projects. Finland also concluded individual agreements on tariffs with certain East European countries, the KEVSOS agreements, modelled on the EEC agreement. The Finnish government assured the USSR that 'the concessions made by Finland to the EEC countries will also be granted immediately to the Soviet Union for any parts not covered by the customs agreement between the two countries'.[82] It could be argued, moreover, that on a political level the extension of Kekkonen's term of office to 1978 by exceptional means, which was approved in parliament in January 1973, was part of this 'balance' or 'compensation' process for a Soviet audience, since Kekkonen had given a personal assurance at Zavidovo that the EEC agreement would not damage the favourable development of Finnish–Soviet relations.

Finnish officials denied that the country's Eastern treaty arrangements formed part of a 'package solution'. They could point out that the small Comecon countries had already for a long time been requesting a free-trade treaty with Finland, and that many issues of economic, technical and scientific cooperation with the USSR had been initiated in the 1960s. One explanation of these simultaneous arrangements may be that Finnish policy-makers considered the country best able to extend economic links to the West just at the time when her trade relations with the USSR were expanding.[83]

The Finns could rely also on a bank of goodwill on the Soviet side arising out of their promotion of the European Security Conference.

This activity may have encouraged Soviet leaders to believe that it would be better for Finland to influence the European system on a general European level than to be left without any connection with the European Community.[84] For some years Finnish spokesmen had been expressing views parallel to those of the USSR about the advantages of general European integration and the benefits of trade with the East for all the Northern countries. At any rate, within a few years of the ratification of the Finnish EEC agreement this document was being described on the Soviet side also as merely a customs agreement which did not influence the earlier international agreements Finland had concluded.[85]

6 The Soviet Interest in Finnish Internal Affairs

The success of the policy of coexistence which has developed between Finland and her great power neighbour ultimately has to be measured against the respect shown for the principle contained in Article 6 of the 1948 FCMA-Treaty. This article, which expresses a classic norm of international law, pledges the parties to the treaty to observe the principle of 'the mutual respect of sovereignty and integrity and that of the non-interference in the internal affairs of the other state'. Some of the gravest doubts in Western minds about the character of post-war Finnish–Soviet relations have arisen in just this area. The Soviet understanding of this principle has not exactly coincided with Western views. In addition, Article 6 of the Finnish treaty has not remained comparable with similarly phrased articles in the Soviet FCMA-treaties with the Eastern bloc countries, since the latter articles were qualified by the Soviet pronouncements regarding the 'socialist commonwealth' towards the end of the 1960s. This thesis, which was popularised in the West as the 'Brezhnev doctrine', gave the notion of 'socialist unity' priority over the principle of non-interference in internal affairs, but bypassed Finland which clearly lay outside the 'socialist commonwealth'.

It is evident that a great power has to lean but slightly on a small neighbouring state to impose pressure on that state. Verbal criticisms by Soviet leaders of developments within Finland cannot be ignored by Finnish statesmen, even if the Finnish response only takes the form of verbal reassurances for Soviet consumption. Finland has only infrequently been subjected to more severe pressures from the East since her post-war settlement. Soviet statesmen have denied that any Soviet interference in Finnish internal affairs has taken place, but when it can most clearly be argued that Finland did come under such pressure, during the period of Khrushchev's dominance in the USSR, the Soviet leader took care to explain that the USSR did have an interest in internal Finnish politics. This was a practical rather than ideological interest; Soviet leaders followed the vicissitudes of Finnish politics with an eye to future developments in Finnish foreign and security policy. The sporadic occasions when Soviet statesmen appear to have wished to influence the course of internal Finnish politics have coincided with periods of political flux in Finland and heightened international tension abroad.

In the immediate post-war years the Soviet concern about internal developments in Finland could be expressed institutionally through the activities and powers of the Allied Control Commission, and it was legally validated by the provisions of the Paris Peace Treaty. During these years Soviet leaders may have had hopes for 'progressive' developments in internal Finnish politics, but they did little actively to promote such tendencies, although they did not hide their hostility to certain Finnish politicians who were regarded as enemies of the Soviet state. The attention the Soviet Union paid to the personalities involved in Finnish politics was largely a legacy of antipathies which had already developed during the war years. Time and again, until the mid-1960s, Soviet spokesmen attacked the political influence of a few Finnish political figures. Soviet leaders sought the removal of those perceived to hold deep-rooted and often ideologically motivated hostility to the Soviet state from the arrangement of political forces in Finland and the Finnish press. This was achieved largely by the mid-1960s through indigenous developments in Finland. With the growth of a new generation of politicians in Finland, lacking what Kekkonen later termed 'old hostile and grudging feelings against the Soviet Union', those political figures who had attracted Soviet distrust and rancour, misplaced or exaggerated though this often had been, gradually withdrew from politics.

Over the last decades Soviet leaders have found little cause to mar the image of Finnish–Soviet relations as a showpiece of East–West relations through heavy-handed criticisms of internal affairs in Finland. They have continued to follow political developments in their neighbour state with care, but they have been quite pragmatic about their expectations for Finland from their policy of peaceful coexistence. Above all Soviet statesmen have not wished to risk losing the advantages derived from trade and a well established security policy *entente* with the Finnish state through clumsy and readily identified attempts to promote ideological goals in Finland.

THE ALLIED CONTROL COMMISSION AND ITS LEGACY 1944–50

The Finnish–Soviet armistice agreement of September 1944 referred to an area of Soviet concern in Finnish internal affairs. The armistice obliged Finland to place those accused of war crimes on trial (Article 13) and to dissolve pro-Hitler organisations situated on Finnish territory, 'as well as other organisations conducting propaganda hostile to the United Nations, in particular to the Soviet Union' (Article 21). In themselves these provisions did not appear exceptionally onerous for Finland, but the establishment of an Allied Control Commission on Finnish soil to ensure the execution of the armistice terms meant that until its departure in 1947 Finland had very much the character of a nation under trial. The Finns were fully aware in whose hands their destiny lay. Although the Control Commission included representatives from Britain, Prime Minister Paasikivi made clear at the end of 1945 that 'they have no material significance, since when the armistice agreement talks of "allies" it is always the Soviet Union in parenthesis'.[1] The Commission tended to act as the vehicle for exchanges between the Finnish and Soviet governments also on matters outside the armistice, but in summer 1945 the Commission pronounced itself satisfied that the armistice conditions had been met sufficiently to warrant the normalisation of diplomatic relations.

Paasikivi claimed that the Control Commission and its chairman, Colonel-General Zhdanov, kept exactly to the provisions of the armistice. This was borne out by the United States representative in Finland in May 1945, who thus far had found 'no evidence' that the Control Commission had 'taken any action *vis-à-vis* the Finnish government which cannot be more or less clearly justified under the armistice terms'.[2] But Paasikivi admitted that differences of interpretation had arisen over the armistice provisions. The speaker of the Finnish parliament, K-A. Fagerholm, disclosed the vulnerability of the Finnish position by declaring that the interpretation given by the Control Commission to the armistice terms was 'final, it cannot be appealed against; neither the Finnish parliament nor the government can refuse to accept it'.[3] The issue of the reparations the armistice imposed on Finland showed this starkly. In December 1944 Finland had to accept the Soviet demand for reparations to be paid at 1938 prices after Zhdanov had threatened to take over all the industrial concerns in eastern Finland if terms were not reached. Finnish leaders could not stand on principle whilst the sovereignty of their country lay in abeyance.

The armistice gave a legal basis for Soviet pressure on Finland to prosecute war criminals. The treatment to be meted out to 'war culprits' was a much more contentious political issue. This was the term Paasikivi used to describe those politicians who were claimed to have led Finland into war in 1941, neglected opportunities to make peace, bound Finland to the side of Germany, and misled the Finnish parliament. The Soviet authorities were inclined to merge these two categories of wrongdoers. At the beginning of 1945 the Soviet political adviser to the Control Commission, Pavel Orlov, complained that Finland was doing nothing about the candidatures of the war criminals in the coming elections, although he admitted that 'no obligation to do so existed under the armistice terms'.[4] At first Prime Minister Paasikivi was insistent that he would not depart from legal and democractic means in dealing with 'war politicians'. In his view the matter constituted an 'internal' Finnish affair, and the Control Commission had maintained that it did not intend to interfere in such affairs.[5] Paasikivi was aware, nevertheless, that if the attempts of compromised war politicians to continue to control much of the Finnish economy and political life were not resisted then all attempts to reorient Finnish policy towards conciliation with the USSR would be defeated. Since even the American Secretary of State sanctioned British and Soviet interference to avert the re-election of the 'men who were primarily responsible for Finland's disastrous war policy',[6] when the Finnish government announced the withdrawal of the candidatures of a dozen prominent war politicians in February 1945 they attracted little sympathy abroad.

The Control Commission also imposed pressure on Finland to bring the Finnish war politicians to trial under Article 13 of the armistice. This required the passage of an enabling act through the Finnish parliament in September 1945. In this fashion an international tribunal was avoided, and although eight men were sentenced, including Risto Ryti the Finnish president from December 1940 to August 1944, none served their full sentences, no-one was executed, and Mannerheim avoided trial. The war-guilt trial of 1945–6 was carried out with obvious reluctance; it was an expression of Paasikivi's 'national realism', which became the prevailing spirit in Finnish policy.

In a speech before the Finnish parliamentary elections in March 1945 Paasikivi had already called for the election of 'new faces . . .

new forces which have not shouldered the ballast of the past', to arouse confidence in Finland's intentions in the USSR as well as the other United Nations.[7] Paasikivi placed his faith in a change in national leadership, but he made clear that he did not anticipate a transformation of Finland's internal economic and social system. The two issues could not, however, so easily be divorced. The Soviet delegation had insisted that full guarantees for political minorities within Finland be written into Article 20 of the armistice agreement. As Foreign Minister Enckell later acknowledged, bearing in mind the fact that the USSR was governed by the Communist Party, this guarantee necessarily imposed additional responsibilities on the Finnish government in its treatment of the internal Communist movement in Finland.[8]

The Finnish Communist Party (SKP) began to function legally once the armistice was signed. In October 1944 Zhdanov took part in the foundation of the Communist dominated Finnish People's Democratic League (SKDL). President Mannerheim appointed the first Communist minister in Finland, Yrjö Leino, the following month; Leino became Minister of Internal Affairs in spring 1945. The Communists won almost one quarter of the seats in parliament after the elections of March 1945. But this success was less a consequence of the presence of the Control Commission on Finnish soil than a reflection of the disillusion of a sizeable number of Social Democrats with their party's wartime leadership and collaboration with what they regarded as 'Right extremism'.[9] A considerable proportion of Social Democrat Party (SDP) members transferred directly to the SKDL. Many influential figures and members who were by ultimate persuasion left-wing remained in the SDP, as indicated by the fact that an opportunity for an electoral alliance with the Communists in 1945 was rejected by just one vote. But in Soviet eyes the SDP was still branded by its previous wartime policies, an association believed to be confirmed in 1948 once right-wing members of the party belonging to the so-called 'Brothers-in-Arms' wing attained the dominant position. The Control Commission refused, therefore, to accept a Social Democrat prime minister for Finland in April 1947.

Zhdanov disclosed the ideological course he anticipated for Finland to the Cominform in September 1947. He described Finland as having 'firmly set foot on the path of democratic development' alongside Romania and Hungary.[10] Zhdanov accordingly supported the Communist Minister of the Interior's continuity in office in Finland in autumn 1947.[11] But Communist and other SKDL ministers, as a rule, responded negatively towards strikes and demonstrations which occurred under Communist leadership or spontaneously after spring 1947, since they feared that these might create difficulties for the coalition they were in. The SKDL Prime Minister, Mauno Pekkala, even condemned unauthorised strikes in parliament.

Full sovereignty returned to Finland once the Control Commission left Finland at the end of September 1947, and Zhdanov himself died the following August. In spring 1948 the Finnish Minister of Defence still regarded the SKP as a Soviet fourth column, ready to 'act upon signals received from Moscow which may be determined by the overall international picture'.[12] But no evidence has emerged of any Soviet designs behind inconclusive rumours of an attempted Communist coup which were aired during this spring.[13] The Finnish Minister of the Interior affirmed that the USSR had brought no pressure, direct or indirect, on the Finnish government in connection with the strike wave which affected Finland in summer 1949.[14] The only Soviet response to the arrest of Communists by the Finnish authorities during these strikes was to be found in hostile Soviet press comments referring to the legal obligation of non-discrimination undertaken by Finland in Article 6 of the peace treaty. The Finnish Foreign Minister concluded in September that he foresaw no signs of extra-legal Soviet pressure on Finland providing the Finns gave no opening for it to be effective. He felt that one of the strengths of the Finnish position lay in the approval and respect felt by Soviet leaders for the strict Finnish adherence to legal obligations. He believed that the present Soviet leadership, from its knowledge of the Finnish people, did not expect any revolutionary political action in Finland.[15] If this was a correct assessment of Soviet views then it is probable that Soviet statesmen actually sought to avoid social disruption in Finland, since this would have affected the Finnish deliveries of goods to the USSR specified in the reparations agreement.

At the end of the 1940s Soviet leaders seem to have been less interested in promoting the Finnish Communist movement than in retarding the discredited right-wing Social Democrats in Finland. The latter objective, of course, tended to work in favour of the SKP, but it could derive some support from the terms of the Paris Peace Treaty. The treaty confirmed the Finnish obligation to bring to trial those 'accused of having committed, ordered, or abetted war crimes and crimes against peace and humanity' (Article 9), and to dissolve organisations conducting 'propaganda hostile to the Soviet Union' (Article 8).

Soviet rancour was directed above all against Väinö Tanner, the long term leader of the Social Democrat Party and Foreign Minister during the Winter War. Tanner had adopted a rigidly uncompromising stance in negotiations with Stalin and Molotov before the Winter War, and after the final armistice with the USSR he proved to be quite unable to accommodate himself to Paasikivi's *Realpolitik*. At the end of 1945 Zhdanov told Paasikivi that his release from trial for war crimes would amount to 'spitting in the face of the Soviet Union'.[16] Tanner was duly convicted in the trials the next year. The SDP leaders of the late 1940s inherited the antipathy which the USSR had felt towards the 'Tannerite adventurists' in earlier years. Soviet commentators paid less attention to the avowed policies of the SDP than to the political character of its leading figures. No distinction was made between 'the old Social Democrat leaders of the Tanner, Fagerholm and Skog brand and the new leaders of the type of Varjonen and Leskinen'.[17] Väinö Leskinen, who became the Secretary of the SDP, was damned for having acted as Secretary of the right-wing 'Brothers-in-Arms' organisation during the war.[18] This Soviet emphasis on personalities and past policy associations meant that for over two decades after the war Soviet leaders distrusted the intentions of any Finnish government under Social Democrat control.

The formation of a minority Social Democrat government in Finland in July 1948, which led the SKDL into opposition, set into motion a torrent of Soviet accusations. Prime Minister Fagerholm was described as 'Tanner's apprentice' (although Tanner was still in prison), while his government was interpreted as a 'signal to all those who support cooperation with the Germans that they will soon get back their former influence'.[19] The principal ministerial posts of the new cabinet had allegedly been assigned to 'Tannerites, collaborationists [a reference to collaboration with Nazi Germany] and members of . . . fascist organisations', set upon creating an 'Atlantic' orientation in Finnish foreign policy.[20] Fagerholm responded with an assurance that his government intended to continue the foreign policy of the former government, of trustworthy cooperation with the USSR, and that the leadership of foreign policy remained in the hands of the president as during the previous four years.[21] The Soviet reaction was to cool relations with Finland on a diplomatic level and claim that Fagerholm's government intended to sabotage the fulfilment of the Finnish–Soviet FCMA-Treaty.[22] But the Soviet authorities made no demands for Communist participation in the Finnish government, and Paasikivi's support for Fagerholm lent his cabinet the strength to weather internal Communist and Soviet criticism.

The approach of the 1950 presidential election placed Paasikivi himself under considerable pressure from the USSR. According to the Soviet press it was natural that Paasikivi 'stood over the cradle' of the Fagerholm government and continued to 'direct its actions', since it represented the continuation of Finnish policy along the 'American channel' which Paasikivi had favoured.[23] Paasikivi was condemned for his leniency toward those convicted of war crimes, and the 'Paasikivi line' was characterised as a 'struggle against the Soviet Union and for support of the Anglo-American instigators of a new war'.[24]

Parallel to this press campaign, the Soviet Deputy Foreign Minister, A. Gromyko, left a note for the Finnish government in December 1949 which demanded that a list of Soviet citizens living in Finland who were described as 'war criminals' should be returned to the USSR, in accordance with Finland's treaty commitments.[25] British diplomats received information that it had been made clear to Paasikivi at least indirectly that the Soviet authorities would regard his re-election as an unfriendly gesture to the USSR, incompatible with the FCMA-Treaty. The Swedish Foreign Ministry even alleged, on the basis of information received from Moscow, that the Soviet Union was planning to revoke the FCMA-Treaty to exert pressure on Paasikivi to withdraw his candidature in the presidential election.[26]

Soviet hostility to Paasikivi was unavailing; he was re-elected president over Kekkonen and Pekkala, both of whom were preferable as candidates in Soviet eyes. Paasikivi's authority as president was fully confirmed, since unlike his earlier election in 1946 and Mannerheim's election in 1944, which had been carried out by the Finnish Parliament, the 1950 election was an endorsement by the Finnish people through the electoral college, as prescribed by the Finnish constitution.

SOVIET ATTITUDES TO FINNISH POLITICAL PARTIES

The Communist dominated SKDL held office in the Finnish government between November 1944 and July 1948, and Mauno Pekkala served as SKDL Prime Minister for the last two and a half years of this period. But the veteran Conservative politician Paasikivi retained the political control of Finland tightly in his own hands, first as Prime Minister from November 1944 until March 1946, and then as President of the Republic. Thus even during the three and a half years the Finnish Communists were represented in the government Soviet statesmen had to deal with the Finnish president over matters of foreign and security policy. After the Finnish elections in June 1948 the SKDL failed to receive the government posts they desired and the party withdrew into opposition. Internal political opposition to the Finnish Communists had strengthened and Paasikivi was now prepared to use his authority to isolate them. The SKDL was to remain in opposition for almost two decades (until May 1966) as a vocal critic of government policy but removed from the levers of power.

Finnish foreign policy is predominantly presidential foreign policy. But even when Soviet confidence in the Finnish president developed later in the 1950s, he alone could not be fully relied on to maintain Finland's line in security policy. Since the war Soviet leaders have revealed an underlying fear of possible negative influences on this line from hostile parliamentary forces. This was plausible since the Finnish president should appoint a government with as broad-based parliamentary support as possible. After the SKDL moved into opposition and conservative forces had been further strengthened by Paasikivi's re-election in 1950 Soviet leaders finally recognised the need to come to terms with the security assurances expressed by bourgeois political parties within a predominantly bourgeois society. They sought reliable political forces in Finland which could ensure the continuity of the presidential line in security relations with the East.

Soviet leaders found it much harder to tolerate or accept the words of the Finnish Social Democrat movement and its party representatives than those of the more staunchly bourgeois Agrarian Party. They preferred to deal with and place their trust in a party which was committed to a practical and restricted social vision and which was indigenously rooted in Finland. The SDP was regarded contrariwise in the late 1940s and the 1950s. The Social Democrats advocated an alternative non-revolutionary path to socialism to the SKDL, for which they fought the Finnish Communists in the trade union movement (SAK) as well as in parliament. In contrast, the Agrarians did not tend openly to compete with the Communists or SKDL for votes. More worrying still to Soviet statesmen were the international links of the Social Democrats; their present Scandinavian orientation, in light of their past pro-German associations, was interpreted as a cover for their basic hostility to the USSR and affinity with the Western states. The SDP was bluntly described by a Soviet commentator in 1950 as 'the "American Party" in Finland', which, alongside the National Coalition Party (the Conservatives), aimed allegedly at the implementation of 'an openly pro-imperialist, anti-popular and anti-Soviet political policy'.[27] The only reference to Finland in the Nineteenth Soviet Party Congress report in 1953 was in fact in association with Scandinavian right-wing socialists, who since the war ostensibly had 'furiously been fighting the peace-loving and democratic forces of the people'.[28] It was clear that the SDP was regarded as an ideological opponent of the Soviet state.

The right-wing Finnish National Coalition Party was grouped together with the SDP in Soviet polemics. Like the SDP the Finnish Conservatives, through their representation of big business, held a variety of international contacts. They were alleged to be 'secretly leading and directing the work of dark forces . . . waging a campaign to revive anti-Soviet revanchist and militarist sentiment'. *Pravda* warned that the participation of the Conservatives in the Finnish government in 1953 for the first time since 1946 would lead to a 'deterioration in Finland's relations with the USSR, which is contrary to the Finnish people's basic vital interests, their security and national independence'.[29] But in fact when a non-party but conservative inclined caretaker government was formed in November 1953 no formal protest was issued by the USSR, and the new Finnish government managed to conclude a new trade treaty with the USSR within weeks of being named.

It became apparent in the early 1950s that Soviet leaders were judging the commitment of Finnish political parties to the new line in security policy with the USSR according to the degree of manifest or latent anti-Sovietism assumed by these parties. As early as 1947 the Supreme Soviet official and specialist on Finland O. W. Kuusinen admitted that 'many who hold Right or conservative views on social and political questions [in Finland] have abandoned . . . the irreconcilable attitude towards the Soviet Union of the extreme Right chauvinists'.[30] Pavel Orlov, one of the primary figures in the Soviet embassy in Helsinki in the immediate post-war years, believed that Paasikivi

> had not agreed with the views of certain of his former Conservative companions about the development of the relations of the Soviet Union and Finland . . . in general his attitude to the Conservatives

was scornful when the issue was one of them and Soviet–Finnish relations.[31]

This helps to account for the confidence eventually aroused in Moscow by Paasikivi's brand of realistic and legalistic conservatism. At the beginning of the 1950s a *Pravda* writer on Finland underlined that 'it is common knowledge that . . . the foreign policy of a country depends on the composition of a government, on its political orientation'.[32] In his second term of office President Paasikivi relied heavily on the Agrarian Party under the premiership of Urho Kekkonen. Kekkonen had originally been converted to understand the necessity of ensuring peaceful and cordial relations with the USSR already during the Continuation War and subsequently had shown his support for the realistic principles of Paasikivi's Eastern policy as Minister of Justice in 1944–6. Between March 1950 and March 1956 Kekkonen headed no fewer than five governments. By the middle of the decade the Agrarian Party in Soviet eyes had assumed the form of a dependable bourgeois force genuinely concerned with promoting conciliation with the USSR and keeping to those security principles enshrined in Finland's post-war treaties. The election of Kekkonen to president in 1956 acted as a further reassurance to Soviet statesmen that these principles would continue to be upheld.

Soviet observers assiduously followed every step taken by Väniö Tanner after he was released from prison in 1949. Tanner was elected once again to chairman of the SDP in 1957 at a time when Soviet leaders were harshly criticising the rearmament and militarisation of West Germany, and soliciting Finnish support for peace initiatives in Central Europe. In June 1957 Khrushchev attacked 'those worthless politicians' who in his view had been driving Finland to destruction alongside Nazi Germany, and when Kekkonen offered Tanner a chance to try and form a government in October the USSR reacted with strong criticism of Tanner and by interrupting trade discussions with Finland. Tanner failed to form a government, but this episode turned out to be only the prelude to a crisis in Finnish–Soviet relations the following year when Soviet leaders exerted pressure on Finland to prevent Finnish foreign policy from falling under the influence of politicians who were regarded as incorrigibly hostile to the Soviet state.

In the late 1950s a clear rightward shift occurred in Finland's domestic policies, which was reflected also in some hostile press speculations about Soviet intentions towards Finland. The Social Democrat writer Arvo Tuominen published allegations, for instance, about a 'conference' ostensibly held in Moscow in 1957 where plans for the intervention of the Soviet army in the internal affairs of Finland were discussed. Finnish Communist Party leaders were accused of 'working to create a situation' to enable them to send an 'appeal for aid' to the Soviet army for the seizure of power in Finland. The Soviet press scorned these allegations,[33] but felt that the anti-Soviet mood which such rumours encouraged could be reflected in the composition of the new Finnish government after the elections of July 1958.[34]

The head of the government formed in August 1958 was the Social Democrat Fagerholm, and it included Conservatives, for the first time in a majority government since the war, Agrarians, and the Social Democrats Väinö Leskinen and Olavi Lindblom, who had led the post-war Social Democrat struggle against domestic Communism in Finland. It quite excluded the SKDL, although the latter had become the strongest parliamentary faction. President Kekkonen was aware that the composition of the new government did not augur well, since the re-ascendancy of Tanner had augmented Soviet distrust of the SDP. In his view Leskinen also had been 'searching for new glory "as an enemy of the Soviet Union" '.[35] In a speech in August Tanner described the USSR as 'a dangerous neighbour' and referred to the 'Communist menace'. From these emotive words and various Conservative Party statements a Soviet writer concluded that 'the Tannerites, in league with the Conservatives, would very much like to push Finland towards her old foreign policy'.[36] Kekkonen wrote to the Agrarian Foreign Minister, J. Virolainen, in mid-September that the Soviet suspicion that a change in the foreign policy course was taking place in Finland 'has to be considered as a fact'. He was particularly alarmed by voices within the Agrarian League itself calling for a 'strong line' and 'direct words' in relations with the USSR, which had led to doubts in the Soviet press about 'certain leaders of the Agrarian League'. Kekkonen stressed that if the belief developed in the USSR that Virolainen wished to adjust Finland's foreign policy it would cause incalculable damage to the Agrarian League and to the country.[37]

Kekkonen tried to reassure the Soviet leadership by stating that so long as he was president he would use the powers vested in the presidency to ensure the continuity of Finland's foreign policy course. Despite Soviet hostility he believed that Fagerholm's government could weather the storm and remain in office, but at the expense of economic difficulties for Finland.[38] In fact, during autumn 1958 the USSR applied a series of varied and increasingly pronounced diplomatic and economic sanctions against Finland.[39] These eventually contributed to a decision by the Agrarians to bring down the coalition by leaving the government in early December, to Fagerholm's resignation, and to the formation of a minority Agrarian government which excluded the Social Democrats.

Soviet leaders had felt a strong aversion to a small coterie of SDP figures represented in Fagerholm's government. From official discussions and private conversations with Soviet leaders Kekkonen later wrote that they held a fixed opinion of 'Tanner and his associates' as enemies of the Soviet Union, based on the public speeches of these men over many years.[40] Khrushchev explained in January 1959 that the advent of a 'night-frost' in Finnish–Soviet relations had coincided with the formation of the Fagerholm government since behind Fagerholm's 'broad back' the Soviet government had detected 'Mr Tanner and his disciple Mr Leskinen, and others well known for their hostility to the Soviet Union'.[41] Yet Soviet antipathies were no longer directed against the SDP as such, as they had been at the beginning of the 1950s. Although Tanner's followers tried to speak in the name of the SDP, Khrushchev stated, 'the Soviet people know very well that Tanner, Leskinen, Lindblom and Pitsinki are still far from being the Finnish Social Democrat Party'.[42]

Since Khrushchev also criticised the 'composition' of Fagerholm's government it came to be widely believed in Finland later that Kekkonen had received a Soviet demand to include the SKDL in the government. The Soviet ambassador, V. Lebedev, was known to have favoured the formation of a broad-based government including the Communists but excluding the Conservatives and the SDP. But no evidence of any such Soviet demands has come to light. Soviet security interests did not require Communists to be included in the Finnish government. The issue was rather the need to form a government strong enough to exclude 'Tanner and his ilk', who in Khrushchev's opinion would 'first and foremost serve the circles in the West' interested in 'drawing Finland into their military-political manoeuvres'.[43] Soviet sensitivity at this time over security issues reflected worries about the growing military strength of West Germany and the increase in East–West tension which could be anticipated in Central Europe. The Agrarian League ministers agreed to withdraw from the Fagerholm government on the same day in fact as the Soviet government issued its 'ultimatum' to the Western states for the demilitarisation of Berlin.

The Soviet leadership denied that any interference in Finnish internal affairs had taken place during the 1958–9 'night-frost' crisis. Khrushchev tried to draw a fine line between the registration of Soviet opinion in anticipation of the policies of a government and pressure against the formation of the government concerned. The kind of government that existed in Finland was, he admitted, the Finnish people's own affair. But he maintained that the USSR could not be indifferent to the policy towards the Soviet Union followed by the government of a neighbouring country. 'It does not depend on us', he told a Latvian audience, 'but we can express our wishes.'[44] Khrushchev probed deeper into the Finnish political fabric by extending this rationale to justify the Soviet interest in Finnish political parties in 1960. While he accepted that Finnish parties and their politics were the internal affair of the Finnish state and the parties in it, he told Kekkonen that as a neighbouring state the USSR could not be impartial over 'what kind of policy this or that party, or these or those of your party leaders, exercises towards the Soviet Union'. Yet the Soviet leader was concerned less with Finnish parties as such than with 'certain public persons' within them.[45]

The lesson Kekkonen drew from the events of 1958 was that so long as Leskinen at least remained in the SDP leadership the Agrarian Party could not risk entering a government with the SDP unless 'the damning judgment of the Soviet Union is reversed'. To include Leskinen again in the Finnish government would threaten to bring Finland's policy line with the USSR 'crashing down'.[46] Kekkonen was prepared to 'assist the Soviet Union' to trust in the continuity of the Finnish policy, which in practical terms meant that he would exercise his presidential powers to prevent governments being named which could encounter a similar Soviet response as in 1958. This exercise of presidential expediency has provided perhaps the best example for those seeking evidence of Finlandisation in Finnish internal affairs, although Kekkonen's systematic exclusion of the SDP from governmental responsibility lasted only a few years.

Within five years of the 'night-frost', internal changes in the SDP, which partly reflected a generational turnover in the party hierarchy, had made a repetition of Soviet political pressure of this kind unlikely. In January 1959 Khrushchev had already expressed confidence in the foreign policy intentions of the majority of Finnish Social Democrats. The organ of the CPSU also recognised the existence of a minority Social Democrat Opposition 'which has openly broken with the reactionary Tanner–Leskinen group', as well as a 'third force' which disagreed with the foreign policy goals of the latter but was hesitant about joining the former.[47] In the early 1960s the SDP began to purge itself of ideological anti-Sovietism. In 1963 the aged Tanner retired as party chairman and Leskinen was removed from the powerful Executive Committee.

By 1964 *Pravda* anticipated a 'real change in political line' and 'a turn from the pro-NATO reactionary course' in the SDP, but affirmed that Leskinen's views remained unchanged: 'as before they contain a great amount of foreign policy provocation against the Soviet Union'.[48] In the following year Leskinen issued a surprising recantation of his former policies and attitudes and explained to Kekkonen his wish to earn Soviet trust personally and for the SDP.[49] The process of reconciliation with the USSR had gone so far by 1966 that after election gains in March the SDP was accepted into the ruling coalition and entrusted by Kekkonen and other Finnish political parties with seats in the government, including the premiership, although these were taken neither by Leskinen nor by any of those Social Democrat leaders who formerly had come under Soviet fire. This SDP led government won Soviet praise, and two years later a full understanding was reached officially between the CPSU and the Finnish SDP.[50] Soviet satisfaction with the realigned foreign policy stand of the SDP ultimately enabled Leskinen himself to become Finnish Foreign Minister.

Throughout the 1970s CPSU–SDP contacts were cultivated, in particular by the SDP chairman, Kalevi Sorsa, who became chairman of the Committee of Disarmament of the Socialist International in 1980. In spring 1982 the first Finnish Social Democrat president, Mauno Koivisto, was welcomed in Moscow; he had appointed Sorsa as Prime Minister. That October, in his capacity as head of a Finnish SDP delegation, Sorsa was distinguished by becoming the first leader of a Western party delegation to meet a CPSU delegation headed by the future leader of the CPSU and Soviet state, Andropov, since the latter had re-entered the Secretariat. SDP–CPSU relations seemed a far cry from those of two decades earlier.

By the 1970s Soviet leaders still looked askance at only one sizeable Finnish party, the National Coalition Party. Before elections in 1971 the Soviet press welcomed a re-examination by this party of its foreign policy views but distrusted its verbal proclamations.[51] Soviet criticism in the 1970s also continued to be levelled against certain maverick figures in Finnish political life, such as Tuure Junnila who was a vocal critic of aspects of official Finnish foreign policy, first in the extreme right-wing (and politically insignificant) Constitutional Party and then among the Conservatives. Another target of Soviet attacks was Veikko Vennamo, the leader of the small poujadist Rural Party in the early 1970s, who had even suggested revisions of the Finnish–Soviet frontier.[52]

In 1973 the Finnish Foreign Minister, Karjalainen, attacked right-wing forces critical of Finland's Eastern policy, which appear 'not only on the extreme Right but to varying extent in several of our parties'.[53] It may be that statements of this kind have fed Soviet apprehensions about the foreign policy unreliability of the Finnish 'Right' despite the expressed support of the Conservatives since the end of the 1960s for the Paasikivi–Kekkonen line, and in so doing have served internal party political objectives. This may help explain why, although a consensus about relations with the USSR included all the major Finnish parties by the mid-1970s, even at the end of the decade the Soviet press was wont to accuse the National Coalition Party of sabotaging Finnish–Soviet relations alongside 'other right-wing groups . . . which do not like Finland's present foreign policy and show an ideological affinity for this party'.[54]

The changes in views and alignments of Finnish political parties in the 1960s did not imply or lead to an emasculation in either their political or social principles. Since the mid-1960s Finnish parties have formed strong coalitions based on mutual interests. One of the largest parties, the National Coalition Party, has admittedly been excluded from the dominant Finnish coalitions, but this has in some respects been a condition of the strength of these coalitions. The Conservatives would simply be unable to build around themselves effective governments capable of producing long-term legislation. The inclusion of the Conservatives would automatically lead also to the refusal of the Finnish Communists to participate in the government, and one of the great political triumphs of post-war Finland has been the extension of parliamentarism to cover the Communists who had previously been excluded from legitimate political involvement.

In the first post-war years Foreign Minister Enckell had felt apprehensive about the relations of the SKP and the CPSU, since he recognised that the latter governed the Soviet state. During these years the Finnish Communists had special channels to influence Soviet views; Zhdanov's influence on Soviet policy towards Finland meant that for ideological reasons the SKP was especially significant to the USSR among Finnish political forces. After his death Soviet leaders continued to maintain special relations with Finnish Communist organisations, but more in their capacity as representatives of the CPSU than as the makers of Soviet policy. Soviet statesmen realised that they could not rely on the SKP or SKDL front to determine Finland's policy, and they began seriously to seek accommodation with additional forces on the Finnish political spectrum. The Finnish Communists were taken by surprise at times, therefore, and forced rapidly to review their policy when, as in the case of the acceptability of Finnish membership in the Nordic Council, the Soviet policy towards Finland had suddenly changed.

The post-Stalin Soviet leadership valued the model of coexistence which Finnish–Soviet relations appeared to illustrate and wished more strongly than before to separate Finnish–Soviet state relations from the relations of the Communist organisations operating within those states. Khrushchev did not instigate the 'night-frost' crisis in order to enhance the role of the SKP and SKDL in Finnish politics so much as to set obstacles before the current Social Democrat leadership. This favoured the Agrarians. Khrushchev did not expect Kekkonen to pander to the Finnish Communists, and he himself was careful not to permit the friendly relations between the CPSU and SKP to jeopardise formal Soviet ties with the dominant trusted bourgeois party, the Agrarian Party, and the Finnish state. An example of Khrushchev's attitude occurred in September 1960 when he was invited by the Finnish Communists to speak at their conference during an official visit to Finland. Khrushchev turned down the offer, explaining that had he gone to the Communist function he would have had to go to speak to every party conference in Finland. The Soviet attitude to the SKP, Kekkonen told the British Prime Minister, Macmillan, had been 'very correct'. On these grounds Kekkonen argued that the large Communist Party in Finland had not been able to influence the foreign policy of Finland in any way.[55] In fact, Kekkonen recognised in 1963 that the Finnish Communists were dissatisfied with Khrushchev's policy towards Finland, 'because it favours the "bourgeoisie" and keeps the Communists in obscurity'.[56]

By the mid-1960s the USSR was beginning to regard internal political developments in Finland as a model for domestic progress also in other Western European countries, particularly France and Italy. Presumably that was one reason why she was glad to see the Communists back in the Finnish government. But there is no evidence that the return of the Communists to government in May 1966, after eighteen years of opposition, was influenced by any Soviet intervention on their behalf; the possibility of their inclusion arose out of internal developments in the Finnish party system.[57] In autumn 1965, moreover, the SKP redefined its relationship to parliamentary democracy and the multi-party system. The old 'Stalinist' leadership of the SKP was replaced at this juncture by a more nationally oriented generation.[58] These changes contributed to a split in the party, and by the late 1960s two factions existed which differed in ideological commitment to the USSR and tactical willingness to participate in Finnish governments. Thus although in 1968 the 'government wing' of the SKP under Party chairman Aarne Saarinen showed clear sympathy with the aims of Dubcek in Czechoslovakia, Taisto Sinisalo's 'opposition wing' of hardliners (the minority faction) loudly approved of the Soviet intervention.

An attempt to reconcile the opposed wings of the SKP was made by the Soviet Ambassador Aleksey Belyakov, who arrived in Helsinki in July 1970. Apparently Belyakov took this role too far and over-stepped the bounds of legal diplomatic activity. Soviet state interests once again were given priority over Communist Party interests in Finland, and since Belyakov's clandestine discussions with the hardline minority SKP faction had apparently been regarded with distaste by Kekkonen among others, he was withdrawn to the USSR in spring 1971. In February 1975 Finnish Communist leaders travelled to the USSR for consultations intended to assist the resolution of their differences. But the only achievement from such talks was the perpetuation of a superficial and fragile unity, which permanently threatened to break down.

In the 1970s this factionalism was reflected in a contradictory view both among the Finnish Communists and CPSU officials about the desirability of SKP participation in Popular Front governments. In 1969 the CPSU representative Arvid Pelshe described SKP's experiences as interesting and declared that 'Soviet Communists observe with feelings of satisfaction that SKP's political line has brought it clear gains'.[59] But in 1971 the Finnish Communists were back in opposition, and by the time the opportunity arose for their re-entry into a ruling coalition in the mid-1970s under the prompting of Saarinen Soviet theoreticians were arguing alongside Sinisalo's minority SKP faction that the Finnish Communists previously had left the government because 'following bourgeois "rules of the game" meant an obligation to carry out a policy which was against the interests of the working class'.[60] Ele Alenius, the non-Communist chairman of the SKDL front, was subject to attacks in the Soviet press; in the early 1980s after he had given up this party post he was accused even of being part of a phenomenon of ' "left-wing" anti-Sovietism' appearing in Finland.[61]

The tendency of the CPSU to lean towards the 'Stalinist' minority faction of the SKP became clearer in the early 1980s. Indeed, a bitter exchange occurred between Saarinen, the retiring chairman of the SKP, and the CPSU during the SKP conference in May 1982. This developed against the background of SKP opposition to increasing the procurement of arms from the USSR, a move supported by the other Finnish governing parties. The CPSU Politburo expressed Soviet concern about the appearance of anti-Sovietism in the SKP, which could have negative results for the continued development of Soviet–Finnish friendship.[62] Saarinen responded by accusing the Soviet Communist Party of provocation calculated to work against the unity of the SKP, and he appealed to Finnish nationalist sentiment in stressing the independence and self-identity of the SKP.[63] The CPSU had supported the minority SKP faction grouped against Saarinen. At no time since the war had ideological differences between the majority of Finnish Communists and the CPSU been expressed so openly. No rapid reconciliation can be anticipated since tensions between the two Communist parties were heightened in spring 1983. The organ of the CPSU, *Pravda*, urged the SKP to rebuff Party members 'who would weaken the principles of the Party's work and its class nature', and supported calls for ending the factional struggle in the Party.[64] But CPSU Politburo member Grigoriy Romanov went further to warn the SKP majority that the CPSU 'will have relations only with a revolutionary Finnish Communist Party'.[65]

From the foregoing it is manifest that Soviet leaders no longer, as they may have done in the 1940s, regard the SKP as an unqualified ideological ally in the Finnish political system. From their reading of the present 'alignment of forces' in Finland they do not expect a radical transformation of Finnish society spearheaded by the Finnish Communists in the near future. Soviet Communist Party leaders still trust that, according to the maxims of peaceful coexistence, the Finnish internal economic and social structure may develop along socialist principles under Communist guidance with the passage of time as an indigenous process. But, contrary to their views in the 1960s they no longer regard the participation of Communists in

Finnish Popular Front governments necessarily as desirable. In December 1982, in fact, the Finnish Communists were excluded from the government for refusing to support the increase in the defence budget partly earmarked for purchases desirable to the USSR.

The affinities between CPSU spokesmen and the more 'revolutionary' minority group in the SKP still exist, but Soviet leaders tend to view the functions of even this more ideologically doctrinaire and pro-Soviet Finnish Communist faction ultimately from the standpoint of Soviet state interests. For the foreseeable future they will continue to rely on the assurances over security policy expressed by dependable non-Communist party and state leaders in Finland. In the early 1980s the healthy Finnish–Soviet state relations were also reflected in CPSU relations with the ruling non-Communist parties in Finland. Thus in April 1982 at a regular meeting in Moscow between the CPSU and the Centre Party (as the Agrarian Party was renamed in 1965), the delegates 'noted the role of the Centre Party in the successful development of Soviet–Finnish relations'.[66] Six months later a CPSU delegation found areas of substantial agreement in discussions with a Finnish SDP delegation. For Soviet statesmen the most useful function the Finnish Communists may currently perform, regardless of their ideological inclinations, is that of an early warning system to ensure that the security policy line followed by Finland does not stray from those principles already established in the late 1940s.

SOVIET INFLUENCES ON THE FINNISH PRESIDENCY

Marshal Mannerheim the veteran military commander, who had become the Finnish president in August 1944 to preside over the armistice negotiations, remained in office until April 1946. His presence, and that of his successor, Paasikivi, helped conservative forces in Finnish society weather the stormy post-war years. But Paasikivi had a grasp of political realities denied to many fellow Finnish conservatives. His insistence on Finland's observance of her legal commitments and on the necessity of reorienting political relations with the USSR was highly valued by Soviet leaders. Although he was a former chairman of the Coalition Party, and there were indirect Soviet moves to block his re-election as president in 1950, by 1954 Paasikivi was awarded the Order of Lenin for his 'outstanding services for the cause of peace'.[67] Soviet spokesmen began to praise the 'Paasikivi line' in Finland's foreign policy, which a month before Paasikivi's final retirement in March 1956 was counterposed to 'the "Mannerheim line" which was and is actively supported by the war criminal Tanner'.[68]

The Soviet press predictably supported the Agrarian Kekkonen against the Social Democrat Fagerholm in the tight presidential election of 1956, and certain Soviet concessions in that year may have partly been intended to boost Finnish electoral support for the 'Paasikivi line'. Kekkonen's victory, by the narrowest possible margin, was welcomed in the USSR,[69] and began an era of not merely correct but cordial relations between the Finnish president and Soviet leaders which mitigated the distrust which still prevailed between the latter and politically active Social Democrat and Conservative figures in Finland. This distrust was vocally expressed again during the presidential election campaign in 1961–2.

When a coalition of five Finnish parties was formed in 1962 by a SDP initiative to prevent the re-election of Kekkonen, the Soviet press claimed that the election of their candidate would lead to Finnish foreign policy falling into the hands of these parties, 'i.e. the leadership of the Social Democrat Party and the extreme rightist elements'. This belief had some substance since their candidate, the retired Chancellor of Justice Olavi Honka, had little political experience to call upon. By extension Soviet commentators portrayed his candidature as 'not merely an attempt to change the supreme leader of the state', but as an attack on the established foreign policy course.[70] Kekkonen's supporters argued that the election of a candidate set up by forces led by Tanner would decisively undermine Soviet confidence in Finland's policy, quite regardless of the foreign policy conducted in reality by the new president.

In retrospect Soviet concern appears inflated, since it is probable that Kekkonen would have been re-elected regardless of subsequent events, and even the Soviet Ambassador in Finland, A. Zaharov, estimated Honka's election chances to be minimal.[71] But it is indisputable that the election front against Kekkonen, which formed against the background of unsettling military developments and plans in Scandinavia, contributed to Soviet uneasiness at the time the decision was made to propose Finnish–Soviet military consultations in September 1961.

A fortnight after the delivery of the Soviet note, in discussions with Foreign Minister Karjalainen, Gromyko referred to the formation of 'a certain political grouping, in Finland intent on trying 'to prevent the continuation of the present foreign policy course'. He delivered a request from the Soviet government for 'the most rapid assurance possible' of the continuation of this course and friendly relations with the USSR.[72] Soviet leaders expected security guarantees from Finland in one form or another. The matter was made more pressing by the fluid political situation in Finland, but as argued earlier the Soviet note was primarily a reaction to developments outside Finland, and when Kekkonen flew to Novosibirsk his intention was to reassure Khrushchev of Finland's stand in regional developments in the North. Yet after this successful meeting many Western observers assumed that Kekkonen had struck a bargain with the Soviet leader about Finnish internal politics, since soon after Kekkonen had left to the USSR Honka announced that he was withdrawing his candidature in the coming presidential election. Kekkonen rejected such allegations that Honka's withdrawal had been some kind of 'price or condition' for the favourable results of the Novosibirsk meeting,[73] although he told Honka later that his decision to stand down had been the right one in the circumstances.[74] Honka was aware that the party front he represented was disintegrating under the pressure of the Soviet note and the recent dissolution of parliament. His decision was a gesture of realism about his election chances as much as a manifestation of support for the Paasikivi line.

At Novosibirsk Khrushchev repeated earlier views during the 'night-frost' crisis about the possible deleterious effect on Finnish foreign policy, in this case through manipulating the presidency, of political forces hostile to the USSR. Before the formal meeting he argued that 'we would be poor politicians were we not attentively to follow the development of the political situation along our borders', and maintained that the USSR could not be indifferent to 'what line is pursued by this or that public figure and the political forces backing him who seek power' in Finland. Khrushchev questioned whether the 'rightist groups' and 'Tannerites' in Finland were not 'seeking to prepare the conditions for restoring the "brotherhood-of-arms" with the West Germans'.[75] At the least Khrushchev implied that the progressive military involvement of West Germany in the Nordic region could be reflected in the policy predilections of Finnish political groups currently striving for the presidency. During the formal discussion between the state leaders the Finnish internal situation was only briefly referred to; Khrushchev expressed renewed confidence in the ability of the Finnish president and government to continue their set foreign policy course. Kekkonen may have impressed on the Soviet leader that whatever the policy ambitions of Tanner and his associates might be they had little chance of implementing them.

In response to an enquiry later by the American Secretary of State, Dean Rusk, about the effects of the Note Crisis on Finnish internal politics, Kekkonen admitted that the Soviet note and the discussion it inspired in Finland could not have failed to influence the internal political situation before the presidential elections. But he argued that if this had been the Soviet intent it should not 'be interpreted as an attempt to change Finland's position, but rather as an attempt to prevent possible changes'.[76] The lesson Kekkonen drew from the Note Crisis in a speech early in 1962 was that in the absence of trust in the intentions of the Finnish political leadership during conditions of international crisis or tension the Soviet authorities would feel obliged to obtain guarantees for their security in the North through the means provided by the 1948 FCMA-Treaty. He argued, therefore, that if the conduct of Finnish foreign policy had been in the hands of the Honka electoral front in autumn 1961, military consultations with the USSR could not have been avoided.[77] But once Soviet military interests in the Finnish quarter are secured through Finnish adherence to the Paasikivi line, he wrote,

the Soviet Union will not take the extra weight on its shoulders that a breach in relations with Finland or continued political pressure directed against Finland, which the whole world would observe and condemn, would then bring about. There is no advantage to the Soviet Union in changing the balance between Finland and the Soviet Union.[78]

The Paasikivi line, with its objective of creating relations of political confidence with the Soviet Union, had been based on the scrupulous fulfilment of Finland's state treaties.[79] Many believed that various examples of post-war Soviet magnanimity towards Finland had reflected a particular personal interest in and favoured view of Finland held by Stalin.[80] A. I. Mikoyan, who in 1954 became the first Soviet leader to visit Finland officially since the Control Commission years, and Prime Minister Bulganin, may also have promoted relations with Finland among the Soviet leadership.[81] It is difficult to assess the influence of such 'patronage', but regardless of its existence President Paasikivi relied on legalistic principles more than personal relations in the conduct of his Eastern policy.

Kekkonen placed still more emphasis than Paasikivi on the role of the president as the personal guarantor of the continuity of the Finnish policy line in relations with the USSR. In his view this was necessary since Finland had often had short-lived and changeable minority governments. But Kekkonen laid himself open to criticism that he was accruing individual political benefits by increasingly becoming identified personally with the Finnish good-neighbour policy with the East. The Honka front had campaigned against power falling into the hands of 'oligarchical political forces'. The collapse of the front and the decisive re-election of Kekkonen showed that the personal confidence felt by Soviet leaders could influence his electoral strength at home. He could even become politically indispensable. Under Kekkonen it was becoming unclear whether the checks and balances in the Finnish constitution could still operate freely, since any attempt to challenge Kekkonen's authority might well be interpreted as an attempt to alter foreign policy and to undermine the 'Paasikivi–Kekkonen line'. For some in the West this was later seen as a symptom of the general malaise of Finlandisation.

Kekkonen responded to such criticisms indirectly by pointing out that since the president cannot form a government which does not enjoy the confidence of parliament, he cannot exercise a foreign policy contrary to the wishes of parliament.[82] But as Finland's Eastern policy is carried out mostly through closed personal discussions with Soviet leaders, and confidence building is assisted by numerous unofficial meetings, it is difficult for parliament to receive a full picture of the manner in which relations with the USSR are being handled. The Finnish parliament has had to rely on Kekkonen's assurances that negotiations with Soviet leaders have been 'correct and matter of fact', that 'no pressure has been exerted', and that 'the agreements concluded have not been contrary to Finland's interests'.[83]

In the longer term Kekkonen did not intend to base Finland's Eastern policy merely on well cultivated personal relations with Soviet leaders, which could only be transient in interstate politics. His central effort, as he wrote in 1963, was to 'ingrain the idea of the special political position and neutrality of Finland so enduringly in the Soviet people and leadership that it will continue also in possible new circumstances'.[84] Once achieved, this would act as a safeguard for Finland were the general line in Soviet international politics to change or the leadership of Finnish foreign policy to be transferred to other hands. In the domestic sphere the continuity of the Finnish policy was assisted by the strengthening of party consensus behind Kekkonen in the 1960s, which ensured that he would encounter no strong electoral opposition.

Before the presidential elections in January 1968 Foreign Minister Karjalainen denied that former presidential elections had been determined significantly by external pressure from the USSR, although he recognised the Soviet interest in the choice of state leaders in neighbouring countries.[85] Since the primary candidate opposing Kekkonen was the Conservative banker M. Virkkunen, Soviet support for Kekkonen could be anticipated. Virkkunen tried to avoid the issue of foreign policy, but *Pravda* declared that he had 'long been known for his extreme hostility to the Soviet Union' and he was accused of calling into question the provisions of the 1948 FCMA-Treaty. Right-wing forces which still wished to 'push Finland on to a path of foreign policy adventures' were discerned in Finland.[86] This was partly a response to the Conservatives' commitment to significantly raise Finland's defence budget, a move Kekkonen was opposed to. Kekkonen himself deplored 'old hostile and grudging feelings against the Soviet Union' which surfaced during the election campaign.[87] Podgorny spoke in favour of Kekkonen's course in a speech in Helsinki, referred to the 'broad mass of citizens' in the election league supporting his candidature, and trusted in 'the continued work of President Kekkonen, of the government and all Finnish progressive forces'.[88]

Kekkonen's re-election in 1968 was a foregone conclusion, regardless of Soviet views, since of the major Finnish parties only the Conservatives opposed him. The modified SDP had indicated already in 1966 that it would support Kekkonen in the coming election since it accepted that the president should represent the interests of the republic above party divisions. The SDP even supported the passage of special legislation to prolong Kekkonen's term of office, but this was shelved once the Conservatives presented a candidate.

In 1973 the governing parties did agree upon an initiative for special legislation to extend Kekkonen's tenure as president until 1978 by a parliamentary vote rather than a popular election. This decision should be assessed against the background of Finland's negotiations for an EEC agreement, since it was revealed after the Zavidovo discussions in September 1972 that Kekkonen had assumed personal responsibility to Soviet leaders for the continuity of Finland's Eastern policy after the ratification of the EEC agreement. Already earlier that year Prime Minister Karjalainen had suggested prolonging Kekkonen's term of office to forestall difficulties in Finland's trade policy negotiations. Nevertheless, Kekkonen threatened to refuse to stand for another term in response to the press leak of the Zavidovo talks. Party consensus behind Kekkonen was so strong by 1978 that none of the major parties ran against him in the presidential elections, which were conducted in the normal manner.[89]

The real test of Kekkonen's Eastern policy arose once he finally relinquished his official duties on grounds of ill-health in October 1981. The conduct of the ensuing presidential election campaign and the aftermath of the elections would illustrate whether the confidence felt by Soviet leaders for the 'Kekkonen line' could outlast the individual in whom it had been vested for a quarter of a century. All the major Finnish political parties presented presidential candidates for the elections, although there existed some degree of unspoken apprehension about the likely Soviet reaction to a range of candidates all professing support for the Paasikivi–Kekkonen line in relations with the USSR.[90]

Soviet views during the 1981–2 election campaign were restrained but audible. The chairman of the Centre (Agrarian) Party, Foreign Minister Paavo Väyrynen, spoke in favour of the long experience of the Centre Party candidate, Ahti Karjalainen, in handling Finnish–Soviet relations. Karjalainen, who had frequently acted as Foreign and Prime Minister under Kekkonen, was considered to be 'known and . . . trusted in the Soviet Union'. On these grounds Väyrynen presented Karjalainen as the candidate best able to continue Kekkonen's foreign policy course.[91] A couple of days later the Soviet Northern European correspondent for *Pravda*, Kuznetsov, indirectly commended Karjalainen by quoting a Finnish statement urging support in the election for those parties and people who actively develop trade with the Soviet Union. For many years Karjalainen had been the Finnish chairman of the Finnish–Soviet trade commission. Kuznetsov expressed indirect disapproval of J. Virolainen, who was competing with Karjalainen for the Centre Party presidential candidature. The ranks of those who oppose Kekkonen's line of friendly relations with the USSR had 'considerably thinned out' he admitted, but in his view they still existed and received 'active support outside Finland'. Therefore, Kuznetsov concluded, 'any miscalculation' by those behind this line 'over whose hands Kekkonen's political tradition falls into may give rise to results which are difficult to predict'.[92]

If this article was intended to influence the outcome of the Centre Party conference to choose the party candidate, it failed. Virolainen, who clearly won more support than Karjalainen, became the official Centre Party candidate for president. The article indicated that although the Soviet authorities had their preferred candidate they did not consider it warranted to pronounce on the unsuitability of any candidate. But Western diplomats interpreted the fact that the Social Democrat candidate, Prime Minister Mauno Koivisto, was left unmentioned as a sign against choosing Koivisto.[93] This may, however, have reflected political discretion, since it would have been difficult for Moscow to evaluate the SDP candidate without also appraising the SKDL candidate fielded by the Finnish Communists.

Koivisto was elected president by a decisive majority, which appeared all the more convincing when compared with Kekkonen's hairbreadth victory in 1956. Although the Finnish Communists had suffered heavily in the elections Radio Moscow interpreted Koivisto's victory as a 'clear shift to the left of the electorate', since it was 'the first time in the history of Finland that a capitalist party candidate has not won the election but the forces of the left'. It was apparent that Koivisto was trusted to continue the foreign policy course of his predecessors from the observation in this Soviet broadcast that 'certain parties failed in their attempts to change the foreign policy course of the country and to lead it from the policy of Paasikivi and Kekkonen'.[94] Kuznetsov confirmed this estimate in *Pravda* a week later.[95]

The election of a new Finnish head of state with a different party background for the first time in a quarter of a decade inevitably led to speculation in Finland and abroad about likely changes of nuance in Finland's foreign policy. Koivisto was perceived, for example, to be more strongly oriented to Scandinavia than Kekkonen had been. But the Soviet Scandinavian specialist, Lev Voronkov, saw 'no reason to conclude, for example on grounds of Soviet criticisms concerning Social Democracy, that a lack of confidence would prevail between Koivisto and the Soviet leadership'. In his view there were no prejudices against Koivisto's foreign policy in the Kremlin, but it was now up to Koivisto himself 'to convince the Kremlin leaders'.[96] Koivisto's first official foreign visit was to the Soviet Union in March 1982, which was successfully conducted. During the visit Brezhnev affirmed that his dialogue with Koivisto 'showed that we have further opportunities for the fruitful development of Soviet–Finnish cooperation'.[97] The Finnish Foreign Minister described the atmosphere of the visit as 'very friendly'.[98] No uneasiness about the change of the Finnish head of state was expressed in Soviet statements after this crucial visit.[99]

The 1982 elections may have rid Finland of a truama in her political consciousness, which in the view of the former Finnish diplomat Max Jakobson had existed since the time of the Note Crisis.[100] It appeared that the party base of the Finnish president, with the possible exception of the Conservatives, was unlikely to create difficulties in future relations with the USSR. Koivisto's election and his reception in Moscow demonstrated that the security and foreign policy principles on which the Paasikivi–Kekkonen course had rested were no longer dependent in either Finnish or Soviet eyes on the far-sightedness of a Finnish head of state with an established past tradition of close relations with Soviet leaders. Before stepping down as president Kekkonen had recognised that 'plenty of capable individuals' could be found in Finland 'who are on the right foreign policy course and in time can take the office of president'.[101] In the 1981–2 election campaign Kekkonen did not name any candidate as more suitable than any other. But the defeat of Karjalainen at the Centre Party congress could be interpreted as a move away from closed personal relations with Soviet leaders, and Koivisto's electoral victory as a move in favour of the open conduct of an established line of relations with the USSR.

The death of Brezhnev in November 1982 provided further evidence that Finland's Eastern relations are not dependent on particular individuals but on policies. According to an apocryphal historical anecdote, when Kekkonen heard that Khrushchev had been replaced by the triumvirate of Soviet leaders, Brezhnev, Kosygin and Podgorny in 1964, he observed 'so far we have had only one good friend in Moscow, now there are three'. The message underlying this tale, as Max Jakobson has pointed out, is that ultimately states do not have friends but interests, and it remains in the Finnish interest to ensure that good relations are maintained with the USSR regardless of who holds power in Moscow.[102] In fact, if Finnish leaders had felt that their relations with the Soviet state were reliant on personal friendships with Soviet leaders then the replacement of A. N. Kosygin as Chairman of the Council of Ministers, and his death two months later in December 1980, would have been a greater loss for Finland than Brezhnev's death. There had long existed warm personal relations between Kosygin and Kekkonen.

From the Finnish point of view the new General Secretary of the

CPSU Central Committee, Yuriy Andropov, had an intriguing past from which it could be assumed that his awareness of the special relations of the USSR and Finland, based on their post-war security *entente*, was at least as great as that of any other current Politburo member. Andropov held posts in the Soviet Komomol and Party apparatus in the Karelo-Finnish Soviet Socialist Republic (the Karelian Autonomous Republic since 1956) during 1940–51. During the Continuation War with Finland he helped to organise partisan detachments to operate behind the Finnish lines, and he maintained an underground intelligence network in the territory occupied by Finland.[103] By historical chance during these years the young Mauno Koivisto was engaged in partisan operations for the Finns. After the armistice with Finland Andropov was required, among other tasks, to organise Party activities in the areas captured from Finland.[104] During his decade in Soviet Karelia Andropov's path repeatedly crossed that of the President of the Karelo-Finnish Republic, the former Finnish Communist leader, O. W. Kuusinen.

Andropov referred to his war experiences in a speech many years later; he regarded the events of the war years as proof of the importance of friendly Finnish–Soviet relations.[105] In October 1982 a Finnish SDP delegation was the first Western party delegation to be received by a CPSU delegation headed by Andropov since he had re-entered the Secretariat nine months earlier. According to the head of the Finnish delegation, K. Sorsa, Andropov gave the impression of being well informed about Finnish affairs.[106] Another member of the delegation has confirmed that Andropov had a 'good understanding' of the situation in Finland, which may have reflected a 'particular interest' in relations with Finland.[107]

There have been a number of indications that the special relations between Moscow and Helsinki have become, if anything, more firmly pronounced since Brezhnev's death. At the Kremlin reception for the sixtieth anniversary of the USSR in December 1982 Andropov singled out Finland for a special mention from the countries of about a hundred delegations present. He referred to the Finnish president's presence and stressed the good-neighbourly relations of Finland and the USSR to this international audience. Koivisto and Andropov held discussions together during this occasion. The first official visit by a Soviet leader to a country outside the Soviet bloc since Brezhnev's death occurred in the same month when the Soviet Prime Minister, N. Tikhonov was received in Helsinki. The joint communique of this visit reaffirmed Finland's position in the Soviet foreign policy outlook.[108] When Koivisto visited Moscow in June 1983 he heard Andropov praise Finnish statesmen in exceptionally warm terms. 'We in the Soviet Union', Andropov declared, 'have developed a deep respect for these leaders of our neighbour country [Paasikivi, Kekkonen, and now Koivisto] as serious politicians, as trustworthy and honest companions, as patriots to their native land, and as people sincerely devoted to the cause of lasting peace'.[109]

In the light of the foregoing some Finnish officials may have been disappointed by Andropov's death after only fifteen months at the head of the Soviet Party, and his replacement in February 1984 by Konstantin Chernenko, who could not be expected to have any particular knowledge of Finland nor of foreign affairs in general. But by now it was apparent that the changes which had taken place at the highest level in the leadership of Finland and the USSR in 1981–2 had left no legacy of uncertainty in bilateral relations, and the Finns could look more calmly to the future. Official cordiality between these states clearly was based on durable political foundations rather than on reliance on the personal relations of statesmen.

THE POLITICS OF THE PRESS: RESTRAINT AND SELFCENSORSHIP IN FINLAND

The existence of Soviet influence over the Finnish media, in particular the press, has been assumed rather generally by Western observers, but this subject has been drawn into a broader political debate which has hindered dispassionate analysis. It remains too easy to forget that some attitudes in Finland continued as a historical legacy of the controls under Tsarist rule, the political extremism of the 1930s, and the restraints imposed by years of total war, all of which reinforced introspective tendencies in the Finnish social and political outlook. It is also easy to overlook the legal restrictions under which Finland left the war and the argument by Finnish statesmen since the early 1960s that neutrality should entail broader commitments for not just the state but also society at large. These factors should be borne in mind before attempts are made to discern the Soviet hand behind each case of Finnish media restraint which favours the USSR. Yet the Finnish press occupies a rather unusual position among those found in Soviet border states, not unrelated to the proximity of Finland's great power neighbour, and this warrants a closer look at this phenomenon.

During the war control of publications in Finland had been based largely on cooperation between editors and the authorities, but the provisions of the armistice agreement and the presence of the Control Commission obliged a prior scrutiny of publications, the telephone and the post. This was done by the Finnish government itself. Unlike other East European armistice agreements there was no provision in the Finnish armistice which gave the Allied (Soviet) command control over publication, the distribution of literature and telecommunications. Finnish censors responded to the wishes of Finnish military officials that sensitive and confidential information about the recently concluded war should not be brought to light prematurely so as to endanger the security of the state. In 1945 Finnish papers were urged to write cautiously about Soviet affairs. The censorship officials stressed that news concerning Soviet leaders or the Red Army should not be published without prior examination, and that news commentary should not adopt an anti-Soviet stand.[110]

The views of Finnish officials and the press over what constituted unsuitable political commentary differed during the conduct of the war-guilt trials. The defence speech of former president Ryti was censored at the demand of the Control Commission, which referred to Article 13 of the armistice to justify this act. In addition, Article 21 expressly forbade Finland to conduct 'propaganda hostile to the United Nations, in particular to the Soviet Union'. The deputy chairman of the Control Commission, Savonenkov, told Paasikivi that such propaganda in the Finnish press had to be 'unconditionally ended', and that the Control Commission would 'not permit the continuation of such fascist propaganda'. Paasikivi told Finnish press representatives that he considered Article 21 to justify Savonenkov's demand. He noted that the armistice placed great obligations on Finland and urged the press to take care not to include material in their papers which could create doubts and suspicions about Finland's sincerity over relations of friendship and confidence with the USSR.[111] Paasikivi recalled Bismarck's comment that the government and people of a country have to pay for the windows broken by journalists.

Paasikivi understood that without a sense of press and media responsibility Finland's nascent Eastern policy could be prejudiced. During his term as ambassador in Moscow in 1940–1 he had already recognised that Soviet leaders were sensitive to foreign views, and that they assumed newspaper reports to correspond more or less to the official attitudes of states. Under Paasikivi the Finnish government encouraged Finnish papers after the war to exercise the same kind of voluntary self-control as the papers of Britain and the United States observed during the war. This was considered necessary until conditions were normalised and the peace treaty signed. Censors were retained until this treaty. For several years Finnish papers handled the USSR very cautiously and preferred to avoid the whole subject. The most important news about Soviet policy consequently was received through Swedish correspondents. In fact non-Communist Finnish papers often sent prepared articles about sensitive subjects to Sweden and then published them as Swedish views.[112] Correspondingly, the Finnish Communist press sent its own information about conditions within Finland directly to the representatives of Soviet publications.[113]

The end of censorship in Finland did not remove the conditions for continued press responsibility. Article 21 of the armistice agreement became Article 8 of the peace treaty, and Soviet observers continued to relate sentiments expressed in the Finnish press with the sincerity of the Paasikivi line. This was important at a time when Finland's security policy was still open to interpretation. 'Since the Fagerholm government came to power', a Soviet correspondent wrote at the end of 1948, 'the Finnish press has been keeping all sails set to the anti-Soviet breeze that blows from across the Atlantic, and that is why Fagerholm's new assurances concerning Finland's "loyalty" to her treaties with the Soviet Union sound anything but convincing'.[114] Some months later Finnish papers were again accused of disseminating 'false information about the Soviet Union' which contravened Fagerholm's assurances that Finland's foreign policy orientation would be continued.[115] Anti-Soviet statements were regarded as evidence of an 'abrupt change of political course' within Finland.[116] In the Soviet view Fagerholm held special responsibility for the character of the press not only because he headed the government but since 'more than ninety per cent of the periodicals are in the hands of big capitalists and their henchmen, the right-wing Social Democrats'.[117] Under this Soviet onslaught Fagerholm admitted that the Finnish press had used 'insulting expression's against the Soviet Union and advised them to exercise care in future.[118]

In September 1948, on the basis of a cabinet motion, Paasikivi prosecuted the editors of two bourgeois newspapers for the publication of statements disparaging the USSR, which had 'endangered Finland's relations with a foreign power'.[119] Any Soviet goodwill gained by this act was lost the following year when the Finnish

Minister of Justice brought to trial the editors of a number of Communist and left-wing papers accused of 'abusing the freedom of the press'.[120] It was difficult to define when such 'abuse' overstepped the rights laid down in Article 6 of the peace treaty. The Soviet view was that 'the reference to the "freedom of the press" is a screen behind which the bourgeois and Social Democrat press conceals its war propaganda, but immediately forgets about freedom of the press when it comes to defence of the peace'.[121] Bourgeois press organs were accused of 'waging a "cold war" against the Soviet Union' in Finland, and of trying to stir up enmity against the Soviet people, by the influential figure O. W. Kuusinen.[122]

Prime Minister Kekkonen warned the Finnish press against attacks on the USSR in 1950, but he believed that 'the only action which the authorities could take . . . was to use their moral influence'. The American Minister in Finland expressed concern to Kekkonen lest the Finnish authorities take 'some action . . . as a result of which one side of the story could be presented to the Finnish public while the other side could not be'.[123] This clearly was an appeal not to act preferentially towards the Communist press by placing the non-Communist press under additional legal restraints. In fact, this was avoided through Paasikivi's strict adherence to the constitutional principles of the Republic.

Throughout the 1950s the Soviet press continued to berate its Finnish counterpart. The Finnish authorities were also condemned for permitting 'American, British and Finnish films which openly propagandise for war and are as a rule anti-Soviet'[124] past the censorship commission. Representatives of the Finnish Left supported these accusations. Former Prime Minister Pekkala spoke in parliament in 1952 against war propaganda in the Finnish press.[125] During the Hungarian crisis in 1956 the SKDL press identified the Finnish government with the commentary of the right-wing press, despite the different line adopted by the government. 'In view of the daily headlines, articles and other writings of our extreme rightist papers', *Vapaa Sana* declared, 'one would be inclined to conclude that the Finnish government was making preparations to break off diplomatic relations with the Soviet Union'.[126] Although Soviet leaders were more likely to judge Finnish intentions by the policy pursued by the government in the United Nations, it is probable that what Finnish papers wrote during the Hungarian crisis helped form the attitudes the USSR assumed towards the different parties in Finland. This was natural since many of the leading Finnish papers were party organs. According to its party composition, Soviet attitudes could then be influenced towards the government as a whole. The issue went beyond mere ideological hostility towards the USSR or affinity with the leading Western states, since in June 1956 Kekkonen had to urge restraint on the Finnish press for speculating about the return of part of Karelia.

Already before the onset of the 'night-frost' in relations with Finland, Khrushchev attacked those who 'opposed the settlement made with the Soviet Union, who have spread absurd entirely unfounded claims about the country of the Soviets', and 'needlessly frighten the Finnish people with senseless stories'.[127] The allegations of the journalist Arvo Tuominen fell into this category. By autumn 1958 the USSR declared itself to be the object of a Finnish propaganda campaign which the Finnish authorities had assisted by lifting the 'ban on anti-Soviet literature, provision for which was made in the peace treaty'.[128] In the Soviet view Finnish correspondents often failed to act as free and independent agents. Khrushchev told Kekkonen during the crucial meeting in January 1959 which resolved the freeze in Finnish–Soviet relations that 'certain journalists and individual organs of the press' in Finland 'have specialised in anti-Soviet utterances and are evidently well paid by reactionary circles; possibly they are subsidised by a third country'. He drew a parallel with the Soviet press: 'if you look through our pages you will find nothing in its pages damaging to the Finnish people or our relations'. Khrushchev concluded with the advice that 'if journalists want to serve their people they should not damage their relations with neighbouring states'.[129]

Kekkonen had little desire no doubt to model the Finnish press on the press principles of the USSR in general, but he recognised on his return from Leningrad that 'without restraint and responsibility on the part of the press, relations between our countries will never attain the degree of confidence that our own interest requires'. He explained that Soviet sensitivity existed probably less 'because our bark might bite' than 'because unfriendly articles are regarded as reflections of public opinion'.[130] Kekkonen's stand was supported by the Agrarian and SKP papers. In an interview for an American journal Kekkonen used a different argument in stating that Finland's right to remain outside the conflicts of interest of the great powers imposed an obligation on the nation's press 'for neutral, objective attitudes' during such conflicts.[131] The relevance of such a commitment for Finnish security was underlined during the Note Crisis, since the only explicit reference to Finland in the Soviet note of October 1961 was to 'Finnish papers, which act as mouthpieces for certain circles' and 'actively support the dangerous military preparations of the member states of NATO'.

In the 1960s Kekkonen came close to advocating an ideological neutrality for Finland. He argued that the credibility of Finland's policy of neutrality abroad required that no distinction should exist between the foreign policy 'exercised by state leaders and the personal foreign policy opinions expressed by private citizens and politicians'.[132] Those who gave priority to international anti-Communism over the Finnish policy of neutrality, 'whether private persons or organisations', Kekkonen laid down, 'have no constructive part in Finnish political life'.[133] The view became established that since the support of Finnish public opinion was necessary to realise the country's policy of neutrality, the published word should be regarded as a component factor of foreign policy. Kekkonen did not believe that this would impede the free flow of news. Indeed, as a European state Finland continued to rely heavily on the news of the European news agencies. Kekkonen's main intention in these years was to consolidate the developing party consensus on Finnish foreign policy, which would 'eliminate baseless accusations and loose demands for changing foreign policy', without limiting the freedom of speech.[134] But it was not until the 1970s that the Finnish media was allotted an institutional role in the nation's Eastern policy.

In the early 1970s the Finnish Communists directed a series of parliamentary questions at the government anticipating the adoption of measures to curtail what was described as a 'right-wing anti-Soviet campaign'. The Finnish government maintained that the basic democratic rights of the freedom of opinion and speech, the details of which were contained in the law on press freedom, prevented any measures being taken in advance against any printed publications. It acknowledged that the Finnish criminal code permitted charges to be brought against printed material which 'by intentionally defaming a foreign state causes a danger that Finland's foreign relations with a foreign state will be injured'. Such prosecutions could only be instigated upon instructions from the president. This law had existed since the war as a potential legal restraint on the Finnish press, but, as Foreign Minister Karjalainen observed in 1973, it had not been resorted to in the 1960s nor thus far in the 1970s.[135]

On the twenty-fifth anniversary of the FCMA-Treaty in April 1973 the official joint Finnish–Soviet communique made a novel reference to the media:

> It is incumbent on the mass information media, displaying the proper responsibility and a businesslike approach, to serve the important cause of the further strengthening of friendship and trust between the peoples of the USSR and Finland and not to harm the development of friendly relations between the two countries.[136]

This important declaration of mutual obligation has been repeated in all subsequent joint communiques of important Finnish–Soviet visits. These communiques have given the media a role in Finland's Eastern relations which hitherto had existed only as a tacit understanding between the neighbour states. But the appeal for responsibility in the 1973 communique was directed at the media rather than at the governments of Finland and the USSR. This had the effect of drawing attention away from Article 8 of the 1947 peace treaty, which was unspecific but remained legally binding on the Finnish state.

In October 1974 the Finnish government was questioned in parliament how it would respond to 'writing idealising fascist thinking and directed . . . against friendly relations between Finland and the Soviet Union' in a fashion 'contrary to the peace treaty'. In reply Karjalainen presumed that the mass media would take into consideration the appeal contained in the 1973 communique. He considered that occasional writings in conflict with Finland's basic foreign policy course could best be dealt with through 'criticism taking place freely within the newspapers themselves',[137] which in his view would strengthen public support for the official line. In the opinion of the Finnish government this was also the appropriate reaction to the publication of a work by Solzhenitsyn in Finland in 1975.[138]

Since works such as those of Solzhenitsyn were written hardly in opposition to Finland's Eastern policy, the government's response indicates that by the mid-1970s a tendency voluntarily to refrain from writing or publishing material critical of the USSR or of Soviet policy in general was officially being encouraged in Finland. Yet Kekkonen did not consider the occasional Soviet article critical of conditions in Finland or Finnish policy as 'anti-Finnish'. In relation to a Soviet article which criticised Finnish economic policy in 1974 Kekkonen recognised that 'in the contemporary world it is a well established custom to refer quite thoroughly to the affairs of a foreign state', and that this often includes 'a strong critical element'. But it was noteworthy that he illustrated this by Finnish press criticism of American rather than of Soviet policy.[139]

The restraint urged on the media and publishers by the Finnish authorities did not reflect nor was it directed at a closer ideological affinity with the USSR. But in practice it was difficult to draw a distinction always between articles critical of the Finnish Communists and ideological anti-Sovietism. The Soviet press attacked a Finnish article in March 1975, for instance, for 'malicious fabrications' about the SKP and 'anti-Soviet slander' calculated to 'undermine friendly Finnish–Soviet relations'.[140] Similarly, *Pravda* claimed that the intention of an 'anti-Communist campaign' conducted in Finland by certain papers in autumn 1981 was to create a situation for changes in Finnish foreign policy by the Finnish Right.[141] But Finnish Communist organisations have been unable to win special treatment in the Finnish press as a whole, although the Communist press has acted partly as a spokesman for Soviet views.

The more vocal insistence by Finnish officials that published criticisms of the USSR were contrary to the Finnish foreign policy line provided much fuel for the Finlandisation debate in the 1970s. Finnish statesmen clearly were ready to make some gestures towards a political accommodation of the persistent Soviet misconception that Finnish publications express public opinion and partly even official views. But these gestures responded to contemporary pressures on Finland's neutral image before and during the European Security Conference in Helsinki; they were designed to further stabilise relations with the USSR with a minimum of social costs for Finland. But certain social costs did arise. Thus in 1974 the Finnish government pronounced on the importance of ensuring that material for instruction in Finnish schools and educational institutions 'which is liable to harm the peace-seeking foreign policy and good-neighbourly relations' of Finland should not be used.[142] Yet since it was difficult to acquire strictly impartial accounts of many areas of Soviet policy and internal life, this kind of political constraint tended to reduce the availability of information in Finland about the Soviet Union. This phenomenon could be regarded as a consequence of a politically legitimised process of self-censorship. One disillusioned Finnish critic argued in 1975 that while the existence of such a process in Finland may permit the development of 'relations of friendship and good-neighbourliness' between the political leaders or statesmen of Finland and the USSR, it may be illusory to expect an extension of such relations down to the individual citizens of the neighbour states without Soviet tolerance of a degree of factual and constructive criticism between these states. The development of genuine international understanding, he concluded, requires a free flow of ideas and information.[143]

Despite the pessimistic views common in the 1970s, the degree to which the Finnish media has become politicised should not be exaggerated. The freedom enjoyed by the mass media in Finland is far greater than that of any other country sharing a lengthy border with the USSR, and by numerous other criteria Finland remains a remarkably open society. The limited restraints which Finnish statesmen had urged the media to adopt early in the 1970s had not tightened but relaxed a decade later. This reflected the disorder among the ranks of the Finnish Communists and the declining influence of the 'Stalinist' faction in parliament, which had been ever-ready to discover and advertise examples of 'anti-Sovietism'. The Finnish authorities were also in general less sensitive about the image of the Finnish media and the expression of Finnish neutrality than during the crucial years of the CSCE process leading to the signing of the Final Act in Helsinki.

Over the last decade Finnish publishers have become aware that Finland's position as an advertisement for peaceful coexistence with the USSR offers them considerable leverage. After all, the principles of peaceful coexistence assume a competition and by implication mutual exchange of ideas between East and West. Gone are the days when Solzhenitsyn's works appeared only in the Swedish language in Finland, although given the small size of the Finnish language market many more esoteric Soviet dissident works remain unpublished in Finnish on commercial grounds. Contemporary Finnish television meets both the approval of Soviet commentators for its ability to present 'truthful documentaries about the USSR' and their condemnation for using 'news and commentary material which is full of attacks against the USSR'.[144] But in this case the Soviet authorities probably remain less worried about the impact of Finnish news reports on Finnish viewers than by the fact that Finnish television is readily visible along the Estonian coast. Indeed, the proximity of Finland to Estonia and Soviet sensitivity to the condition of the Baltic republics was expressed in a Soviet allegation early in 1984 that United States intelligence services were using Finland for the printing and dissemination of material meant to foment nationalism and anti-Sovietism in Estonia.[145] This claim reflected Soviet concern lest the Baltic republics become amenable to influences from and the example of not so much Finland as their neighbour Poland.

The independent press in Finland, which accounts for about 60 per cent of newspaper circulation, does not eschew publishing reports on political and economic mismanagement in the Soviet bloc but avoids political diatribes against the Soviet system. Even so, Soviet officials still find it possible to protest that, looking through the pages of the primary Finnish 'bourgeois' papers 'it is difficult to find information in their news about the social achievements and economic development of the USSR or truth about the Soviet political and social life'.[146] If this is a sincerely held belief in the Soviet Union and not merely polemics then it reflects the continued division in outlook on fundamental issues between Soviet spokesmen and the considerable majority of Finns, even after several decades of Finnish–Soviet 'peaceful coexistence'. In other words most Finns feel no closer to the Soviet system than in the 1940s and 1950s. But in some areas the division between Finland and the Soviet Union may be artificially perpetuated. It is undeniable, therefore, that considering the importance for Finland of trade relations with the USSR and the significance of Soviet scientific and technical research, the Russian language remains surprisingly under-studied in Finland. This still acts as a practical hindrance to further technical, cultural and media exchanges between the neighbour states.

Conclusion: Finnish–Soviet Relations, a Model?

Many Western observers have tended to regard Finland as lying within an extended and loosely defined Soviet sphere of influence. Finnish policies and political practices have often been interpreted simply as responses to the proximity of Soviet power. Such assumptions underlie the notion of Finlandisation. But as this study reveals, the influences which have determined Finland's domestic and foreign policies have been multifarious, and the Soviet Union has been far less intrusive in its relations with Finland than is commonly believed. These Finnish policies have frequently been misconstrued by those who have little knowledge of Finland but have been intent on uncovering the hidden Soviet hand in this country. Western commentators attracted to the model of Finlandisation have downgraded the importance of historical factors and have greatly underestimated the resilience and diversity of Finnish political life. They have often overlooked the broader interests behind Finland's neutral foreign policy and failed to appreciate the role of Finland's post-war treaties. The priority given to the maintenance of cordial relations and a positive dialogue with the USSR in the spirit, and in some areas the letter, of these treaties, has resulted at times in peculiarities or anomalies in Finnish politics. Certain restraints have also been observed by Finland in her external relations. But the assertion that these features of Finland's position can be drawn together to form a model suitable for general applicability remains unwarranted.

The proponents of the Finlandisation thesis have been inclined to draw a simple analogy between Soviet policy towards or influence over Finland and Western Europe. But it is misconceived to equate the power potential, geographical vulnerability, and historical experience of Finland and Western Europe.[1] Since Finnish foreign policy is formulated and conducted under the assumption that a strong Western position is maintained, and since this policy is intended to conform to and make use of both West and East, it is also a misconception to view Finland's present policy as a negative model for a future decline of Western Europe.[2] Any comparison of more or less fixed demographic and historical preconditions does not favour analogies between Soviet–Finnish and other Soviet–European relationships. A more sophisticated Western view has been that such analogies can instead be based on behavioural traits which may arise from similar sets of psychological conditions. Yet even if some degree of anticipatory deference can be identified in Finnish policies or political practices there is no reason to suppose that this will be duplicated elsewhere in Europe if it is determined by conditions and perceptions unique to Finland.

The basic determinants of Finland's position in the political order of post-war Europe were Finland's peace treaty and the 1948 FCMA-Treaty with the Soviet Union. Both treaties imposed enduring political and military commitments on a small state defeated by a great power neighbour, and the conditions of the FCMA-Treaty remain unique in Europe.[3] The commitments of these treaties have shaped many of the political perceptions Finnish statesmen share, but they were reinforced by deep internal characteristics of Finnish society only indirectly related to Finnish–Soviet relations, in particular a traditional authoritarian outlook.[4] These social tendencies have formed the traits characteristic of the Finnish political culture rather than Soviet influence.

Western critics of *détente* who have employed the Finlandisation argument have interpreted *détente* alongside the broader Soviet strategy of peaceful coexistence as a means of Soviet advancement by stealth. Since the Soviet view of peaceful coexistence presumes a continuation if not an intensification of the ideological competition between East and West, Soviet descriptions of Finnish–Soviet relations since the mid-1950s as a paragon of peaceful coexistence, or even as a model for a new order East–West relations, have aroused deep suspicions in the West about Finland's position. But already in 1955 Prime Minister Kekkonen had strongly affirmed that Finland could preserve its state and social system unimpaired in an era of peaceful coexistence through demonstrating that the prevailing democratic system 'best suits our people, our conditions and our social development'.[5] Indeed, at the end of the 1958–9 'night-frost' crisis in Finnish–Soviet relations Khrushchev reassured the Finns that 'the internal structure of your state does not concern us; it is your people's own affair'.[6] What became apparent in the 1950s and 1960s was that Soviet leaders held different expectations of the political conduct and social development of neutral Finland, a developed European state with an established market economy, to those of neutralist or 'non-capitalist road' countries in the Third World. Consequently they have not been disillusioned unduly by Finland's political progress and they have refrained from exploiting ideologically motivated pressures within Finland.

What has remained of enduring political importance for the USSR, as Khrushchev reiterated in January 1959 for example, is that Finland should adhere to the policy line in her Eastern relations laid down in the 1947 peace treaty and the 1948 FCMA-Treaty. Finland's commitment to this line and to the obligations of these treaties has met Soviet security needs in the direction of Finland comprehensively, and this distinguishes Soviet–Finnish relations from Soviet relations with any other border state outside the Soviet bloc. Indeed, in June 1983 the security principles and priorities of Soviet–Finnish relations were reinforced by the prolongation of the FCMA-Treaty for a further twenty years. Soviet leaders have also had to consider the broader Nordic regional implications of any undue political pressure on Finland. With these considerations in mind it is evident that analogies between the positions of Finland and, for example, Afghanistan obscure Soviet policy rather than clarify it.

Although post-war Soviet policy towards Finland has had a very particular and individual character, in response to regional influences and bilateral treaty arrangements, broad changes in the general Soviet foreign policy outlook have been reflected in Finnish–Soviet relations. Such a shift in Soviet perceptions, for instance, preceded the Soviet acknowledgement of Finland's neutral stand in foreign affairs in the mid-1950s. But since the bedrock of Finnish–Soviet security relations had already been laid down by the late 1940s, fluctuations in the Soviet reliance on military and political instruments in the conduct of national policy in the 1950s and 1960s, which were expressed more clearly elsewhere in the world in regions of political flux and security sensitivity for the USSR, were identifiable only by changes of nuance in Soviet policy towards Finland. The three main periods of strained Finnish–Soviet relations, 1948–9, 1958–9, and 1961–2, occurred against the background of heightened East–West tension in general. Their incidence did not constitute evidence of a reappraisal of the underlying policy conducted by Soviet leaders *vis-à-vis* Finland; they were contingent on political developments within the Nordic region in general and they left the structure of bilateral Finnish–Soviet relations intact.

Since the mid-1970s there has been a reassertion in Soviet policy of the priority given to military defence in questions of security relations. With respect to Finland this prompted an emphasis on the role and significance of the military articles of the 1948 FCMA-Treaty. It also underlay the debate which developed at the end of the 1970s over the implications of cruise missiles and the apparent Soviet suggestion for joint Finnish–Soviet military exercises. In the Nordic context this Soviet 'security drive' fuelled current controversy about the formation of a Northern nuclear-free zone, inspired Soviet polemics against developments in Norwegian policy, and may have been behind Soviet submarine intrusions into Nordic territorial waters.

This shift in the focus of Soviet policy partly reflected changes in the Soviet policy outside Europe towards the countries lying outside the great power alliance systems. Soviet disillusion with the developmental prospects of these countries has been expressed in a reduced emphasis on political and economic coordination with them and a greater concentration on the narrower issue of military access. This may be one strand in a developing 'globalist approach' in Soviet foreign policy, encouraged by the growing naval power and airlift capability of the USSR, and marked by an emphasis on access and influence.[7] The military provisions of the Finnish–Soviet FCMA-Treaty provide an ideal channel for increasing such access and influence in part of the Nordic region, but only in certain specified circumstances and under certain conditions. Soviet statements since the mid-1970s indicate that the USSR does not intend to forego this option if it becomes necessary for reasons of military security.

In Soviet policy the non-military provisions of the 1948 treaty, and the principles behind peaceful coexistence and Finland's active policy of neutrality were invoked in the 1970s to urge on Finnish–Soviet political coordination in the international arena. Since Finland will continue to share a common interest with the USSR over at least European *détente* and the fruits of the CSCE process, relations between the two states can be expected to develop in this field later in the 1980s, while the development of further Soviet political coordination on international issues with other non-European states with neutralist or neutral policies is less assured. Soviet leaders can use the example of Finland to exhort the other European neutral and non-aligned countries to continue their work for the consolidation of European security. The Soviet Union also derives appreciable long-term benefits from its trade with Finland, and the character of this trade and the forms of Finnish–Soviet economic cooperation have a broader role in Soviet policy since they can be commended as a model for Soviet–West European trade links.

For these reasons Finland's political and economic relations with the Soviet Union have not suffered from the Soviet emphasis over the last decade on issues of military defence in the Soviet definition of state security, nor have they been gravely affected by the general militarisation of great power relations in the early 1980s. The history of these relations since 1944 shows that they have at times undeniably been subject to serious strain, and such strain may recur in the future. But the broad structure of post-war Finnish–Soviet relations, formed by a pragmatic policy of coexistence based on a well established security policy *entente*, has served both states overall most satisfactorily. Neither Finland nor the Soviet Union will hasten to upset this arrangement.

Appendix 1

EXTRACTS FROM: TREATY OF PEACE WITH FINLAND

(signed in Paris, 10 February 1947)

Article 2

In accordance with the Armistice Agreement of September 19 1944 Finland confirms the return to the Soviet Union of the province of Petsamo (Pechenga) voluntarily ceded to Finland by the Soviet State under the Peace Treaties of October 14 1920, and March 12 1940.

Article 4

1. In accordance with the Armistice Agreement, the Soviet Union confirms the renunciation of its right to the lease of the Peninsula of Hangö, accorded to it by the Soviet–Finnish Peace Treaty of March 12 1940, and Finland for her part confirms having granted to the Soviet Union on the basis of a fifty years lease . . . the use and administration of territory and waters for the establishment of a Soviet naval base in the area of Porkkala–Udd . . .

2. Finland confirms having secured to the Soviet Union, in accordance with the Armistice Agreement, the use of the railways, waterways, roads and air routes necessary for the transport of personnel and freight dispatched from the Soviet Union to the naval base at Porkkala–Udd and also confirms having granted to the Soviet Union the right of unimpeded use of all forms of communication between the Soviet Union and the terrritory in the area of Porkkala–Udd.

Article 5

The Åland Islands shall remain demilitarised in accordance with the situation as at present existing.

Article 6

Finland shall take all measures necessary to secure to all persons under Finnish jurisdiction, without distinction as to race, sex, language or religion, the enjoyment of human rights and of the fundamental freedoms, including freedom of expression, of press and publication, of religious worship, of political opinion and of public meeting.

Article 7

Finland, which in accordance with the Armistice Agreement has taken measures to set free, irrespective of citizenship and nationality, all persons held in confinement on account of their activities in favour of or because of their sympathies with, the United Nations or because of their racial origin, and to repeal discriminatory legislation and restrictions imposed thereunder, shall complete these measures and shall in future not take any measures or enact any laws which would be incompatible with the purposes set forth in this Article.

Article 8

Finland, which in accordance with the Armistice Agreement has taken measures for dissolving all organisations of a Fascist type or para-military, as well as other organisations conducting propaganda hostile to the Soviet Union or to any of the other United Nations, shall not permit in future the existence and activities of organisations of that nature which have as their aim the denial to the people of their democratic rights.

Article 9

1. Finland shall take all necessary steps to ensure the apprehension and surrender for trial of:

(a) Persons accused of having committed, ordered or abetted war crimes and crimes against peace or humanity;
(b) Nationals of any Allied or Associated Power accused of having violated their national law by treason or collaboration with the enemy during the war.

Article 13

The maintenance of land, sea and air armaments and fortifications shall be closely restricted to meeting tasks of an internal character and local defence of frontiers. In accordance with the foregoing, Finland is authorised to have armed forces consisting of not more than:

(a) A land army, including frontier troops and anti-aircraft artillery, with a total strength of 34 400 personnel;
(b) A navy with a personnel strength of 4500 and a total tonnage of 10 000 tons;
(c) An airforce, including any naval air arm, of 60 aircraft, including reserves, with a total personnel strength of 3000. Finland shall not possess or acquire any aircraft designed primarily as bombers with internal bomb-carrying facilities.

These strengths shall in each case include combat, service and over-head personnel.

Article 15

Personnel not included in the Finnish Army, Navy or Airforce shall not receive any form of military training, naval training or military air training . . .

Article 17

Finland shall not possess, construct or experiment with any atomic weapon, any self-propelled or guided missiles or apparatus connected with their discharge (other than torpedoes . . .), sea mines or torpedoes of non-contact types . . ., submarines or other submersible craft, motor torpedo boats, or specialised types of assault craft.

Article 18

Finland shall not retain, produce or otherwise acquire, or maintain facilities for the manufacture of, war material in excess of that required for the maintenance of the armed forces permitted under Article 13 of the present Treaty . . .

Article 20

Finland shall cooperate fully with the Allied and Associated Powers with a view to ensuring that Germany may not be able to take steps outside German territory toward rearmament.

Article 23

1. Losses caused to the Soviet Union by military operations and by the occupation by Finland of Soviet territory shall be made good by Finland to the Soviet Union . . . compensation for the above losses shall be made by Finland . . . in the amount of $300 000 000 payable over eight years from September 19 1944 in commodities (timber products, paper, cellulose, sea-going and river craft, sundry machinery, and other commodities).

Appendix 2

THE TREATY OF FRIENDSHIP, COOPERATION AND MUTUAL ASSISTANCE BETWEEN THE REPUBLIC OF FINLAND AND THE UNION OF SOVIET SOCIALIST REPUBLICS

The President of the Republic of Finland and the Presidium of the Supreme Soviet of the USSR; desiring further to develop friendly relations between the Republic of Finland and the USSR:

Being convinced that the strengthening of good-neighbourly relations and cooperation between the Republic of Finland and the USSR lies in the interest of both countries;

Considering Finland's desire to remain outside the conflicting interests of the Great Powers; and expressing their firm endeavour to collaborate towards the maintenance of international peace and security in accordance with the aims and principles of the United Nations Organisation;

Have for this purpose agreed to conclude the present treaty and have appointed as their plenipotentiaries:

The President of the Republic of Finland: Mauno Pekkala, Prime Minister of the Republic of Finland; the Presidium of the Supreme Soviet of the USSR: Vyacheslav Mikhailovich Molotov, Vice-Chairman of the Council of Minister of the USSR, and Minister for Foreign Affairs,

who, after exchange of their full powers, found in good and due form, have agreed on the following provisions:

Article 1

In the eventuality of Finland, or the Soviet Union through Finnish territory, becoming the object of an armed attack by Germany or any state allied with the latter, Finland will, true to its obligations as an independent state, fight to repel the attack. Finland will in such cases use all of its available forces for defending its territorial integrity by land, sea and air, and will do so within the frontiers of Finland in accordance with obligations defined in the present treaty and, if necessary, with the assistance of, or jointly with, the Soviet Union.

In the cases aforementioned the Soviet Union will give the help required, the giving of which will be subject to mutual agreement between the Contracting Parties.

Article 2

The High Contracting Parties shall confer with each other if it is

174

established that the threat of an armed attack as described in Article 1 is present.

Article 3

The High Contracting Parties give assurance of their intention loyally to participate in all measures towards the maintenance of international peace and security in conformity with the aims and principles of the United Nations Organisation.

Article 4

The High Contracting Parties confirm their pledge, given under Article 3 of the Peace Treaty signed in Paris on 10 February 1947, not to conclude any alliance or join any coalition directed against the other High Contracting Party.

Article 5

The High Contracting Parties give assurance of the decision to act in a spirit of cooperation and friendship towards the further economic develop-ment and consolidation of economic and cultural relations between Finland and the Soviet Union.

Article 6

The High Contracting Parties pledge themselves to observe the principle of the mutual respect of sovereignty and integrity and that of non-interference in the internal affairs of the other state.

Article 7

The execution of the present treaty shall take place in accordance with the principles of the United Nations Organisation.

Article 8

The present treaty shall be ratified and remain in force ten years after the date of its coming into force. The treaty shall come into force upon the exchange of the instruments of ratification, the exchange taking place in the shortest possible time in Helsinki.

Provided neither of the High Contracting Parties has denounced it one year before the expiration of the said ten-year period, the treaty shall remain in force for subsequent five year periods until either High Contracting Party one year before the expiration of such five-year periods in writing notifies its intention of terminating the validity of the treaty.

In witness hereof the Plenipotentiaries have signed the present treaty and affixed their seals.

Done in City of Moscow on the sixth day of April 1948 in two copies, in the Finnish and Russian languages, both texts being authentic.

Notes and References

INTRODUCTION

1. See J. P. Vloyantes, *Silk Glove Hegemony: Finnish–Soviet Relations 1944–1974. A Case Study of the Theory of the Soft Sphere of Influence* (Kent, Ohio: 1975).
2. N. Ørvik, *Sicherheit auf Finnisch* (Stuttgart-Degerloch: 1972).
3. Interview of Professor M. Woslenski, former Secretary of the disarmament commission of the Soviet Academy of Sciences, in *Der Spiegel*, 7 October 1980. Woslenski left the USSR in 1977.
4. S. Harrison, 'Dateline Afghanistan: Exit through Finland?', *Foreign Policy*, 41 (Winter 1980–81) 183 and 186.
5. D. Vital, *The Survival of Small States* (Oxford: 1971), ch. 4.
6. G. Maude, 'The Further Shores of Finlandization', *Cooperation and Conflict*, XVII (1982) 6.
7. Interview in *Newsweek*, 3 September 1973.
8. Speech on 4 April 1973, *Ulkopoliittisia Lausuntoja ja Asiakirjoja* (Helsinki: Ministry of Foreign Affairs) (henceforth *ULA*) 1973, 104.
9. See ULA, 1974, 158–9.
10. H. Hakovirta, *Suomettuminen* (Jyväskylä: 1975) pp. 162–3.
11. W. Laqueur, 'Europe: The Specter of Finlandization', *Commentary*, 64, no. 6 (1977) 40.
12. For example, T. Junnila, *Suomen Itsenäisyydestä on Kysymys* (Porvoo: 1971) pp. 109–11.
13. W. Lacqueur, *A Continent Astray, 1970–1978* (New York: 1979) p. 223.
14. See *Uusi Suomi*, 31 March 1978.
15. For this period see D. G. Kirby, *Finland in the Twentieth Century* (London: 1979) ch. 3.
16. See ibid., p. 117
17. For an analysis of the institutional factors contributing to the particularly strong position of the Finnish president, see P. Kastari, 'The Position of the President in the Finnish Political System', *Scandinavian Political Studies*, 4 (1969).
18. See J. Nousiainen, *The Finnish Political System* (Cambridge, Mass.: 1971) ch. 7.

1 THE RECONSTRUCTION OF POST-WAR FINNISH–SOVIET SECURITY RELATIONS

1. US Representative in Finland (Hamilton) to Secretary of State,

Helsinki, 8 March 1945. *Foreign Relations of the United States 1945*, IV (Washington: 1968) 605.
2. O. Apunen, *Paasikiven-Kekkosen Linja* (Helsinki: 1977) p. 15.
3. Hamilton to State Department, 10 January 1947. J. R. Ylitalo, *Salasanomia Helsingistä Washingtoniin: Muistelmia ja Dokumentteja Vuosilta 1946–48* (Keuruu: 1978) pp. 26–7.
4. T. Palm, *Moskova 1944: Aselepo Neuvottelut Maaliskuussa ja Syyskuussa 1944* (Helsinki: 1972) pp. 120–1.
5. Ibid., pp. 132–3.
6. Ibid., p. 135.
7. Chief of North European Department of State Department (H. Cumming) in a political summary of the peace treaty written on 16 September 1946, referred to this British disclosure. Ylitalo, *Salasanomia Helsingistä Washingtoniin*, p. 18.
8. Palm, *Moskova: 1944*, p. 61.
9. US Chargé in Finland (Hulley) to the Secretary of State, Helsinki 16 October 1945. *Foreign Relations of the United States 1945*, IV, 657.
10. Interview in *Time*, 25 November 1946. Ylitalo, *Salasanomia Helsingistä Washingtoniin*, p. 40.
11. H. Rautkallio, *Suomen Suunta 1945–1948* (Savonlinna: 1979) p. 67.
12. Ibid., p. 70.
13. T. Polvinen, *Jaltasta Pariisin Rauhaan: Suomi Kansainvälisessä Politiikassa III 1945–1947* (Porvoo-Helsinki: 1981) pp. 96–9.
14. Speech on 25 September 1944. T. Vilkuna (ed.), *Urho Kekkonen Puheita ja Kirjoituksia I: Puheita Vuosilta 1936–1956* (Helsinki: 1967) p. 140.
15. Speeches on 6 December 1944 and 15 March 1945. J. K. Paasikivi, *Paasikiven Linja I* (Porvoo: 1962) pp. 9–10 and 14.
16. Statement to newspaper representatives, December 1945. Ibid., pp. 35–6.
17. Cited by Paasikivi in ibid., pp. 44–5.
18. Rautkallio, *Suomen Suunta 1945–1948*, p. 176.
19. Ibid.
20. Interview in paper of Finnish–Soviet Society in February 1947. Cited in T. Karvonen, *Neljännesvuosisata YYA-Sopimusta* (Helsinki: 1973) p. 84.
21. Cited by Kekkonen in speech on 4 April 1973. *ULA*, 1973, 96.
22. These initiatives were explained by Foreign Minister Enckell to Ambassador Warren. The US Minister in Finland (Warren) to Secretary of State, 2 March 1948. *Foreign Relations of the United States 1948*, IV (Washington: 1974) 768.
23. Described in S. Jägerskiöld, *Från Krig till Fred: Gustaf Mannerheim 1944–1951* (Helsinki: 1981); reviewed in *Helsingin Sanomat*, 15 November 1981.
24. See discussion between Enckell and US Ambassador Hamilton. Ylitalo, *Salasanomia Helsingistä Washingtoniin*, pp. 55–6.
25. Enckell to Scott. Rautkallio, *Suomen Suunta 1945–1948*, p. 155.
26. US Ambassador in Sweden (Matthews) to Secretary of State, Stockholm 20 February 1948. *Foreign Relations of the United States 1948*, IV, 761.

27. US Minister in Finland (Warren) to Secretary of State, 20 February 1948. Ibid., 762.
28. Text of letter published in *Vapaa Sana*, 3 March 1948.
29. J. O. Söderhjelm, *Kolme Matkaa Moskovaan* (Helsinki: 1970) p. 113.
30. Mannerheim to Count Bernadotte; related to US Ambassador in Sweden. Document of 5 March 1948, reproduced in Ylitalo, *Salasanomia Helsingistä Washingtoniin*, p. 224.
31. Speech on 8 April 1948. Cited in *Vapaa Sana*, 9 April 1948.
32. *Pravda*, 8 April 1948.
33. Speech on 8 April 1948. Cited in *Vapaa Sana*, 9 April 1948.
34. L. Ingul'skaya, *V bor'be demokratizatsiyu finlyandii 1944–1948* (Moscow: 1972) p. 245.
35. *Suomen Sosialidemokraatti*, 8 April 1948.
36. Speech on 14 April 1948. *Helsingin Sanomat*, 15 April 1948.
37. Paasikivi, *Paasikiven Linja I*, pp. 99–100.
38. Constitutional Committee of Parliament, Report no. 9 to the Foreign Affairs Committee, Helsinki 22 April 1948. Cited in *Helsingin Sanomat*, 1 November 1961.
39. J. Triska and R. Slusser, *The Theory, Law and Policy of Soviet Treaties* (Stanford: 1962). See also Y. Koloskov, 'International Treaties: Theory and Practice', *International Affairs* (Moscow), 12 (1973) 114.
40. Letter on 9 March 1965. M. Tyrkkö and K. Korhonen (eds), *Urho Kekkonen Kirjeitä Myllystäni I* (Helsinki: 1976) pp. 227–8.
41. Ibid., p. 228.
42. Foreign Affairs Committee of Parliament, Report no. 20, Helsinki 26 April 1948. Cited in O. Apunen, *Kansallinen Realismi ja Puolueettomuus Suomen Ulkopoliittisina Valintoina* (Tampere: 1972) appendix 2. See also B. Broms, *Eduskunnan Ulkoasianvaliokunta* (Turku: 1967) pp. 343–8.
43. N. Petersen, 'Britain, Scandinavia and the North Atlantic Treaty 1948–49', *Review of International Studies*, 8, no. 4 (October 1982) 251.
44. Cited in G. Lundestad, *America, Scandinavia and the Cold War 1945–1949* (Oslo: 1980) p. 88.
45. Ibid., p. 108.
46. Ibid., p. 209.
47. Director of Office of European Affairs (Hickerson) to Minister of Finland (K. Jutila), 14 March 1949. *Foreign Relations of the United States 1949*, v (Washington: 1976) 437.
48. Conversation in Washington, 26 October 1948. *Foreign Relations of the United States 1948*, III (Washington: 1974) 268–9.
49. Lundestad, *America, Scandinavia and the Cold War 1945–1949*, pp. 261–2.
50. US Ambassador in Soviet Union (Kirk) to Secretary of State, Moscow 23 August 1949. *Foreign Relations of the United States, 1949* v, 441.
51. Rautkallio, *Suomen Suunta 1945–1948*, p. 161.
52. Ibid., p. 205.
53. Ibid., p. 204.
54. Smith to Secretary of State, Moscow 1 March 1948. *Foreign Relations of the United States 1948*, IV, 766.

55. Secretary of State to Legation in Finland, Washington 1 March 1948. Ibid., 767.
56. Top secret telegram on 23 March 1948. Reproduced in Ylitalo, *Salasanomia Helsingistä Washingtoniin*, p. 267.
57. Airgram on 16 October 1950. *Foreign Relations of the United States 1950*, IV (Washington: 1980) 586. And conversation by Minister in Finland (Cabot), Helsinki 26 September 1950, p. 587.
58. Minister in Finland (Warren) to Secretary of State, 6 March 1948. *Foreign Relations of the United States 1948*, IV, 770.
59. *Izvestiya*, 9 March 1948.
60. For example, *Literaturnaya Gazeta*, 25 December 1948.
61. Memorandum from Director of Office of European Affairs (L. E. Thompson) to Under Secretary of State (T. Webb), 29 June 1949. *Foreign Relations of the United States 1949*, V, 440.
62. Washington, 1 December 1949. Ibid., 443.
63. Ibid., 445.
64. Smith to Secretary of State, Moscow 1 April 1948. *Foreign Relations of the United States 1948*, V, 775.
65. Y. Kallinen in discussions with Ambassador Warren. US Minister in Finland to Secretary of State, 27 April 1948. Ibid., 779.
66. Recounted by Kekkonen in interview on 8 April 1975. *ULA*, 1975, 398.
67. R. Svento, *Ystäväni Juho Kusto Paasikivi* (Helsinki: 1960) p. 66.
68. Smith to Secretary of State, Moscow 4 May 1948. *Foreign Relations of the United States 1948*, IV, 845.
69. Comment on Radio Moscow, 23 January 1949. Cited in *Helsingin Sanomat*, 24 January 1949.
70. *New Times* (Moscow), 50 (1948) 17–18.
71. *New Times* (Moscow), 15 (1949) 18.
72. *Pravda*, 2 October 1951.
73. O. W. Kuusinen, 'The Finnish Foes of Peace and their Artifices', *New Times* (Moscow), 25 (1951), 9.
74. Memorandum by Secretary of State, 9 February 1950, of meeting with the President. *Foreign Relations of the United States 1950*, IV, 575.
75. *New Times* (Moscow), 15 (1949). See also *Pravda*, 14 August 1949.
76. *Krasnaya Zvezda*, 27 March 1949. See also *Pravda*, 19 February 1949; *Izvestiya*, 24 March 1949.
77. *Izvestiya*, 14 June 1950.
78. R. Väyrynen, *Conflicts in Finnish–Soviet Relations. Three Comparative Case Studies* (Tampere: Acta Universitatis Tamperensis, ser A, 47, 1972) p. 126.
79. Report on 26 February 1949. Noted in memorandum by Director of US Office to European Affairs (Hickerson) to Secretary of State. *Foreign Relations of the United States 1949*, V, 435.
80. *Izvestiya*, 8 December 1951.
81. *Pravda*, 18 February 1953.
82. A. Päärnilä, 'Ahvenanmaan Takuut Ulkopolitiikan Ongelman', *Helsingin Sanomat*, 19 August 1979.
83. *New Times* (Moscow), 50 (1948), 17–18.
84. *Izvestiya*, 14 February 1950.

85. *Literaturnaya Gazeta*, 7 June 1951. See also *Izvestiya*, 7 June 1950.
86. *Helsingin Sanomat*, 19 August 1979.
87. *Izvestiya*, 14 October 1951.
88. See K. Törnudd, *Soviet Attitudes Towards Non-Military Regional Cooperation* (Helsinki: 1961) pp. 110–17.
89. *Izvestiya*, 9 January 1955.
90. Speech on 26 January 1955. T. Vilkuna (ed.), *Urho Kekkonen Puheita ja Kirjoituksia I*, p. 335.
91. *Khrushchev Remembers II: The Last Testament*, trans. and ed. S. Talbott (London: Penguin, 1977), pp. 268–70.
92. Speech broadcast on 22 September 1955. J. K. Paasikivi, *Paasikiven Linja I*, 192–3. For a similar Soviet appraisal, see *Pravda*, 17, 25 and 27 January 1956.
93. *Helsingin Sanomat*, 18 September 1955.
94. M. Lazarev, *Imperialist Military Bases on Foreign Territories and International Law* (Moscow: 1963).
95. A. Piradov, 'Bases and International Law', *International Affairs* (Moscow), 5 (1964) 99.
96. *Karjala*, cited in *Uusi Suomi*, 28 October 1955.
97. O. Apunen, *Paasikiven-Kekkosen Linja*, p. 96.
98. *Literaturnaya Gazeta*, 22 March 1955.
99. *Izvestiya*, 13 July 1956.
100. Max Jakobson, *Veteen Piirretty Viiva: Havaintoja ja Merkintöjä Vuosilta 1953–1965* (Keuruu: 1981) p. 72.
101. N. S. Hruštšev, *Neuvostoliitto ja Pohjola: Puheita ja Lausuntoja Vuosilta 1956–63* (Helsinki: 1964) p. 63.

2 THE 1961 NOTE CRISIS

1. *Izvestiya*, 9 July 1955.
2. Soviet–Norwegian communique of visit 10–16 November 1955; *Pravda*, 16 November 1955.
3. Soviet–Swedish communique of visit 29 March–4 April 1956; *Pravda*, 4 April 1956.
4. Interview in *Dansk Folkestyren; Pravda*, 15 January 1958. See also *Pravda*, 18 February 1959.
5. *Izvestiya*, 11 February 1959.
6. See, for example, *Izvestiya*, 14 August 1959.
7. A. Pogodin, 'Dangerous Plans', *International Affairs* (Moscow), 4 (1960) 78.
8. *Izvestiya*, 14 August 1959.
9. Pogodin, 'Dangerous Plans', 79.
10. *Izvestiya*, 4 May 1961. See also earlier criticisms, for example in *Izvestiya*, 19 February 1959; Soviet government note to Norwegian government, *Pravda*, 20 April 1959.
11. Speech in Rovaniemi on 27 September 1961. *Helsingin Sanomat*, 28 September 1961. Brezhnev held the post of Chairman of the Presidium of the Supreme Soviet of the USSR.

12. *Helsingin Sanomat*, 24 October 1959.
13. Cabinet meeting on 9 August 1961. Max Jakobson, *Veteen Piirretty Viiva*, p. 217.
14. Meeting in the White House on 16 September 1961. Ibid., pp. 234–5.
15. *ULA*, 1961, 211–12. For the complete Soviet note, see *ULA*, 1961, 210–13.
16. APN comment on 6 November 1961. *Maakansa*, 8 November 1961.
17. Government communique of discussions in Moscow on 14 November 1961. *ULA*, 1961, 178.
18. Speech broadcast on 14 November 1961. *ULA*, 1961, 179–80.
19. Government communique of discussions in Moscow on 17 November 1961. *ULA*, 181.
20. Speech on 19 November 1961. *ULA*, 1961, 182.
21. Radio Moscow on 21 November 1961. *Päivän Sanomat*, 22 November 1961.
22. Jakobson, *Veteen Piirretty Viiva*, pp. 263–4.
23. Speech on 24 November 1961. N. S. Hruštšev, *Neuvostoliitto ja Pohjola*, pp. 150–1.
24. Government communique of discussions on 25 November 1961. *ULA*, 1961, 183.
25. The account of the discussions which follows draws from the official communique in Hruštšev, Neuvostoliitto ja Pohjola, pp. 155–6; and from Jakobson, *Veteen Piirretty Viiva*, pp. 275–8.
26. Interview on 7 February 1962. *ULA*, 1962, 11–12.
27. Speech on 26 November 1961. *ULA*, 1961, 187.
28. Interview on 7 February 1962, *ULA*, 1962, 11.
29. Jakobson, *Veteen Piirretty Viiva*, p. 297.
30. Ibid., pp. 258–60, 278–9.
31. *Pravda*, 14 December 1961.
32. Speech on 10 December 1961. *ULA*, 1961, 191.
33. See A. Brundtland, 'The Nordic Balance', *Cooperation and Conflict*, II (1966). Brundtland's thesis is updated in another paper, *The Nordic Balance* (Norsk Utrenrikspolitisk Institutt, NUPI notat no. 229, December 1981).
34. A. Brundtland, 'The Nordic Balance' (1966) 45.
35. Cited in *Suomen Kuvalehti*, 14 November 1964.
36. Cited in H. Särkiö and G. Hägglund, *Mitä Tapahtuu jos . . .* (Helsinki: 1975) p. 155.
37. See G. Maude, 'Finland's Security Policy', *The World Today* (October 1975) 409.
38. S. Lindberg, 'The Illusory Nordic Balance: Threat Scenarios in Nordic Security Planning', *Cooperation and Conflict*, 1 (1981) 59.
39. See O. Apunen, *Paasikiven-Kekkosen Linja*, p. 258.
40. Yu. Goloshubov, *Skandinaviya i problemy poslevoennoy Yevropy* (Moscow: 1974) p. 238; see pp. 235–40. See also Y. Simonov, 'The Concept of a "Nordic Balance" and Reality', *International Affairs* (Moscow), 6 (1974) 99.
41. Interview in *Helsingin Sanomat*, 27 February 1982.

3 THE SCOPE OF FINNISH SECURITY POLICY 1961–84

1. V. V. Pokhlebkin, *SSSR-Finlyandiya 260 let otnosheniy* (Moscow: 1975).
2. Interview on 27 September 1966. *ULA*, 1966, 24.
3. The 'Pyjama pocket' speech, published on 23 January 1957. T. Vilkuna (ed.), *Urho Kekkonen Puheita ja Kirjoituksia I*, p. 241.
4. *Pravda*, 27 January 1952. See also *Literaturnaya Gazeta*, 2 February 1952.
5. Address in Oslo on 30 June 1964. *Pravda*, 1 July 1964. See also press conference for A. Mikoyan in Oslo, *Pravda*, 1 July 1964; and A. S. Kan, 'Neytralistskie traditsii vo vneshney politike skandinavskikh gosudarstv', *Novaya i noveyshaya istoriya*, 4 (1962) 63–4.
6. See Nordic commentators in O. Vänttinen (ed.), *Itsenäinen Suomi, Puolueeton Pohjola* (Tampere: 1967).
7. Speech on 29 November 1965. T. Vilkuna (ed.), *Urho Kekkonen Puheita ja Kirjoituksia II: Puheita Presidenttikaudelta 1956–1967* (Helsinki: 1967) 402.
8. Ibid. See also A. Pajunen, 'Finland's Security Policy', *Cooperation and Conflict* (1968) 90–1.
9. G. Maude, *The Finnish Dilemma: Neutrality in the Shadow of Power* (London: 1976) p. 72.
10. Notes on 10 December 1957, 4 April 1958 and 15 July 1958. *ULA*, 1956–58, 187ff., 193ff., 195ff.
11. See A. Rapacki, 'The Polish Plan for a Nuclear-Free Zone Today', *International Affairs* (London), 39, no. 1 (January 1963).
12. Speech in Riga on 11 June 1959. N. S. Hruštšev, *Neuvostoliitto ja Pohjola*, p. 87. See also pp. 91–7 for a similar proposal in greater detail made in a speech in Stettin on 17 July 1959.
13. *Izvestiya*, 14 August 1959. This contains a full account of the contemporary Soviet position towards a nuclear-free North.
14. *Pravda*, 1 July 1960.
15. *Pravda*, 26 June 1964.
16. V. Golubkov, 'President Kekkonen's Important Initiative', *International Affairs* (Moscow), 8 (1963) 107.
17. Interview at end of visit by Gromyko to Finland. *Uusi Suomi*, 27 March 1964.
18. For example, Pokhlebkin, *SSSR-Finlyandiya 260 let otnosheniy*, p. 239.
19. Speech in Moscow on 3 December 1963. T. Vilkuna (ed.), *Urho Kekkonen Puheita ja Kirjoituksia II*, 309–10.
20. O. Apunen, *Paasikiven-Kekkosen Linja*, p. 239.
21. *Izvestiya*, 16 December 1965. See also Pokhlebkin, *SSSR-Finlyandiya 260 let otnosheniy*, p. 361.
22. See, for example, *Pravda*, 19 April 1965.
23. Top secret memorandum of Discussions on the Present World Situation, Washington 25 July 1950. *Foreign Relations of the United States 1950*, III (Washington 1977) 1666.
24. Memorandum of conversation by the Minister in Finland (Cabot), 26 September 1950. *Foreign Relations of the United States 1950*, IV, 588.

25. J. Wuorinen, 'Finland', in S. Kertesz (ed.), *The Fate of East Central Europe* (Notre Dame: 1956) p. 337.
26. *Pravda*, 21 May 1964.
27. Speech in Kremlin on 7 November 1963. *Pravda*, 8 November 1963.
28. Report on 29 March 1966. M. Rush, *The International Situation and Soviet Foreign Policy* (Columbus, Ohio: 1970) p. 311.
29. *Helsingin Sanomat*, 21 November 1968.
30. *Pravda*, 28 November 1968.
31. P. Vasilyev, 'Scandinavian and European Security', *International Affairs* (Moscow), 8 (1969) 46–7.
32. *Uusi Suomi*, 26 and 27 November 1968. See R. Väyrynen, 'Finland's Role in Western Policy since the Second World War', *Cooperation and Conflict*, 2 (1977) 101.
33. Kekkonen under pseudonym Liimatainen, 29 November and 5 December 1968. M. Tyrkkö and K. Korhonen (eds), *Urho Kekkonen Nimellä ja Nimimerkillä 1* (Keuruu: 1977) pp. 276–7, 281.
34. Answer to parliamentary question on 5 October 1978. *ULA*, 1978, 41–2. See also *The Times*, 17 October 1978.
35. Interview in *Helsingin Sanomat*, 27 February 1982.
36. Interview in *Dagbladet*, 18 and 20 November 1978. *ULA*, 1978, 152.
37. *ULA*, 1978, 41–2.
38. See letter by Ambassador Tötterman in the *Daily Telegraph*, 4 May 1978.
39. Reports on 22 January 1980. Referred to in *Yearbook of Finnish Foreign Policy* (1980), 73.
40. For text of this treaty signed in December 1978, see *Pravda*, 6 December 1978.
41. Interview on 22 February 1980. *ULA*, 1980, 162.
42. Statement on 16 September 1980. Ibid., 74.
43. See interview on 16 March 1982. *ULA*, 1982, 181.
44. T. Bartenev and J Komissarov, *Kolmekymmentä Vuotta Hyvää Naapuruutta* (Keuruu: 1977) pp. 95, 102, 98.
45. See article by J. Iloniemi, *ULA*, 1979, 149.
46. See O. Apunen, 'Geographical and Political Factors in Finland's Relations with the Soviet Union', *Yearbook of Finnish Foreign Policy* (1977) 29.
47. W. H. Halsti, *Me, Venäjä ja Muut* (Helsinki: 1969) p. 43.
48. See arguments by the Finnish naval officer (in 1984 Commander-in-Chief of the navy) J. Klenberg, *The Cap and the Straits: Problems of Nordic Security* (Cambridge, Mass: 1968). See also review of this work by A. Brundtland, *Cooperation and Conflict*, 3 (1968) 254–5.
49. *Parlamentaarisen Puolustuskomitean Mietintö*, Komiteanmietintö 1971, A 18 (Helsinki: 1971) pp. 19–20.
50. *Report of Second Parliamentary Defence Committee*, Committee Report 1976, 37 (Helsinki: 1976).
51. Kolmannen *Parlamentaarisen Puolustuskomitean Mietintö*, Komiteanmietintö 1981, 1 (Helsinki: 1981) pp. 21, 19.
52. See A. Pajunen, 'Suomi Sotilaspoliittisessa Voimakentässä', in I.

184 Notes and References

Hakalehto (ed.), *Suomi Kansainvälisen Jännityksen Maailmassa* (Porvoo: 1969) p. 40.
53. Komiteanmietintö 1971, A18, p. 19.
54. See *Pravda*, 22 April and 30 April 1978.
55. *Pravda*, 4 September and 10 September 1983.
56. R. Nyberg, 'Finnish Security Policy', *Nya Argus*, 12 (1981); this was a lecture to the Swedish Defence College. Such scenarios are explored, however, in S. Lindberg, 'The Illusory Nordic Balance: Threat Scenarios in Nordic Security Planning', *Cooperation and Conflict*, 1 (1981).
57. Komiteanmietintö 1981, 1, p. 22.
58. Ibid.
59. Interview in *Helsingin Sanomat*, 4 January 1983.
60. S. Serbin, 'USSR–Finland: Good Neighbourly Relations', *International Affairs* (Moscow), 5 (1983) 55.
61. Komiteanmietintö 1971, A18, p. 18.
62. For the scenarios of a Soviet attack on Sweden, see A. Roberts, *Nations in Arms: The Theory and Practice of Territorial Defence* (London: 1976) pp. 85–91.
63. See R. Nyberg, *Security Dilemmas in Scandinavia* (Cornell Univ. Peace Studies Programme occasional paper no. 17, June 1983) pp. 32–4; G. Maude, 'Suomalainen Dilemma Tänääñ: Lapin Puolustus', *Kanava*, 3 (1983) 242–5.
64. Komiteanmietintö 1981, 1, p. 19.
65. Address in Oslo on 30 June 1964. *Pravda*, 1 July 1964.
66. *Pravda*, 9 April 1963.
67. V. Golubkov, 'Peaceful Cooperation in Northern Europe', *International Affairs* (Moscow), 11 (1965) 65; *Izvestiya*, 21 January 1968.
68. Y. Golovin, 'Nordic Europe: Security and Cooperation', *International Affairs* (Moscow), 2 (1971) 54.
69. Interview on 22 May 1969. *ULA*, 1969, 159.
70. *Pravda*, 8 April 1977.
71. See *Pravda*, 17 January 1974.
72. *Suomen Sosialidemokraatti*, 17 March 1977.
73. A. Brundtland, *The Nordic Balance* (1981) pp. 12–13.
74. *Izvestiya*, 6 April 1979.
75. K. Voronkov, 'Norway and NATO's Nuclear Strategy', *International Affairs* (Moscow), 2 (1980) 135; reviewing N. Gleditsch, I. Botnen, S. Lodgaard, and O. Wilkes, *Norge i Atomstragian: Atompolitikk, Alliansepolitikk, Basepolitikk* (Oslo: 1978).
76. *Pravda*, 19 February 1980. For Soviet views on the US–Norwegian rapid deployment agreement, see also *Pravda*, 1 April 1980, 5 July 1980.
77. *Pravda*, 22 November 1980. See also *Pravda*, 11 August 1980.
78. Interview in *Dagbladet*, 10 June 1980. *ULA*, 1980, 178.
79. Interview on 17 September 1980. Refered to in *Yearbook of Finnish Foreign Policy* (1980) 72.
80. O. Apunen, in *Suomen Sosialidemokraatti*, 30 November 1979.
81. Report in the *Guardian*, 27 October 1982; see also report on 29 December 1983.

82. This incident is fully covered in *Helsingin Sanomat*, 29 October–7 November 1981.
83. See *Helsingin Sanomat*, 7 November 1981.
84. C. Bildt, 'Sweden and the Soviet Submarines', *Survival* (July/August 1983) 167.
85. Report in the *Guardian*, 12 November 1981.
86. Attack in *Pravda*, 1 February 1982. For Swedish response, see *Helsingin Sanomat*, 3 February 1982.
87. See *Pravda*, 30 March 1982, 12 October 1982.
88. See *Helsingin Sanomat*, 16–21 October 1981.
89. Speech on 8 May 1978. *Helsingin Sanomat*, 9 May 1978.
90. See speech by N. Podgorny in *Pravda*, 5 April 1973; and joint Finnish–Soviet statement in *Pravda*, 8 April 1973.
91. *Helsingin Sanomat*, 10 May 1978.
92. Interview on 14 March 1979. *ULA*, 1979, 128.
93. See debate over this point in mid-1970s in G. Maude, 'Finland's Security Policy', *The World Today* (October 1975) 413–14.
94. Y. Komissarov, 'The Future of a Nuclear Weapon-Free Zone in Northern Europe', *Yearbook of Finnish Foreign Policy* (1978) 30.
95. L. Voronkov, 'Rauhan ja Turvallisuuden Näköalat Pohjois-Euroopassa', *Ulkopolitiikka*, 1 (1981) 35.
96. *Pravda*, 27 June 1981; *New Times* (Moscow), 27 (1981) 8–9. See also K. Borisov, 'Nuclear-Free Zones: From the Idea to its Realisation', *New Times* 41 (1981) 6.
97. *Helsingin Sanomat*, 26 September 1981.
98. *Helsingin Sanomat*, 1 October 1981.
99. *Helsingin Sanomat*, 18 November 1981. For an argument in favour of such a plan, see *Helsingin Sanomat*, 25 April 1982.
100. *Helsingin Sanomat*, 27 April 1982.
101. Finnish–Soviet communique of visit by Prime Minister Tikhonov to Finland, *Pravda*, 12 December 1982.
102. Speeches by Koivisto and Andropov on 6 June 1983. *Helsingin Sanomat*, 7 June 1983.
103. *Helsingin Sanomat*, 8 June 1983.
104. Report in the *Guardian*, 18 November 1983.
105. See speech by Prime Minister O. Palme on 1 June 1983, in K. Möttölä (ed.), *Nuclear Weapons and Northern Europe* (Helsinki: 1983) p. 85.
106. Speech on 20 January 1984. Finnish Foreign Ministry press release.
107. J. Komissarov, 'NATO'n Eurostrategia ja Pohjois-Eurooppa', *Suomen Kuvalehti*, 47 (1979) 42–6.
108. *Helsingin Sanomat*, 10 May 1978.
109. Speech on 10 December 1979 by Paavo Väyrynen. See S. Härkönen, 'Eurostrategic Weapons, Northern Europe and Finland', *Yearbook of Finnish Foreign Policy* (1979) 25.
110. Komiteanmietintö 1981, 1, pp. 20, 46.
111. R. Väyrynen, *Stability and Change in Finnish Foreign Policy* (Helsinki: Research Reports Department of Political Science, University of Helsinki, Series A, 62, 1982) p. 69.
112. Speech on 3 March 1983. *Finnish Features* 5/4 March 1983, 2.

113. *Helsingin Sanomat*, 26 June 1980.
114. V. Smirnov, *Hyvän Naapuruuden Tiellä* (Tampere: 1983) p. 69.
115. See ibid., and *Helsingin Sanomat*, 3 May 1981.
116. Report in the *Guardian*, 29 November 1983.
117. See report in the *Observer*, 5 February 1984.
118. Confirmed through discussions in the Political Department of the Finnish Foreign Ministry.
119. Statement on 30 August 1980. Referred to in *Yearbook of Finnish Foreign Policy* (1980) 74.
120. Cited in *Dagens Nyheter*, 11 November 1980.
121. Lev Voronkov in interview by *Helsingin Sanomat*, 27 February 1982.
122. Cited in T. Vaahtoranta, 'Nuclear Weapons and the Nordic Countries: Nuclear Status and Policies', in Möttölä, *Nuclear Weapons and Northern Europe*, p. 54.
123. O. Bykov, 'A Nuclear-Weapon Free Zone in the North of Europe – A Soviet View', in Möttölä, *Nuclear Weapons and Northern Europe*, p. 31.
124. Answer to question at press conference on 2 July 1983. Cited in Möttölä, *Nuclear Weapons and Northern Europe*, p. 87.

4 FINNISH NEUTRALITY: THE TOUCHSTONE OF RELATIONS WITH THE EAST

1. Lecture by Foreign Minister Merikoski on 29 March 1963. *ULA*, 1963, 12.
2. Letter from Paasikivi and Tanner handed in Moscow on 10 November 1939 to M. Molotov. *The Development of Finnish–Soviet Relations During the Autumn of 1939* (Helsinki: Ministry of Foreign Affairs of Finland) p. 69.
3. Enckell in talks with French Minister in Helsinki (Coulet). *Foreign Relations of the United States 1948*, IV, 761.
4. A. Rosas, *Sodanaikanen Puolueettomuus ja Puolueettomuuspolitiikka* (Turku: Publications of Univ. of Turku Department of Public Law, 12, 1978) p. 108.
5. Position paper on 'The Position of Finland in the Event of a General War'. *Foreign Relations of the United States 1950*, IV, 584.
6. J. O. Söderhjelm, *Kolme Matkaa Moskovaan* (Helsinki: 1970) p. 118.
7. *Ibid.*, pp. 183–4.
8. Speech on 9 April 1948. J. K. Paasikivi, *Paasikiven Linja I*, p. 98.
9. Söderhjelm, *Kolme Matkaa Moskovaan*, p. 189. The preamble discussions were between delegates Kekkonen and Vyshinski.
10. Ibid., p. 188.
11. Letter to Stalin, in *Suomen Sosialidemokraatti*, 16 March 1948.
12. See speeches in *Helsingin Sanomat*, 15 April and 17 April 1948.
13. Instructions on 9 October 1939 for discussions to be held in Moscow. *The Development of Finnish–Soviet Relations During the Autumn of 1939*, pp. 46–7.

14. Ibid., p. 49.
15. Memorandum of Soviet government handed to Paasikivi and Tanner in Moscow on 23 October 1939. Ibid., p. 54. See also K. Korhonen, *Turvallisuuden Pettäessä: Suomi Neuvostodiplomatiassa Tartosta Talvisotaan 2 1933–1939* (Helsinki: 1971) p. 213.
16. *Pravda*, 24 October 1949.
17. Report on 22 September 1947. M. Rush (ed.), *The International Situation and Soviet Foreign Policy*, p. 130.
18. *Foreign Relations of the United States 1950*, IV, 584–5.
19. J. Wuorinen, 'Finland', in S. Kertesz (ed.), *The Fate of East Central Europe*, p. 336.
20. Report on 14 February 1956. Rush, *The International Situation and Soviet Foreign Policy*, p. 185.
21. Speech on 7 June 1957. T. Vilkuna (ed.), *Urho Kekkonen Puheita ja Kirjoituksia II*, p. 38.
22. Communique on 2 February 1957. *ULA*, 1956–8, 124.
23. Speech on 8 June 1957. N. S. Hruštšev, *Neuvostoliitto ja Pohjola*, p. 21.
24. Cited in O. Apunen, *Paasikiven–Kekkosen Linja*, pp. 220–1.
25. Communique issued on 27 October 1962. *ULA*, 1962, 102.
26. U. Wagner, *Finnlands Neutralität: Eine Neutralitätspolitik mit Defensivallianz* (Hamburg: 1974) p. 58.
27. Apunen, *Paasikiven-Kekkosen Linja*, pp. 217–18.
28. See D. Woker, *Die Skandinavischen Neutralen: Prinzip und Praxis der Schwedischen und der Finnischen Neutralität* (Series of Swiss Society for Foreign Policy, 5, 1978) p. 56.
29. Speech by J. Virolainen in Berne on 13 March 1968. *ULA*, 1968, 18.
30. See S. Verosta, *Die Dauernde Neutralität* (Vienna: 1967) pp. 21–5, 35. Verosta uses the term 'Faktische dauernde Neutralität' in relation to Sweden and Finland.
31. Lecture on 29 March 1963. *ULA*, 1963, 12.
32. See Wagner, *Finnlands Neutralität*, p. 64.
33. N. Ørvik, *Sicherheit auf Finnisch*, pp. 180–1, 30.
34. This argument follows A. Rosas, *Sodanaikanen Puolueettomuus*, pp. 116–23.
35. Verosta, *Die Dauernde Neutralität*, p. 33. Verosta accepts Max Jakobson's claim that the FCMA-Treaty is not in conflict with neutrality.
36. See Wagner, *Finnlands Neutralität*, p. 37ff.: Woker, *Die Skandinavischen Neutralen*, pp. 35–6.
37. In addition to Rosas, *Sodanaikanen Puolueettomuus*, see J. Kalela, 'Puolueettomuus ja Suomen Idänsuhteet', *Politiikka*, 1 (1971); M. Elovainio, 'YYA-Sopimuksen Synty sekä Sopimuksen Merkitys Suomen Puolueettomuudelle Sopimusoikeudellisesti Tarkasteltuna', *Politiikka*, 2 (1979).
38. S. B. Krylov and V. N. Durnenevski, *Mezhdunarodno-pravovye formy mirnogo sosushchestvovaniya gosudarstv i natsii* (Moscow: 1957) p. 133.
39. *Pravda*, 6 April 1960.
40. *Mirovaya ekonomika i mezhdunarodnye otnosheniya*, 3 (1962); cited in *ULA*, 1963, 15–16.
41. Lecture on 29 March 1963. *ULA*, 1963, 15–16.

42. See, for example, I. Rozdorozhny and V. Fedorov, *Finlyandiya – nash severny sosed* (Moscow: 1966) p. 148.
43. See J. Komissarov, *Suomi Löytää Linjansa* (Helsinki: 1974) p. 148.
44. L. Oppenheim and H. Lauterpacht, *International Law II* (Edinburgh: 1960) p. 663. Referred to by G. Maude in unpublished paper, 29 November 1978.
45. Report to Finnish cabinet on 9 August 1961. M. Jakobson, *Veteen Piirretty Viiva*, pp. 217–18.
46. Speech by M. Jakobson, head of the Political Department of the Foreign Ministry, on 13 November 1963. *ULA*, 1963, 41.
47. R. Nyberg, *Security Dilemmas in Scandinavia*, p. 27.
48. For example, visit to Finland by Marshal of the Soviet Union A. Grechko, Soviet Minister of Defence, in January 1971. *Pravda*, 30 January 1971.
49. For example, *Krasnaya Zvezda*, 6 April 1965.
50. S. Serbin, 'USSR–Finland: Good Neighbourly Relations', *International Affairs* (Moscow), 5 (1983) 52.
51. See, for example, Soviet view of presence of US military attachés at Finnish army manoeuvres in *Izvestiya*, 17 October 1958.
52. M. Jakobson in letter to the Finnish Defence Council in summer 1964. Jakobson, *Veteen Piirretty Viiva*, pp. 301–2.
53. K. Orvik, 'The Limits of Security: Defence and Foreign Trade in Finland', *Survey*, 24 (Spring 1979) 95–6.
54. For the character of Finnish arms sales, see *Helsingin Sanomat*, 13 October 1981.
55. See H. Hakovirta, 'YYA-Sopimuksen Konsultaatio- ja Avunantokysymys Suomen Puolueettomuuden Uskottavuusproblematiikassa', *Politiikka*, (1970) 245–52.
56. For example, M. Kemppainen, 'Kestääkö Puolueettomuutemme?', *Suomalainen Suomi*, 36 (1968) 330.
57. J. Kalela, 'Puolueettomuus ja Suomen Idänsuhteet', *Politiikka*, 1 (1971) 71–2.
58. See Örvik, 'The Limits of Security', 93–5.
59. T. Bartenev and J. Komissarov, *Kolmekymmentä Vuotta Hyvää Naapuruutta*, p. 104.
60. For this statement and the surrounding debate, see H. Särkiö, *Vuoden 1948 YYA-Sopimus Suomalaisten Komenttien Valossa Kiinnittäen Erityisesti Huomiota sen Sotilaallisen Puoleen* (Hämeenlinna: 1973) pp. 86–90.
61. Letter on 27 January 1969. M. Tyrkkö and K. Korhonen (eds), *Urho Kekkonen Kirjeita Myllystäni 2* (Helsinki: 1976) pp. 32–3.

5 EXTERNAL AFFAIRS

1. Speech on 27 November 1954. *Helsingin Sanomat*, 28 November 1954.
2. *Novaya Vremya*, 16 August 1956.
3. Speech on 30 January 1957. *ULA*, 1956–8, 126.

4. Speech on 20 July 1970. *Tass*, 20 July 1970.
5. Speech by Foreign Minister K. Korhonen on 26–7 November 1976. *ULA*, 1976 II, 126.
6. See speech by Prime Minister Bulganin on 17 September 1955, *Helsingin Sanomat*, 18 September 1955; and Kekkonen's speech on 18 September 1955, T. Vilkuna (ed.), *Urho Kekkonen Puheita ja Kirjoituksia I*, p. 361.
7. Speech on 27 November 1954. *Helsingin Sanomat*, 28 November 1954.
8. Note on 10 December 1957. *ULA*, 1956–8, 187–93.
9. *Helsingin Sanomat*, 24 May 1958.
10. Speech on 8 June 1957. N. Hruštšev, *Neuvostoliitto ja Pohjola*, p. 21.
11. *Helsingin Sanomat*, 22 March 1964.
12. Speech on 16 November 1966. *Helsingin Sanomat*, 17 November 1966.
13. *Helsingin Sanomat*, 18 July 1970.
14. See G. Maude, *The Finnish Dilemma*, pp. 83–91.
15. See J. Blomberg and P. Joenniemi, *Kaksiteräinen Miekka – 70 Luvun Puolustuspolitiikka*, (Helsinki: 1971) pp. 45–7.
16. Kekkonen under pseudonym Liimatainen, 11 February 1972. M. Tyrkkö and K. Korhonen (eds), *Urho Kekkonen Nimellä ja Nimimerkillä I*, p. 228.
17. M. Seglin, 'USSR–Finland: Thirty Years of Good Neighbourliness', *International Affairs* (Moscow), 12 (1974) 25–6.
18. Soviet–Danish protocol on consultations, Copenhagen 6 October 1976. *Pravda*, 8 October 1976.
19. Interview on 4 May 1981. *ULA*, 1981, 124–5.
20. Report by Brezhnev on 23 February 1981. Cited in *New Times* (Moscow), 9 (1981) 26; and *Pravda*, 24 February 1981.
21. Speech on 5 August 1978. Y. V. Andropov, *Speeches and Writings*, 2nd ed. (Oxford, New York: 1983) p. 189.
22. Speech on 22 December 1982. Cited in S. Serbin, 'USSR–Finland: Good Neighbourly Relations', *International Affairs* (Moscow), 5 (1983) 51–2.
23. V. Smirnov, *Hyvän Naapuruuden Tiellä*, p. 85.
24. Speech on 9 December 1982. *ULA*, 1982, 283.
25. Cited in Serbin 'USSR–Finland: Good Neighbourly Relations', 53.
26. See joint communique in *Helsingin Sanomat*, 11 June 1983.
27. See communique of meeting between Finnish and Soviet CSCE delegations on 14 January 1982. *ULA*, 1982, 308.
28. Speech on 6 June 1983. *Helsingin Sanomat*, 7 June 1983.
29. See speech by P. Väyrynen on 20 January 1984. Finnish Foreign Ministry press release.
30. See *Izvestiya*, 21 February 1980; *Helsingin Sanomat*, 11 August 1981.
31. Smirnov, *Hyvän Naapuruuden Tiellä*, p. 22.
32. In Thirty-Second Sitting of the UN General Assembly, autumn 1977.
33. Smirnov, *Hyvän Naapuruuden Tiellä*, pp. 26, 86.
34. See speech by Kekkonen on 9 November 1972. *ULA*, 1972, 60–1.
35. See *Yhidstyneiden Kansakuntien 11 Yleiskokous New Yorkissa*, (Helsinki: 1957), pp. 14–17; and for special sitting on Hungary and resolutions thereon, pp. 69–70. See also K. Törnudd, *Suomi ja Yhdistyneet Kansakunnat* (Helsinki: 1967) pp. 66–9.
36. Ibid. (*Yhdistyneiden Kansakuntien*), pp. 26–7.

37. Speech on 7 October 1968. *ULA*, 1968, 207. See also pp. 246–7 for Foreign Ministry communiques.
38. Communique on 31 December 1979. *Helsingin Sanomat*, 2 January 1980.
39. See explanation of Finnish vote in UN by Ambassador I. Pastinen on 15 January 1980. *Helsingin Sanomat*, 16 January 1980.
40. Communique of meeting on 5–6 September 1983. *Finnish Features*, 10/9 September 1983, 1.
41. *Helsingin Sanomat*, 1 February 1982.
42. H. Kyröläinen, *Talous ja Politiikka eri Järjestelmän Omaavien Valtioiden Suhteissa: Suomi ja Neuvostoliitto 1944–1979* (Tampere: Univ. of Tampere Department of Political Science Research Reports 62, 1981) p. 167.
43. Speech on 22 October 1959. *Helsingin Sanomat*, 23 October 1959.
44. See R. Väyrynen, 'Talous ja Politiikka Suomen ja Neuvostoliiton Suhteissa Vuosina 1945–1970', in H. Hakovirta and R. Väyrynen (eds), *Suomen Ulkopolitiikka* (Jyväskylä: 1975) pp. 315–74.
45. R. Väyrynen, *Conflicts in Finnish–Soviet Relations*, pp. 94–6.
46. Speech on 4 April 1973. *ULA*, 1973, 105.
47. Interview on 6 April 1975. *ULA*, 1975, 397.
48. H. Kyröläinen, 'Economics and Politics in the Relations between States of Different Social Systems: Finland and the Soviet Union 1944–1979', in O. Apunen (ed.). *Détente – a Framework for Action and Analysis* (Tampere: Univ. of Tampere Department of Political Science Research Reports, 61, 1981) p. 227.
49. See D. Anckar, 'Finnish Foreign Policy Debate: The Saimaa Canal Case', *Cooperation and Conflict*, 4 (1970).
50. Speech on 23 September 1955. T. Vilkuna (ed.), *Urho Kekkonen Puheita ja Kirjoituksia I*, p. 354.
51. Ya. Il'inskiy, 'Liniya Paasikivi: zavoevanie finlyandskogo naroda', *Mirovaya ekonomika i mezhdunarodnye otnosheniya*, 3 (1963) 59–60.
52. For the early debate surrounding this project, see P. Kähkölä and A-K. Ripatti, *Suomen Idänkauppa* (Helsinki: 1971) pp. 155–64. For a symposium of Soviet and Finnish views on such cooperation. See A. Inkari and L. Talypin (eds), *20 Vuotta Suomalais-Neuvostoliittolaista Tieteellis-Teknillistä Yhteistoimintaa* (Helsinki: Publications of the Soviet Institute, series B, 20, 1976). See also K. Möttölä; O. Bykov and S. Korolev (eds), *Finnish–Soviet Economic Relations* (London: 1983).
53. See *Soviet News*, 29 February 1984, 76.
54. H. Kyröläinen, 'Economics and Politics', pp. 237–8.
55. G. Maude, *The Finnish Dilemma*, p. 106.
56. T. Miljan, *The Reluctant Europeans: the Attitudes of the Nordic Countries Towards European Integration* (London: 1977) p. 73. For a Soviet argument in this vein, see J. Piskulov, *Neuvostoliitto ja Pohjola* (Jyväskylä: 1976) pp. 124–5.
57. Smirnov, *Hyvän Naapuruuden Tiellä*, p. 35.
58. Kekkonen writing under pseudonym Liimatainen, 6 April 1974. M. Tyrkkö and K. Korhonen (eds), *Urho Kekkonen Nimellä ja Nimimerkillä 2*, 362–3.
59. See *Helsingin Sanomat*, 9 March 1982.

60. Communique in *Helsingin Sanomat*, 11 June 1983.
61. For the debate in Finland, see O. Apunen, *Kansallinen Realismi ja Puolueettomuus Suomen Ulkopoliittisina Valintoina*, pp. 115–33.
62. Note sent to British and French embassies on 11 July 1947. *Helsingin Sanomat*, 12 July 1947.
63. H. Hakovirta, *Puolueettomuus ja Integraatiopolitiikka* (Tampere: Acta Universitatis Tamperensis, ser A, 78, 1976) p. 205.
64. Ibid.
65. Communique of visit by Khrushchev to Helsinki on 4 September 1960. *ULA*, 1960, 104.
66. See also speech by Khrushchev on 23 November 1960. N. Hruštšev, *Neuvostoliitto ja Pohjola*, pp. 134–6.
67. See H. Kyröläinen, *Talous ja Politiikka*, pp. 217–18.
68. Interview on 22 May 1969. *ULA*, 1969, 160–1.
69. P. Korpinen, 'Suomen Nordek-politiikka', *Katsaus*, 1 (1975). See also Maude, *The Finnish Dilemma*, pp. 116–17.
70. Speech on 23 July 1970. *ULA*, 1970, 219–20.
71. *Pravda*, 18 November 1971.
72. *Izvestiya*, 25 December 1971. See R. Väyrynen, *EEC ja Ulkopolitiikka* (Hämeenlinna: 1973) p. 77.
73. Quotes of discussions published in *Dagens Nyheter*, 31 October 1972.
74. O. Apunen, *Paasikiven-Kekkosen Linja*, pp. 330–1.
75. R. Väyrynen, *EEC ja Ulkopolitiikka*, pp. 62–8.
76. Interview on 2 April 1973. *ULA*, 1973, 92.
77. Speech on 9 November 1972. *ULA*, 1972, 53–8.
78. Interview on 3 September 1973. *ULA*, 1973, 364.
79. Kekkonen under pseudonym Liimatainen, 26 October 1973. M. Tyrkkö and K. Korhonen (eds), *Urho Kekkonen Nimellä ja Nimimerkillä 2*, 347.
80. Interview on 2 April 1973. *ULA*, 1973, 92.
81. O. Apunen, *Paasikiven-Kekkosen Linja*, p. 333.
82. Motion to parliament on 16 October 1973. Cited in F. Singleton, 'Finland, Comecon, and the EEC', *The World Today*, 30 (1974) 68.
83. H. Hakovirta, *Puolueetomuus ja Integraatiopolitiikka*, pp. 293, 325.
84. See E. Antola, 'Finland and the Prospects for Western European Integration in the 1980s', *Yearbook of Finnish Foreign Policy* (1981) 45–8.
85. Piskulov, *Neuvostoliitto ja Pohjola*, p. 97.

6 THE SOVIET INTEREST IN FINNISH INTERNAL AFFAIRS

1. J. K. Paasikivi, *Paasikiven Linja I*, pp. 37–8.
2. US representative in Finland (Hamilton) to Secretary of State, 17 March 1945. *Foreign Relations of the United States 1945*, IV, 609.
3. Speech broadcast on 19 February 1946. *Suomen Sosialidemokraatti*, 20 February 1946.
4. Reported in telegram on 12 January 1945 by Secretary of US Mission in Finland (Higgs). *Foreign Relations of the United States 1945*, IV, 603.

5. Discussions with Secretary of US Mission. Higgs to Secretary of State, 25 January 1945. Ibid., 598–9.
6. US Secretary of State to Secretary of US Mission in Finland, Washington 3 February 1945. Ibid., 603.
7. Speech broadcast on 15 March 1945. Paasikivi, *Paasikiven Linja I*, pp. 15–16. See O. Apunen, *Kansallinen Realismi ja Puolueettomuus*, pp. 50–90.
8. The Minister in Finland (Warren) to Secretary of State, 31 August 1949. *Foreign Relations of the United States 1949*, v, 442.
9. J. H. Hodgson, *Communism in Finland: a History and Interpretation* (Princeton: 1967) pp. 202–14.
10. Report on the international situation, 22 September 1947. M. Rush (ed.), *The International Situation and Soviet Foreign Policy*, p. 130.
11. See Y. Leino, *Kommunisti Sisäministerinä* (Helsinki: 1958) p. 242. For Zhdanov's view that the USSR had made 'a mistake in not occuyping Finland', see M. Djilas, *Conversations with Stalin* (New York: 1961) p. 155.
12. US Minister in Finland (Warren) to Secretary of State, 27 April 1948. *Foreign Relations of the United States 1948*, iv, 779.
13. See A. Upton, *The Communist Parties of Scandinavia and Finland* (London: 1973) pp. 285–93.
14. Minister in US Legation (Simonen) in telegram on 19 July 1949. *Foreign Relations of the United States 1949*, v, 442.
15. Enckell in talks with Warren. US Minister in Finland (Warren) to Secretary of State, 31 August 1949. Ibid., 442.
16. US Chargé in Finland (Hulley) to Secretary of State, 26 November 1945. *Foreign Relations of the United States 1945*, iv, 622.
17. *New Times* (Moscow), 4 (1950) 10.
18. See, for example, *Pravda*, 26 November 1952.
19. *Literaturnaya Gazeta*, 11 August 1948.
20. *New Times* (Moscow), 34 (1948) 16.
21. Speeches on 30 September 1948, *Helsingin Sanomat*, 1 October 1948; and on 5 October 1948, *Helsingin Sanomat*, 6 October 1948.
22. *Pravda*, 24 October 1949; and *Literaturnaya Gazeta*, 14 January 1950.
23. *Literaturnaya Gazeta*, 14 January 1950; and *New Times* (Moscow), 4 (1950) 11.
24. *Literaturnaya Gazeta*, 15 February 1950.
25. See *Pravda*, 1 January 1950.
26. Meeting of Swedish Ambassador in London (Hägglöf) in British Foreign Ministry, 3 February 1950. H. Rautkallio, 'Vuoden 1950 Presidentinvaalien Ulkoiset Paineet eli Kuinka Paasikivi Yritettiin Kaataa Ulkopolitiikalla', *Suomen Kuvalehti*, 10 (1982) 24–7.
27. *Bolshevik*, 22 (1950) 63–8.
28. Report by G. M. Malenkov. L. Gruliow (ed.), *Current Soviet Policies: The Documentary Record of the 19th Communist Party Congress and the Reconstruction after Stalin's Death* (New York: 1953) p. 103.
29. *Pravda*, 5 July 1953. See also *Pravda*, 21 July 1953.
30. O. W. Kuusinen, 'Finland's New Foreign Policy', *New Times* (Moscow), 15 (1947) 7–8.

31. Interview in the late 1960s. V. V. Pohlebkin, *J. K. Paasikivi ja Neuvostoliitto* (Espoo: 1980) pp. 112–13.
32. *Pravda*, 12 December 1950.
33. *Pravda*, 3 and 4 July 1958.
34. *Izvestiya*, 13 July 1958.
35. Letter to J. Virolainen on 17 September 1958. M. Tyrkkö and K. Korhonen (eds), *Urho Kekkonen Kirjeitä Myllystäni 1*, pp. 45–6.
36. D. Borisov, 'A New Government', *International Affairs* (Moscow), 10 (1958) 98.
37. Letter to on 17 September 1958. Tyrkkö and Korhonen, *Urho Kekkonen Kirjeitä Myllystäni 1*, pp. 44–5.
38. Discussions in Washington on 16 September 1961. M. Jakobson, *Veteen Piirretty Viiva*, p. 235.
39. These are well documented in R. Väyrynen, *Conflicts in Finnish–Soviet Relations*, pp. 129–41.
40. Letter on 10 April 1963. Tyrkkö and Korhonen, *Urho Kekkonen Kirjeitä Myllystäni 1*, p. 157.
41. Speech in Leningrad on 23 January 1959. *Pravda*, 24 January 1959.
42. *Pravda*, 8 May 1959.
43. Ibid.
44. Speech in Riga on 11 June 1959. N. S. Hruštšev, *Neuvostoliitto ja Pohjola*, p. 89.
45. Speech on 3 September 1960. Ibid., pp. 114–15.
46. Tyrkkö and Korhonen, *Urho Kekkonen Kirjeitä Myllystäni 1*, pp. 160–1. See also pp. 250–1.
47. *Pravda*, 29 September 1959.
48. *Pravda*, 9 February 1964.
49. Meeting on 17 October 1965, described by Kekkonen in letter on 6 January 1966. Tyrkkö and Korhonen, *Urho Kekkonen Kirjeitä Myllystäni 1*, pp. 250–1.
50. Joint statement, in *Pravda*, 21 May 1968.
51. *Izvestiya*, 26 December 1971.
52. See *Izvestiya*, 26 December 1971.
53. Lecture on 5 November 1973. *ULA*, 1973, 60.
54. *Izvestiya*, 16 March 1979.
55. Meeting with Macmillan during official visit to Britain in May 1961. Cited in Jakobson, *Veteen Piirretty Viiva*, pp. 207–8.
56. Tyrkkö and Korhonen, *Urho Kekkonen Kirjeitä Myllystäni 1*, p. 160.
57. O. Borg and J. Paastela, *Communist Participation in Governmental Coalitions: The Case of Finland* (Tampere: Univ. of Tampere Department of Political Science Research Reports, 59, 1981) pp. 17–18.
58. Ibid., p. 22.
59. Cited in ibid., p. 37.
60. Ibid.
61. V. Smirnov, *Hyvän Napuruuden Tiellä*, p. 91.
62. *Helsingin Sanomat*, 13 May 1982.
63. *Kansan Sana*, 18 May 1982.
64. *Pravda*, 26 April 1983.
65. Cited in J. Iivonen, *A Ruling Non-ruling Communist Party in the West:*

the *Finnish Communist Party* (Tampere: Univ. of Tampere Department of Political Science occasional papers, 32, 1983) p. 26.
66. S. Serbin, 'USSR–Finland: Good Neighbourly Relations', *International Affairs* (Moscow), 5 (1983) 53.
67. *Pravda*, 19 September 1954.
68. *Pravda*, 13 February 1956.
69. *Pravda*, 22 August 1956.
70. *Izvestiya*, 16 March 1961.
71. Jakobson, *Veteen Piirretty Viiva*, p. 268.
72. Government communique of discussions on 14 November 1961. *ULA*, 1961, 178.
73. Letter on 19 October 1963. Tyrkkö and Korhonen, *Urho Kekkonen Kirjeitä Myllystäni 1*, p. 173.
74. Letter on 19 January 1962. Ibid., p. 138.
75. *Pravda*, 25 November 1961.
76. Cited in Jakobson, *Veteen Piirretty Viiva*, p. 297.
77. Speech on 7 January 1962. T. Vilkuna (ed.), *Urho Kekkonen Puheita ja Kirjoituksia II*, p. 220.
78. Letter to Ambassador R. Seppälä on 20 January 1962. Tyrkkö and Korhonen, *Urho Kekkonen Kirjeitä Myllystäni 1*, pp. 133–4.
79. See speech by Paasikivi on being inaugurated into office on 1 March 1950. J. K. Paasikivi, *Paasikiven Linja I*, p. 131.
80. See speech by Kekkonen in memory of Stalin on 6 March 1953. T. Vilkuna (ed.), *Urho Kekkonen Puheita ja Kirjoituksia I*, p. 285.
81. See speech by N. A. Bulganin in Lahti. *Helsingin Sanomat*, 11 June 1957.
82. For example, in interview on 27 September 1966. *ULA*, 1966, 25.
83. Speech on 25 September 1964. T. Vilkuna (ed.), *Urho Kekkonen Puheita ja Kirjoituksia II*, p. 342.
84. Letter on 29 April 1963. Tyrkkö and Korhonen, *Urho Kekkonen Kirjeitä Myllystäni 1*, p. 164.
85. Speech on 22 November 1967. *ULA*, 1967, 75.
86. *Pravda*, 11 January 1968.
87. Letter on 23 January 1968. M. Tyrkkö and K. Korhonen (eds), *Urho Kekkonen Kirjeitä Myllystäni 2*, p. 10.
88. Speech in Helsinki. *Helsingin Sanomat*, 7 December 1967.
89. See R. Wihtol, 'The 1978 Finnish Presidential Elections', *Yearbook of Finnish Foreign Policy* (1977) 59–64.
90. For the foreign policy views of the candidates, see R. Lehtinen, 'Foreign Policy in the Presidential Election Campaign', *Yearbook of Finnish Foreign Policy* (1981).
91. *Helsingin Sanomat*, 18 November 1981.
92. Article by Yu. Kuznetsov, *Pravda*, 20 November 1981. Assessed in Finnish papers: *Uusi Suomi*, 21 November 1981; *Helsingin Sanomat*, 21 November 1981.
93. *Uusi Suomi*, 21 November 1981.
94. *Helsingin Sanomat*, 23 January 1982.
95. Yu. Kuznetsov in *Pravda*, 29 January 1982.
96. Interview in *Helsingin Sanomat*, 27 February 1982.

97. Speech on 9 March 1982. *Helsingin Sanomat*, 10 March 1982. See also official joint communique, *Helsingin Sanomat*, 12 March 1982.
98. *Helsingin Sanomat*, 11 March 1982.
99. For example, Tass assessment of Koivisto's visit, on 12 March 1982, *Helsingin Sanomat*, 13 March 1982; and comment by Soviet Deputy Prime Minister N. Talyzin on anniversary of the FCMA-Treaty, *Helsingin Sanomat*, 6 April 1982.
100. *Uusi Suomi*, 6 November 1981.
101. U. K. Kekkonen, *Tamminiemi* (Helsinki: 1980) pp. 59–60.
102. Jakobson, *Veteen Piirretty Viiva*, p. 339.
103. See J. Steele and E. Abraham, *Andropov in Power: From Komsomol to Kremlin* (Oxford: 1983) pp. 24–35.
104. See ibid., pp. 36–8.
105. Speech in Petrozavodsk in 1968. Referred to in *Helsingin Sanomat*, 21 November 1982.
106. *Helsingin Sanomat*, 13 November 1982. The meeting was held in Moscow on 26 October 1982.
107. Interview of E. Liikanen, Parliamentary Secretary of the SDP, in June 1983.
108. Communique issued on 11 December 1982. *ULA*, 1982, 288ff.
109. Speech on 6 June 1983. *Helsingin Sanomat*, 7 June 1983.
110. E. Salminen, *Aselevosta Kaappaushankkeeseen: Sensuuri ja Itsesensuuri Suomen Lehdistössä 1944–48* (Keuruu: 1978) pp. 54–5, 60.
111. Statement on 11 February 1946. Paasikivi, *Paasikiven Linja I*, pp. 42–3.
112. Salminen, *Aselevosta Kaappaushankkeeseen*, pp. 196–9.
113. Ibid., p. 71.
114. *New Times* (Moscow), 52 (1948) 16.
115. *New Times* (Moscow), 4 (1949).
116. *Literaturnaya Gazeta*, 12 March 1949.
117. *Bolshevik*, 22 (1950) 68.
118. *New Times* (Moscow), 52 (1948) 16.
119. R. Väyrynen, *Conflicts in Finnish–Soviet Relations*, p. 199.
120. Condemned in *Pravda*, 24 October 1949.
121. *Trud*, 28 December 1951.
122. O. Kuusinen, 'The Finnish Foes of Peace and their Artifices', *New Times* (Moscow), 25 (1951) 11.
123. Conversation with US Minister in Finland (Cabot), 23 March 1950. *Foreign Relations of the United States 1950*, IV, 580–1.
124. *Trud*, 17 May 1952.
125. Noted in *Krasnaya Zvezda*, 1 June 1952.
126. *Vapaa Sana*, 18 November 1956. See K. Killinen, 'The Press and Foreign Policy', in *Finnish Foreign Policy* (Helsinki: Finnish Political Science Association, 1963) p. 210.
127. Speech on 8 June 1957. N. S. Hruštšev, *Neuvostoliitto ja Pohjola*, p. 23.
128. *Izvestiya*, 21 November 1958.
129. Speech in Leningrad on 23 January 1959. *Pravda*, 24 January 1959.
130. Speech broadcast on 25 January 1959. *ULA*, 1959, 77–8.
131. Interview by *New York Times* on 5 March 1959. *ULA*, 1959, 10–11.
132. Interview on 5 May 1963. *ULA*, 1963, 25.

133. Speech on 27 November 1962. T. Vilkuna (ed.), *Urho Kekkonen Puheita ja Kirjoituksia II*, p. 259.
134. See speech concerning the foreign policy 'opposition' on 25 September 1964. Ibid., pp. 338–9.
135. Answer on 23 October 1973 to parliamentary question put on 2 October 1973. *ULA*, 1973, 319–20. See also responses to similar questions in *ULA*, 1973, 296–7; and *ULA*, 1974, 403.
136. Communique issued on 6 April 1973. *Pravda*, 8 April 1973; *Helsingin Sanomat*, 6 April 1973.
137. Answer to parliamentary question on 15 November 1974. *ULA*, 1974, 403–4.
138. Answer to parliamentary question on 27 November 1975. *ULA*, 1975, 333–4.
139. Kekkonen writing under pseudonym Liimatainen, 6 April 1974. M. Tyrkkö and K. Korhonen (eds), *Urho Kekkonen Nimellä ja Nimimerkillä 2*, pp. 261–3.
140. *Pravda*, 21 March 1975.
141. *Pravda*, 20 October 1981.
142. Answer to parliamentary question on 9 December 1974. *ULA*, 1974, 406–7.
143. C-G. Lilius, 'Suomalainen Itsesensuuri', *Kanava*, 1 (1975) 27.
144. V. Smirnov, *Hyvän Naapuruuden Tiellä*, p. 89. For the restraints on Finnish broadcasting and television, see D. Fields, 'Finland: How Much Self-Censorship Remains?', *Index on Censorship*, 2 (1982) 16–18.
145. Report in the *Guardian*, 24 January 1984.
146. Smirnov, *Hyvän Naapuruuden Tiellä*, p. 89.

CONCLUSION: FINNISH–SOVIET RELATIONS, A MODEL?

1. See G. Kennan, 'Europe's Problems, Europe's Choices', *Foreign Policy*, 14 (1974) 7–9.
2. G. Maude, *The Finnish Dilemma*, p. 47.
3. See G. Maude, 'Has Finland been Finlandized?', in G. Ginsburgs and A. Rubinstein (eds), *Soviet Foreign Policy Toward Western Europe* (New York: 1978) pp. 45–53.
4. See G. Maude, 'The Further Shores of Finlandization', *Cooperation and Conflict*, XVII (1982) 10–12.
5. Speech on 28 August 1955, T. Vilkuna (ed.), *Urho Kekkonen Puheita ja Kirjoituksia I*, pp. 358–9.
6. Speech on 23 January 1959. N. S. Hruštšev, *Neuvostoliitto ja Pohjola*, p. 81.
7. Argued by J. Erickson, March 1980. Cited in F. Halliday, *Threat From the East? Soviet Policy from Afghanistan and Iran to the Horn of Africa* (London: 1982) p. 148.

Bibliography

1 OFFICIAL DOCUMENTS, SPEECHES, WRITINGS

Foreign Relations of the United States 1945 (1968) IV (Washington).
Foreign Relations of the United States 1948 (1974) IV (Washington).
Foreign Relations of the United States 1949 (1976) V (Washington).
Foreign Relations of the United States 1950 (1980) IV (Washington).
Hruštšev, N. S. (1964) *Neuvostoliitto ja Pohjola: Puheita ja Lausuntoja Vuosilta 1956–63* (Helsinki).
Karjalainen, A. (1970) *Minun Näkökulmastani: Vuosikymmen Ulko-, Kauppa- ja Talouspolitiikkaa* (Helsinki).
Kolmannen Parlamentaarisen Puolustuskomitean Mietintö (1981) Komiteanmietintö 1981, 1 (Helsinki).
Paasikivi, J. K. (1962) *Paasikiven Linja I: Puheita Vuosilta 1944–1956* (Porvoo).
Parlamentaarisen Puolustuskomitean Mietintö (1971) Komiteanmietintö 1971, A 18 (Helsinki).
Rönkä, R. (ed.) (1972) *Suomen ja Neuvostoliiton Väliset Voimassa Olevat Sopimukset* (Helsinki: Publications of the Soviet Institute, series B 11).
Rush, M. (1970) *The International Situation and Soviet Foreign Policy: Reports of Soviet Leaders* (Columbus, Ohio).
The Development of Finnish–Soviet Relations During the Autumn of 1939 (Helsinki: Ministry of Foreign Affairs of Finland).
Toisen Parlamentaarisen Puolustuskomitean Mietintö (1976) Komiteanmietintö 1976, 36 (Helsinki).
Tyrkkö, M. and Korhonen, K. (eds) (1976) *Urho Kekkonen Kirjeitä Myllystäni 1 1956–1967* (Helsinki).
Tyrkkö, M. and Korhonen, K. (eds) (1976) *Urho Kekkonen Kirjeitä Myllystäni 2 1969–1975* (Helsinki).
Tyrkkö, M. and Korhonen, K. (eds) (1977) *Urho Kekkonen Nimellä ja Nimimerkillä 1* (Keuruu).
Tyrkkö, M. and Korhonen, K. (eds) (1977) Urho Kekkonen Nimellä ja Nimimerkillä 2 (Keuruu).
Ulkopoliittisia Lausuntoja ja Asiakirjoja (1957–) (Helsinki: Finnish Ministry of Foreign Affairs).
Vilkuna, T. (ed.) (1967) *Urho Kekkonen Puheita ja Kirjoituksia I: Puheita Vuosilta 1936–1956* (Helsinki).
Vilkuna, T. (ed.) (1967) *Urho Kekkonen Puheita ja Kirjoituksia II: Puheita Presidenttikaudelta 1956–1967* (Helsinki).

Yhidistyneiden Kansakuntien Yleiskokouksen- (1959–) (Helsinki: Finnish Ministry of Foreign Affairs).

Ylitalo, J. R. (1978) *Salasanomia Helsingistä Washingtoniin: Muistelmia ja Dokumentteja Vuosilta 1946–1948*, trans. and ed. L. Toiviainen (Keuruu).

2   SOVIET BOOKS AND ARTICLES

Bartenev, T. and Komissarov, J. (1977) *Kolmekymmentä Vuotta Hyvää Naapuruutta* (Helsinki).

Bartenev, T. and Komissarov, Yu. (1976) *Tridtsat' let dobrososedstva k istorii sovetsko-finlyandskikh otnosheniy* (Moscow).

Bartenev, T. and Komissarov, Yu. (1978) *SSSR-finlyandiya: orientiry sotrudnichestva* (Moscow).

Goloshubov, Yu. I. (1974) *Skandinaviya i problemy poslevoennoy Yevropy*, (Moscow).

Goloshubov, Yu. I. (1971) *Skandinaviya i yevropeyskaya bezopasnost'* (Moscow).

Gorov, Yu. A. (1959) 'Nekotorye fakty iz istorii neytral'noy politiki Skandinavskikh stran', *Skandinavskiy sbornik* (Tallin), IV.

Il'inskiy, Ya. (1963) ' "Liniya Paasikivi": zavoevanie finlyandskogo naroda', *Mirovaya ekonomika i mezhdunarodnye otnosheniya*, 3.

Ingul'skaya, L. A. (1972) *V bor'be za demokratizatsiyu finlyandii (1944–1948)* (Moscow).

Kan A. S. (1962) 'Neytralistskie traditsii vo vneshney politike skandinavskikh gosudarstv', *Novaya i noveyshaya istoriya*, 4.

Kan, A. S. (1970) *Neuvostoliiton ja Suomen Väliset Suhteet Leniniläisen Kansallisuuspolitiikan Valossa* (Helsinki: Offprint from Yearbook of the Soviet Institute, 22).

Khrushchev Remembers II: The Last Testament (1977) Trans. and ed. S. Talbott (London: Penguin).

Komissarov, J. (1974) *Suomi Löytää Linjansa* (Helsinki).

Komissarov, J. (1978) 'The Future of a Nuclear Weapon-Free Zone in Northern Europe', *Yearbook of Finnish Foreign Policy*.

Komissarov, J. (1979) 'NATOn Eurostrategia ja Pohjois-Eurooppa', *Suomen Kuvalehti*, 47.

Komissarov, J. (1981) 'Paasikiven-Kekkosen Linja', *Ulkopolitiikka*, 2.

Koronen, M. M. (1960) *Sovetsko-finlyandskie otnosheniya – primer mirnogo sosushchestvovaniya* (Leningrad).

Möttölä, K.; and Bykov, O. and Korolev, S. (eds) (1983) *Finnish–Soviet Economic Relations* (London).

Piskulov, J. *Neuvostoliitto ja Pohjola* (1976) (Helsinki).

Pohlebkin, V. V. (1969) *Suomi Vihollisena ja Ystävänä 1714–1967* (Porvoo).

Pohlebkin, V. V. (1980) *J. K. Paasikivi ja Neuvostoliitto* (Espoo).

Pokhlebkin, V. V. (1961) *Finlyandiya i sovetskiy soyuz* (Moscow).

Pokhlebkin, V. V. (1975) *SSSR-finlyandiya 260 let otnosheniy (1713–1973)* (Moscow).

Rozdorozhny, I. and Fedorov, V. (1966) *Finlyandiya – nash severny sosed* (Moscow).

Rosdoroznyi, I. (1969) *Rauhanomainen Rinnakkainolo, Keskinäinen Luottamus ja Ystävyys: Neuvostoliiton ja Suomen Suhteiden Kehityksestä* (Moscow).

Smirnov, V. (1983) *Hyvän Naapuruuden Tiellä* (Tampere).

Tomasevsky, D. (1973) *European Détente and Soviet–Finnish Relations* (Helsinki: The Finnish Institute of International Affairs, INFO 39).

Voronkov, L. S. (1976) *Severnaya Yevropa: obshchestvennost' i problemy vneshney politiki* (Moscow).

Voronkov, L. S. (1978) 'Vuoden 1948 Sopimuksen Merkitys Neuvostoliittolais-Suomalaisten Suhteiden Nykyvaiheessa', *Ulkopolitiikka*, 1.

Voronkov, L. S. (1980) *Strany severnoy Yevropy v sovremennykh mezhdunarodnykh otnosheniyakh* (Moscow: znanie 8).

Voronkov, L. S. (1981) 'Rauhan ja Turvallisuuden Näköalat Pohjois-Euroopassa', *Ulkopolitiikka*, 1.

Voronkov, L. S. and Senyukov, Yu. P. (1977) *Finlyandiya – nash severny sosed* (Moscow: znanie, 5).

3 WESTERN BOOKS

Apunen, O. (1972) *Kansallinen Realismi ja Puolueettomuus Suomen Ulkopoliittisina Valintoina* (Tampere: Univ. of Tampere Department of Political Science Research Reports, 28).

Apunen, O. (1975) *Suomen Ulkopoliittinen Doktriini Toiminnallisia Perspektiivejä* (Jyväskyla: Univ. of Tampere Department of Political Science offprint series, 3).

Apunen, O. (1978) *Ulkopolitiikamme Kiinnekohtia*, 2nd ed. (Tampere: Univ. of Tampere Department of Political Science mimeograph, 2).

Apunen, O. (1977) *Paasikiven-Kekkosen Linja* (Helsinki).

Bjøl, E. (1983) 'Nordic Security', *Adelphi Papers*, 181 (London).

Blinnikka, A. (1969) *Valvontakomissian Aika* (Porvoo).

Blomberg, J. and Joenniemi, P. (1971) *Kaksiteräinen Miekka – 70 Luvun Puolustuspolitiikkaa* (Helsinki).

Brundtland, A. O. (1981) *The Nordic Balance* (Norsk Utrenrikspolitisk Institutt, NUPI notat no. 229, December).

Castrén E. (1954) *The Present Law of War and Neutrality* (Helsinki: Annals of the Finnish Academy of Science, series B, 85).

Essays on Finnish Foreign Policy (1969) (Helsinki: Finnish Political Science Association).

Finnish Foreign Policy: Studies in Foreign Politics (1969) (Helsinki: Finnish Political Science Association).

Ginsburgs, G. and Rubinstein, A. Z. (eds) (1978) *Soviet Foreign Policy Toward Western Europe* (New York).

Ginther, K. (1975) *Neutralität und Neutralitätspolitik: Die Österreichische*

Neutralität Zwischen Schweizer Muster und Sowjetischer Koexistenzdoktrin (Vienna and New York).

Hakalehto, I. (ed.) (1966) *Suomen Ulkopolitiikan Kehityslinjat 1809–1966* (Porvoo).

Hakalehto, I. (ed.) (1969) *Suomi Kansainvälisen Jännityksen Maailmassa* (Porvoo).

Hakovirta, H. (1975) *Suomettuminen: Kaukokontrollia vai Rauhanomaista Rinnakkaiseloa* (Jyväskylä).

Hakovirta, H. (1976) *Puolueettomuus ja Integraatiopolitiikka* (Tampere: Acta Universitatis Tamperensis, ser A, 78).

Hakovirta, H. and Väyrynen, R. (eds) (1975) *Suomen Ulkopolitiikka* (Helsinki).

Halliday, F. (1982) *Threat from the East? Soviet Policy from Afghanistan and Iran to the Horn of Africa* (London).

Halsti, W. H. (1976) 'Finlandization', in Urban, G. R. (ed.), *Détente* (London).

Halsti, W. H. (1969) *Me, Venäjä ja Muut* (Helsinki).

Heikkilä, T. (1965) *Paasikivi Peräsimessä – Pääministerin Sihteerin Muistelmat 1944–1948* (Keuruu).

Hyvämäki, L. (1957) *Vaaran Vuodet 1944–1948* (Helsinki).

Holloway, D. (1982) 'Foreign and Defence Policy', in Brown A. and Kaser, M. (eds), *Soviet Policy for the 1980s* (Oxford).

Holloway, D. (1983) *The Soviet Union and the Arms Race* (New Haven and London).

Iivonen, J. (1983) *A Ruling Non-ruling Communist Party in the West: The Finnish Communist Party* (Tampere: Univ. of Tampere Department of Political Science occasional papers, 32).

Inkari, A. (ed.) (1978) *Tieteelis-Tekninen ja Taloudellinen Yhteistoiminta Suomen ja Neuvostoliiton Välillä* (Helsinki: Committee for Scientific-Technical Cooperation between Finland and the Soviet Union, series 3).

Jakobson, M. (1968) *Finnish Neutrality: A Study of Finnish Foreign Policy since the Second World War* (London).

Jakobson, M. (1968) *Kuumalla Linjalla: Suomen Ulkopolitiikan Ydin Kysymksiä 1944–1968* (Porvoo).

Jakobson, M. (1980) *Veteen Piirretty Viiva: Havaintoja ja Merkintöjä Vuosilta 1953–1965* (Keuruu).

Junnila, T. (1962) *Nootikriisi Tuoreeltaan Tulkittuna* (Porvoo).

Junnila, T. (1964) *Suomen Taistelu Turvallisuudestaan ja Puolueettomuudestaan* (Helsinki).

Junnila, T. (1971) *Suomen Itsenäisyydestä on Kysymys* (Porvoo).

Karvonen, T. (1973) *Neljännesvuosisata Yya-Sopimusta* (Helsinki).

Killinen, K. (1964) *Puoluettomuuden Miekka: Suomen Puolustuskysymyksen Tarkastelus* (Porvoo).

Kirby, D. G. (1979) *Finland in the Twentieth Century: a History and Interpretation* (London).

Korhonen, K. (1971) *Suomi Neuvostodiplomatiassa Tartosta Talvisotaan 2 1933–1939: Turvallisuuden Pettäessä* (Helsinki).

Korhonen, K. (ed.) (1975) *Urho Kekkonen – A Statesman for Peace* (London).

Krosby, H. P. (1978) *Kekkosen Linja: Suomi ja Neuvostoliito 1944–1978* (Jyväskylä).

Kyröläinen, H. (1981) *Talous ja Politiikka eri Järjestelmän Omaavien Valtioden Suhteissa: Suomi ja Neuvostoliitto 1944–1979* (Tampere: Univ. of Tampere Department of Political Science Research Reports, 62).

Kyröläinen, H. (1981) 'Economics and Politics in the Relations Between States of Different Social Systems: Finland and the Soviet Union 1944–1979', in Apunen, O. (ed.), *Détente – A Framework for Action and Analysis* (Tampere: Univ. of Tampere Department of Political Science Research Reports, 61).

Küng, A. (1976) *Mitä Suomessa Tapahtuu* (Helsinki).

Kähköla, P. and Ripatti, A-K. (1971) *Suomen Idänkauppa* (Helsinki).

Laqueur, W. (1979) 'Finlandization', in *A Continent Astray 1970–1978* (New York).

Lafond, J-M. (1974) 'Finlandisation – La Finlande Incomprise', Dijon Univ. Ph.D. thesis.

Lundestad, G. (1980) *America, Scandinavia, and the Cold War 1945–1949* (Oslo).

Luoto, R. T. (1978) *Sopimus Ystävyydestä: Suomen ja Neuvostoliiton Välisen YYA-Sopimuksen Merkitys Suomen Turvallisuuspolitiikassa 1948–1978*, 2nd ed. (Tampere).

Lyon, P. (1963) *Neutralism* (Leicester).

Manerkorpi, M. (ed.) (1970) *J. K. Paasikivi* (Hämeenlinna).

Maude, G. (1976) *The Finnish Dilemma: Neutrality in the Shadow of Power* (London).

Maude, G. (1978) 'Has Finland been Finlandized?', in Ginsburgs, G. and Rubinstein, A. (eds), *Soviet Foreign Policy Toward Western Europe* (New York).

Mazour, A. G. (1956) *Finland Between East and West* (Princeton, NJ).

Miljan, T. (1977) *The Reluctant Europeans: The Attitudes of the Nordic Countries Towards European Integration* (London).

Möttölä, K. (ed.) (1983) *Nuclear Weapons and Northern Europe – Problems and Prospects of Arms Control* (Helsinki: The Finnish Institute of International Affairs).

Möttölä, K.; Bykov, O. and Korolev, S. (eds) (1983) *Finnish–Soviet Economic Relations* (London).

Nousiainen, J. (1971) *The Finnish Political System* (Cambridge, Mass).

Nyberg, R. (1983) *Security Dilemmas in Scandinavia: Evaporated Nuclear Options and Indigenous Conventional Capabilities* (Cornell Univ. Peace Studies Programme occasional paper no. 17, June).

Paile, G. (1967) *Pelin Säänöt: Suomen ja Neuvostoliiton Suhteet Vuodesta 1944* (Helsinki).

Palm, T. (1972) *Moskova 1944: Aselepo Neuvottelut Maaliskuussa ja Syyskuussa 1944* (Helsinki).

Pohjoinen, T. (1973) *25 Vuotta Rauha ja Ystävyyttä* (Oulu).

Polvinen, T. (1981) *Jaltasta Pariisin Rauhaan: Suomi Kansainvälisessä Politiikassa III 1945–1947* (Porvoo).

Puntila, L. A. (1974) *The Political History of Finland 1809–1966* (Helsinki).

Rautkallio H. (1979) *Suomen Suunta 1945–1948* (Savonlinna).

Rintala, M. (1969) *Four Finns. Political Portraits of Four Major Leaders of the Finnish Government: Mannerheim, Tanner, Ståhlberg and Paasikivi* (Berkeley).

Roberts, A. (1976) *Nations in Arms: the Theory and Practice of Territorial Defence* (London).

Rosas, A. (1978) *Sodanaikainen Puolueettomuus ja Puolueettomuuspolitiikka: Tutkimus Kahden Puolueettomuusmallin Asemasta Kansainvälisessä Oikeudessa* (Turku: Publications of Univ. of Turku Department of Public Law, 12).

Salminen, E. (1979) *Aselevosta Kaappaushankkeeseen: Sensuuri ja Itsesensuuri Suomen Lehdistössä 1944–1948* (Keuruu).

Salonen, A. M. (1972) *Linjat* (Helsinki).

Steele, J. (1983) *World Power: Soviet Foreign Policy under Brezhnev and Andropov* (London).

Steele, J. and Abraham, E. (1983) *Andropov in Power: From Komsomol to Kremlin* (Oxford).

Suomen Tunallisuuspolitiikan Käsikirja (1977) (Helsinki).

Suomi, J. (ed.) (1980) *Näkökulmia Suomen Turvallisuuspolitiikkaan 1980– Luvulla* (Keuruu).

Särkiö, H. (1973) *Vuoden 1948 YYA-Sopimus Suomalaisten Komenttien Valossa Kiinnittäen Erityisesti Huomiota sen Sotilaallisen Puoleen* (Hämeenlinna).

Särkiö, H. and Hägglund, G. (1975) *Mitä Tapahtuu jos . . .* (Helsinki).

Söderhjelm, J. O. (1970) *Kolme Matkaa Moskovaan* (Helsinki).

Triska, J. and Slusser, R. (1962) *The Theory, Law and Policy of Soviet Treaties* (Stanford).

Turner, B. and Nordquist, G. (1982) *The Other European Community: Integration and Cooperation in Nordic Europe* (London).

Törnudd, K. (1967) *Suomi ja Yhdistyneet Kansakunnat* (Helsinki).

Törnudd K. (1961) *Soviet Attitudes Towards Non-Military Regional Cooperation* (Helsinki: Soc. Sc. Fennica).

Upton, A. F. (1973) *The Communist Parties of Scandinavia and Finland* (London).

Upton, A. F. (1977) 'Finland', in McCauley, M. (ed.), *Communist Power in Europe 1944–1949* (London).

Verosta, S. (1967) *Die Dauernde Neutralität: Ein Grundriss* (Vienna).

Vigor, P. (1975) *The Soviet View of War, Peace and Neutrality* (London).

Vital, D. (1971) 'Finland – a Paradigm for the Future', in *The Survival of Small States* (Oxford).

Vloyantes, J. P. (1975) *Silk Glove Hegemony: Finnish–Soviet Relations 1944–1974. A Case Study of the Soft Sphere of Influence* (Kent, Ohio).

Vänttinen, O. (ed.) (1967) *Itsenäinen Suomi – Puolueeton Pohjola* (Tampere).

Väyrynen, R. (1970) *Yöpakkaset v. 1958–59 Neuvostoliiton Ulkopoliittisen Käyttätymisen Kuvastajana* (Helsinki: INFO, Finnish Institute for International Affairs mimeograph series, 19).

Väyrynen, R. (1972) *Conflicts in Finnish–Soviet Relations* (Tampere: Acta Universitatis Tamperensis, ser A, 47).

Väyrynen, R. (1973) *EEC ja Ulkopolitiikka* (Hämeenlinna).

Väyrynen, R. (1982) *Stability and Change in Finnish Foreign Policy* (Helsinki: Univ. of Helsinki Department of Political Science Research Reports, series A, 60).
Wagner, U. (1974) *Finnlands Neutralität: Eine Neutralitätspolitik mit Defensivallianz* (Hamburg).
Wahlbäck, K. (1968) *Mannerheimista Kekkoseen: Suomen Politiikan Päälinjoja 1917–1967* (Helsinki).
Woker, D. (1978) *Die Skandinavischen Neutralen: Prinzip und Praxis der Schwedischen und der Finnischen Neutralität* (Series of Swiss Society for Foreign Policy, 5).
Wolfe, T. W. (1970) *Soviet Power and Europe 1945–1970* (Baltimore and London).
Wuorinen, J. (1956) 'Finland', in Kertesz, S. (ed.), *The Fate of East Central Europe* (Notre Dame).
Ørvik, N. (1963) *Europe's Northern Cap and the Soviet Union* (Cambridge, Mass.).
Ørvik, N., (1972) *Sicherheit auf Finnisch* (Stuttgart-Degerloch).

4 WESTERN ARTICLES

Anckar, D. (1970) 'Finnish Foreign Policy Debate: The Saimaa Canal Case', *Cooperation and Conflict*, 4.
Anckar, D. (1973) 'Party Strategies and Foreign Policy: The Case of Finland 1955–1963', *Cooperation and Conflict*, 1.
Antola, E. (1981) 'Finland and the Prospects of Western European Integration in the 1980s', *Yearbook of Finnish Foreign Policy*.
Apunen, O. (1981) 'Some Conclusions about the Komissarov Debate', *Yearbook of Finnish Foreign Policy*.
Apunen, O. (1977) 'Geographical and Political Factors in Finland's Relations with the Soviet Union', *Yearbook of Finnish Foreign Policy*.
Apunen, O. (1978) 'Nuclear Weapon-Free Areas, Zones of Peace and Nordic Security', *Yearbook of Finnish Foreign Policy*.
Apunen, O. (1980) 'Three "waves" of the Kekkonen Plan and Nordic Security in the 1980s', *Bulletin of Peace Proposals*, 1.
Apunen, O. and Rytövuori, H. (1982) 'Ideas of "Survival" and "Progress" in the Finnish Foreign Policy Tradition', *Journal of Peace Research*, XIX, 1.
Barnes, R. I. (1974) 'Swedish Foreign Policy: a Response to Geopolitical factors', *Cooperation and Conflict*, IX.
Bildt, C. (1983) 'Sweden and the Soviet Submarines', *Survival*, July/August.
Blomberg, J. (1970) 'YYA-Sopimuksen Ydinajatus', *Ydin*, 1.
Brodin, K. (1975) 'Suomettumista', *Kanava*, 5.
Brodin, K. and Goldmann, K.; and Lange, C. (1968) 'The Policy of Neutrality: Official Doctrines of Finland and Sweden', *Cooperation and Conflict*, I.
Brundtland, A. O. (1966) 'The Nordic Balance', *Cooperation and Conflict*, II.

Elovainio, M. K. (1979) 'YYA-Sopimuksen Synty sekä Sopimuksen Merkitys Suomen Puolueettomuudelle Sopimusoikeudellisesti Tarkasteltuna', *Politiikka*, 2.

Fields, D. (1982) 'Finland: How Much Self-Censorship Remains?', *Index on Censorship*, 11, 2 (April).

Forster, K. (1962) 'Finland's Policy in the United Nations and the Paasikivi Line', *Journal of Central European Affairs*, 21, 4 (January).

Forster, K. (1968) 'Finland's 1966 Elections and Soviet Relations', *Orbis*, 12, 3.

Gilberg, T. *et al.* (1981) 'The Soviet Union and Northern Europe'. *Problems of Communism*, (March–April).

Ginsburgs, G. (1960) 'Neutrality and Neutralism and the Tactics of Soviet Diplomacy', *The American Slavic and East European Review*, 19.

Guiton, R-J. (1969) 'Die Beziehungen zwischen Finnland und der Sowjetunion im Spiegel der Finnischen Regierungskrise vom Herbst 1958', *Europa Archiv*, 14.

Hakovirta, H. (1970) 'Yya-Sopimuksen Konsultaatio- ja Avunantokysymys Suomen Puoluettomuuden Uskottavuusproblematiikassa', *Politiikka*.

Hakovirta, H. (1975) 'Neuvostoliitto Suomen Tarkkailijana', *Turvallisuuspolitiikkaa*, 4.

Hakovirta, H. (1981) 'Neuvostoliitto ja Puolueettomuus Lansi-Euroopassa', *Politiikka*, 2.

Hodgson, J. H. (1959) 'The Paasikivi Line', *American Slavic and East European Review*, 18, 2 (April).

Hodgson, J. H. (1962) 'Postwar Finnish Foreign Policy: Institutions and Personalities', *Western Political Quarterly*, 15, 1.

Hodgson, J. H. (1967) 'The Finnish Communist Party and Neutrality', *Government and Opposition*, 2, 2.

Hodgson, J. H. (1974) 'Finnish Communism and Electoral Politics', *Problems of Communism* (January–February).

Holst, J. J. (1966) 'Norwegian Security Policy: The Strategic Context', *Cooperation and Conflict*, II.

Holsti, K. J. (1964) 'Strategy and Techniques of Influence in Soviet–Finnish Relations', *Western Political Quarterly*, 17, 1 (March).

Härkönen, S. (1979) 'Eurostrategic Weapons, Northern Europe and Finland: New Weapons Technology as a Finnish Security Problem', *Yearbook of Finnish Foreign Policy*.

Jakobson, M. (1962) 'Finland's Foreign Policy', *International Affairs* (London), 38, 2 (April).

Jakobson, M. (1975) 'Itsesensuurista', *Kanava*, 2.

Jakobson, M. (1980) 'Substance and Appearance: Finland', *Foreign Affairs*, 58 (Summer)

Kalela, J. (1971) 'Puolueettomuus ja Suomen 'Idänsuhteet', *Politiikka*.

Kemppainen, M. J. (1968) 'Kestääkö Puolueettomuutemme?', *Suomalainen Suomi*, 36 (August).

Kennan, G. F. (1974) 'Europe's Problems, Europe's Choices', *Foreign Policy*, 14.

Klenberg, J. (1976) 'A Parliamentary View on Finnish Security Policy', *Yearbook of Finnish Foreign Policy*.

Korhonen, K. (1976) 'Finland as a Neighbour of the Soviet Union', *Yearbook of Finnish Foreign Policy*.

Krosby, H. P. (1960) 'The Communist Power Bid in 1948', *Political Science Quarterly*, 76 (June).

Kuusisto, A. (1959) 'The Paasikivi Line in Finland's Foreign Policy', *Western Political Science Quarterly*, 12, 1 (March).

Laqueur, W. (1977) 'Europe: The Specter of Finlandization', *Commentary*, 64, 6 (December).

Lehtinen, R. (1981) 'Foreign Policy in the Presidential Election Campaign', *Yearbook of Finnish Foreign Policy*.

Lilius, C-G. (1975) 'Self-Censorship in Finland', *Index on Censorship* (Spring).

Lindberg, S. (1980) 'Towards a Nordic Nuclear-Weapons-Free Zone', *Yearbook of Finnish Foreign Policy*.

Lindberg, S. (1981) 'The Illusory Nordic Balance: Threat Scenarios in Nordic Security Planning', *Cooperation and Conflict*, 1 (March).

Linnainmaa, H. (1975) 'Finland's Economic Cooperation with CMEA-Member Countries and the Agreement Between Finland and the CMEA', *Co-existence*, 12, 1 (May).

Maude, G. (1975) 'Finland's Security Policy', *The World Today* (October).

Maude, G. (1979) 'Tutkijan Dilemma', *Ulkopolitiikka*, 3.

Maude, G. (1982) 'The Further Shores of Finlandization', *Cooperation and Conflict*, XVII.

Maude, G. (1983) 'Suomalainen Dilemma Tänään: Lapin Puolustus', *Kanava*, 3.

Mäentakanen, E. (1978) 'Western and Eastern Europe in Finnish Trade Policy, 1957–1974: Towards a Comprehensive Solution?', *Cooperation and Conflict*, XIII, 1.

Nurmi, L. (1981) 'YYA-Keskustelua PPK:N Julkistamisen Jälkeen', *Ulkopolitiikka*, 2.

Nyberg, R. (1981) 'Finnish Security Policy, *Nya Argus*, 12.

Pajunen, A. (1968) 'Finland's Security Policy', *Cooperation and Conflict*.

Pajunen, A. (1972) 'Finland's Security Policy in the 1970s: Background and Perspectives', *Cooperation and Conflict*, 7, 3/4.

Petersen, N. (1982) 'Britain, Scandinavia and the North Atlantic Treaty 1948–49', *Review of International Studies*, 8, 4 (October).

Rautkallio, H. (1982) 'Vuoden 1950 Presidentinvaalien Ulkoiset Paineet eli Kuinka Paasikivi Yritettiin Kaataa Ulkopolitiikalla', *Suomen Kuvalehti*, 10.

Sariola, S. (1982) 'Finland and Finlandization', *History Today*, 32 (March).

Singleton, F. (1974) 'Finland, Comecon, and the EEC', *The World Today*, 30 (February).

Singleton, F. (1981) 'The Myth of "Finlandisation" ', *International Affairs* (London), 57, 2 (Spring).

Singleton, F. (1982) 'Finland after Kekkonen', *The World Today* (March).

Sundqvist, U. (1973) 'Suomen ja Neuvostoliiton Tiede- ja Kulttuuriyhteis-työstä, *Ulkopolitiikka*, 2.

Tarschys, D. (1971) 'Neutrality and the Common Market: the Soviet View', *Cooperation and Conflict*, 2.

Tuomioja, E. and Tarkka, J. (1981) 'Suomen Turvallisuus – Mitä on Tehtävä?', *Ulkopolitiikka*, 2.

Törngren, R. (1961) 'The Neutrality of Finland', *Foreign Affairs*, 39, 4 (July).

Vesa, U. (1979) 'Determining Finland's Position in International Crises', *Yearbook of Finnish Foreign Policy*.

Välilehto, H. (1973) 'YYA-Sopimus Sanomalehdistössä', *Ydin*, 3.

Väyrynen, R. (1969) 'A Case Study of Sanctions: Finland and the Soviet Union in 1958–59', *Cooperation and Conflict*, 3.

Väyrynen, R. (1977) 'Finland's Role in Western Policy Since the Second World War', *Cooperation and Conflict*, 2.

Wahlbäck, K. (1969) 'Finnish Foreign Policy: Some Comparative Perspectives', *Cooperation and Conflict*, 4.

Wagner, U. (1975) 'Finnland und die UdSSR: Das Sogenannte Finnlandisierungsproblem', *Osteuropa*, 25.

Wilhelmus, I. (1966) 'Finnlands Neutralitätspolitik', *Deutsche Aussenpolitik*, 11.

Örvik, K. E. (1979) 'The Limits of Security: Defence and Foreign Trade in Finland', *Survey*, 107, 24 (Spring).

Örvik, K. E. (1983) 'Finnish Foreign Policy and the Kekkonen Tradition', *Survey*, 118–119, 27 (Autumn–Winter).

Index